The
Intrepid Guerrillas
of North Luzon

BERNARD NORLING

THE UNIVERSITY PRESS OF KENTUCKY

The University Press of Kentucky
Scholarly publisher for the Commonwealth,
serving Bellarmine University, Berea College, Centre College of
Kentucky, Eastern Kentucky University, The Filson Historical
Society, Georgetown College, Kentucky Historical Society,
Kentucky State University, Morehead State University, Murray
State University, Northern Kentucky University, Transylvania
University, University of Kentucky, University of Louisville,
and Western Kentucky University.
All rights reserved.

Editorial and Sales Offices: The University Press of Kentucky
663 South Limestone Street, Lexington, Kentucky 40508-4008
www.kentuckypress.com

09 08 07 06 05   5   4   3   2   1

The Library of Congress has cataloged the hardcover edition as
follows:

Norling, Bernard, 1924-
      The intrepid guerrillas of North Luzon / Bernard Norling.
            p.   cm.
      Includes bibliographical references and index.
      ISBN 0-8131-2118-3 (cloth : alk. paper)
      1. World War, 1939-1945—Underground movements—
Philippines—Luzon. 2. United States. Army. Cavalry, 26th.
Troop C—History. 3. Cagayan-Apayao Forces (Guerrilla
organization : philippines)—History. 4. Guerrillas—
Philippines—Luzon—Biography. 5. Guerrillas—United States—
Biography.   6. World War, 1939-1945—Personal narratives,
American. 7. Luzon   (Philippines)—History, Military. I. Title.
D802.P52L8965   1999
940.53'5991—dc21   99-17356
      ISBN 0-8131-9134-3 (pbk. : acid-free paper)

This book is printed on acid-free recycled paper meeting
the requirements of the American National Standard
for Permanence of Paper for Printed Library Materials.

∞ ⊛

Manufactured in the United States of America

 Member of the Association of
American University Presses

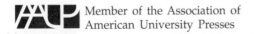

Contents

Preface

Much has been written by or about most of the major Filipino and American leaders of guerrilla resistance to the Japanese occupation of the Philippines, 1942-1945. Ramon Magsaysay, Ferdinand Marcos, Manuel Roxas, Marcos Augustin (code-named Marking), Eleuterio "Terry" Adeviso, Wendell Fertig, Russell Volckmann, Donald Blackburn, Robert Lapham, Ray Hunt, Edwin Ramsey, and others have written their memoirs or been the subjects of biographies. All these men succeeded in living through the war (no mean feat in itself); all contributed variously to Allied victory. Many less well-known American and Filipino leaders of irregulars also resisted the enemy, but either they did not survive the war, or they left no records, or they simply returned to civilian life and forgot the war. Thus it is that their achievements, often brief but significant, have attracted much less attention.

A fair number of these were men of courage and ability who strove as manfully as any to vex the Japanese, protect Filipino civilians, and collect intelligence for Gen. Douglas MacArthur's headquarters in Australia. Prominent among them on Luzon were Claude Thorp, Joseph Barker, Ralph Praeger, Thomas Jones, William Bowen, Walter Cushing, Roque Ablan, Marcelo Adduru, Juan Pajota, Guillermo Nakar, and Arthur Furagganan, to cite a representative sampling. They were not cut from the same cloth. Cushing was a meteoric success but survived only until September 1942. Ablan, able and determined, badgered the Japanese for a year, then simply vanished to an unknown fate. Barker showed brilliant promise but took one risk too many. Bowen eventually surrendered to save the lives of the families of his men. Thorp's character and purposes have been the subject of much controversy. Pajota's deeds were never adequately recognized. Several of those named were betrayed to the Japanese and subsequently executed. Ablan was probably murdered. Only two, Jones and Pajota, survived the war.

The primary purpose of this book is to record what is known of the wartime deeds of Troop C, 26th Cavalry, and of the Cagayan-Apayao Forces (hereafter referred to as CAF), both of which were commanded by Capt. Ralph Praeger. Praeger's organization lasted longer than any other in North Luzon, but it was eventually destroyed by the Japanese in August-September 1943. The second objective of the narrative is to recount what is known of the activities of Walter Cushing, Roque Ablan, Guillermo Nakar, Manuel Enriquez, Romulo Manriquez, and other leaders of the ephemeral irregular forces in North Luzon.

The principal problem involved in attempting to record the history of Praeger's organization is the simple lack of information. A notation in the U.S. National Archives explains it: "virtually all Troop 'C' records had been destroyed at the time its leaders were captured and the unit dispersed."[1] Moreover, only one American from Praeger's outfit lived through the war, his executive officer, Capt. Thomas S. Jones. Luckily for the historical record, Jones was conversant with everything that had gone on in Troop C and the CAF between December 8, 1941, and his own capture by the enemy on September 4, 1943. Nevertheless, Jones did not keep either a diary or any personal records. To have done so before his capture would have violated army regulations. After his capture he spent much of the rest of the war languishing in Japanese army prisons and prison hospitals. There, even had his health been better, he would not have dared to write anything because he would have had no place to hide it. In his circumstances, it almost certainly would have been discovered by the Japanese. They could then have used the information for their own purposes when dealing with other CAF members who had been captured with Jones and of whose fate Jones had no current knowledge.

To compound difficulties for historians, the CAF was headquartered in jungle-covered mountains in far northern Luzon, in probably the poorest province in the whole Philippines. It was a region so isolated that there was only a horse trail into its "capital city," a hamlet consisting of a few score semiliterate mountaineers. Aside from walking or riding a horse, the CAF's only contacts with the outside world were by a radio that was inoperative much of the time or a telephone line to a CAF outpost on the north coast. Most of the time the CAF had no regular contact with other guerrilla organizations in adjoining provinces.

For all these reasons most of what is known about the day-to-day existence and activities of the Praeger organization comes from a single source: an unpublished seventy-page monograph, entitled "Operations of Troop C, 26th Cavalry Philippine Scouts in Northern Luzon: The First Two Years," which Jones wrote entirely from memory in 1946.

Yet matters are not as dark as they might seem. Thomas Jones was an unusual man. Always an omnivorous reader, in the middle 1930s he was a student at that ancient citadel of British learning, Oxford University. From early youth Jones had also been keenly interested in military affairs, so much so that he enlisted in the 121st Cavalry, New York National Guard, in his teens. In 1935, at the age of twenty, he was commissioned in the Cavalry Reserve. Two years later he enlisted in the Regular Army, fully expecting that general war would break out in Europe no later than the autumn of 1938.[2]

Jones was on the staff of the Philippine Department's headquarters when he was ordered to active duty with the 26th Cavalry in July 1940. He was promoted to captain shortly after the war began in December 1941, and soon became Praeger's executive officer and chief confidant.

He wrote his history of Troop C, 26th Cavalry and the CAF, in February 1946, less than three years after his capture by the Japanese. It was written to fulfill academic requirements at the Cavalry School, Fort Riley, Kansas, where it was scrutinized by knowledgeable and critical people. Although details about many things easily become distorted in human memories, it is probably safe to assume major events witnessed by a thirty-year-old officer of intelligence, experience, and character—events in which he was personally involved—would surely be recalled with general accuracy only three or four years after they occurred.

Two quotations, taken together, from Jones's narrative sum up the essentials of the Filamerican resistance movement in the Philippines during World War II.

> Defeat is a terrible thing. Its full significance cannot be grasped merely through the material losses which are part of it. It brings down with it the whole structure about which a nation or an army has been built. It subjects men to the most severe of moral tests at a time when they are physically least able to meet them. Defeat brings to light weaknesses heretofore unsuspected or ignored so that everyone sees them. Respect is replaced by contempt. Loyalty disintegrates. On the battlefield [human] fear is accepted as natural and passed over, but the failings in character which defeat exposes cannot be passed over.
>
> Leadership, in part, may properly be regarded as an acquired technique under normal circumstances, but it must be rooted in character if it is to survive a major disaster. For it is only the man of character who has the courage to stand fast when everything is crashing around him. He alone possesses the spirit of self sacrifice which is necessary to keep alive the loyalty of his men when disloyalty becomes an everyday occurrence. He alone has the impelling sense of devotion which causes him to discharge his duty as he understands it when the chain of command has been destroyed, in a situation without precedents, when others counsel him to the contrary of what he believes is right. Under normal circumstances, it is difficult to discern the true character of a man, but in the midst of defeat character cannot be concealed.
>
> It was the good fortune of [Troop C, 26th Cavalry] that its commander was a man of character. He held his men together when he had nothing to offer them

except privation and danger. He taught them by his own example the lesson of duty. . . .

Their battle record . . . was inconsiderable in terms of a world war. Yet to achieve even very little made heavy demands on the leadership qualities of the commander. This is not a story of combat successes. Battles cannot be fought and wars won without materiel. Spirit alone is insufficient. The liberation of the Philippines ultimately could be accomplished only by great forces coming from outside those islands. But insofar as their task was made easier during 1942 and 1943 by enemy troops being detained in the Philippines [when they] might have otherwise been used elsewhere, and insofar as the guerrilla forces contributed to the intelligence that made the actual invasion less difficult, the primary credit must go to the Filipino and American leaders . . . who kept alive the spirit of resistance in a conquered country.[3]

None of them typified this spirit better than Captain Ralph Praeger.

That any of the . . . guerrilla bands [who resisted the Japanese in the Philippines were] able to survive and continue resisting . . . during the long years between the fall of Corregidor and the invasion of Leyte [was] due almost solely to the efforts of the ordinary people of the Philippines. They—men, women, and children— made heroic sacrifices to keep the resistance movement alive. Whatever credit may go to the actual guerrillas themselves can never be so great as that which belongs to the civilians who supported them, and who bore the brunt of the enemy's anger and reprisals.[4]

In addition to Jones's account, there are also some scattered archival materials that contain peripheral information about the CAF, radiograms that passed between Praeger in North Luzon and MacArthur's headquarters in Australia, and occasional fleeting references to the CAF in the memoirs and biographies of a few other Luzon guerrillas.

Readers of this account will surely be puzzled, perhaps exasperated, at times by seemingly inconsistent references to the military ranks of persons mentioned in the text. Unhappily, it is unavoidable. Regular Army personnel often had a permanent rank and a temporary (usually higher) one at the same time. Nearly everyone was promoted at least once during the war. Both American and Filipino guerrillas assumed certain ranks on their own, promoted each other, or were promoted by higher authority. Sometimes these promotions were officially recognized after the war; often they were not. Thus it was possible for an individual to have a regular rank, a temporary one, and a guerrilla rank at the same time. Hence reference to the rank of anyone below General MacArthur himself is only approximate.

Anyone who undertakes serious research and writing incurs debts along the way. As noted before, I am particularly indebted to Col. Thomas S. Jones, USA (Ret.), for his memoir. He also helped me greatly by discussing with me his experiences in World War II and answering many questions about guerrilla life in North Luzon. I also owe a great deal to William E. Bowen Jr. of Neenah, Wisconsin, the son of Lt. William E. Bowen, who figures prominently in this account. He suggested this whole subject to me, persistently encouraged me to undertake it, and provided me with materials he had already collected concerning it. I am also grateful to Col. Ralph B. Praeger Jr., USAF (Ret.), who allowed me to use his family's collection of letters, newspaper clippings, and other materials related to Ralph B. Praeger Sr., which had been saved over half a century. I would also like to thank staff members at the National Archives II and the Ernie Pyle Museum for assisting me in research; members of the University of Notre Dame Interlibrary Loan Office for securing books for me; and Cheryl Reed, who has by now typed manuscripts for me so many times that I should list her as coauthor.

Abbreviations

BMA—Bulacan Military Area (district north of Manila dominated by Bernard Anderson's guerrillas)

CAF—Cagayan-Apayao Forces (North Luzon guerrilla force commanded by Ralph Praeger, 1942-1943)

C.G.—Commanding General

CINC—Commander in Chief

C.O.—Commanding Officer

CP—Command Post

DSC—Distinguished Service Cross

ECLGA—East Central Luzon Guerrilla Army (Edwin Ramsey's organization)

GHQ—General Headquarters (usually in reference to MacArthur's SWPA headquarters)

KAZ—Call letters of GHQ SWPA radio station

LGAF—Luzon Guerrilla Armed Forces (Robert Lapham's guerrillas; north central Luzon)

MP—military police

NA II—National Archives II (in College Park, Maryland)

PAC—Philippine Archives Collection (in National Archives II)

PC—Philippine Constabulary (national police force)

PHILRYCOM—U.S. Army Philippine—Ryuku Islands Command

RAG—Records of the Adjutant General's Office (in National Archives II)

RG—Record Group (in National Archives II)

SWPA—Southwest Pacific Area (The geographical area that

included Australia, Guadalcanal, the Philippines, and
environs)

Troop C—Unit of the 26th Cavalry, commanded by Ralph
Praeger, 1941-1943

USAFFE—U.S. Army Forces, Far East (the ground forces
commanded by General MacArthur)

USAFIP—U.S. Army Forces in the Philippines (General
Wainwright's command in the Philippines after
MacArthur departed for Australia, taking the designa-
tion USAFFE with him)

USAFIP NL—U.S. Army Forces in the Philippines, North
Luzon (Guerrilla organization founded by Colonels
Moses and Noble; subsequently commanded by Russell
Volckmann)

USPIF—U.S. Philippine Islands Forces (the Merrill-Calyer
guerrilla forces)

WYY—Call letters of Praeger's radio station (changed to
WWAL in August 1943)

The Guerrilla War Begins

On December 8, 1941, Walter Cushing, the American manager of a gold mine in the mountains of the northern Philippine island of Luzon, heard that the Japanese had launched surprise attacks on U.S. installations at Clark Field, Iba Field, and several other places on the island. Always a volatile man, Cushing was both enraged and outraged. Within two days he began to organize a private army and to make plans to attack the enemy. About a month later he sent for two hundred of his assorted followers, then being given rudimentary military training by a footloose American army officer in Abra Province in north-central Luzon. They were to assemble at Baugen in nearby Ilocos Sur Province on January 14 for the purpose of ambushing a large Japanese convoy.

By the middle of the night on January 18 the troops were moving in previously acquired trucks down Highway 3 to Candon, one of the larger towns in Ilocos Sur. There the main highway went through the center of town. All traffic had to move on it because the high, steep Ilocos Mountains rose immediately to the east. The few Filipinos still living there had been persuaded to leave town the evening before. The guerrillas arrived before dawn and Cushing placed them in all the stores, residences, and other buildings for half a mile along the east side of the road. The Japanese were expected to come in two sections some twenty minutes apart. About 9:00 A.M. the northern outpost signaled that a ten-truck convoy was approaching. When the lead truck reached the center of town a prearranged signal initiated the ambush and everyone fired at once from a distance variously estimated at fifteen to thirty feet—point-blank range. The column was almost annihilated. Trucks were hastily pushed out of sight and corpses carried behind buildings, and the trap was reset. The second enemy group was similarly shot up and all the trucks were burned. The few Japanese who escaped the fusillade fled into nearby fields, where they were dispatched by civilians with bolos, the long, heavy knives Filipinos use to cut sugarcane and for other kinds of light chopping and slashing. Other civilians rushed from hiding places to mutilate the corpses lying in the street. Those who took part in the massacre were exultantly unanimous afterward that the most memorable feature of the whole enterprise was the sight of Cushing himself rushing up and down the street, a .45-caliber pistol in each hand and a stick of dynamite in each rear pants pocket, shouting something like, "Give it to 'em boys! They'd do the same to you." The day was a disaster for the enemy. Sixty-nine were killed, fifty-eight of them air force officers, and fourteen trucks were captured or destroyed. Only one guerrilla was wounded. It was a model guerrilla operation, the heaviest blow the Japanese suffered anywhere in North Luzon in the first month of World War II.

Unfortunately for the victors, an enemy bomber returning from the south observed the second attack and reported it to Japanese forces in Vigan, twenty-five miles north. A larger enemy force soon burned the whole town of Candon and began to chase Cushing. The latter waged a skillful delaying action in which the enemy suffered still more casualties and Cushing's forces escaped with the loss of only one man.[1]

The varied responses of the parties involved in the Candon raid are interesting. Radio Tokyo howled about the hit-and-run tactics of the "sons of bitches" as though Cushing had cheated at some sporting event. Cushing himself, impetuous and filled to bursting with nervous energy, wanted to launch another raid immediately, but his subordinates were simply not up to it. Footsore and weary, they wanted only to rest. Cushing had to console himself with devising a system of detachments to be stationed at various points in and near Ilocos. He planned to attack at one point, then hurriedly leave that detachment and rush with one or two hundred hardened natives to another point, then use them to attack there, thus giving his foes no rest physically and no respite psychologically.

This scheme never got off the ground, but news of the Candon massacre spread rapidly. It made Cushing a hero to Americans and Filipinos alike all over North Luzon, and greatly impressed Col. John P. Horan, who had begun the war as commandant of Camp John Hay at Baguio—the summer capital of the Philippines located high in the mountains 125 miles north of Manila—and who was attempting to establish a guerrilla organization of his own. Horan immediately proclaimed Cushing a major in his guerrilla troop-to-be. Cushing soon began to travel all over Ilocos Sur, Abra, and La Union Provinces, rallying the populace, restoring disrupted local government, and recruiting more guerrillas.

The Japanese, concluding that they must act decisively, launched a four-pronged offensive into Mountain Province to capture the subprovincial capital of Bontoc. One drive was to go through the town of Cervantes in Ilocos Sur. Cushing scouted the town alone at midnight. After learning that several hundred enemy troops would soon be billeted in several concrete buildings, he sat down to await dynamite he had thoughtfully ordered from the Lepanto Mine and which he planned to bury under the buildings. But, before the trap could be sprung, the Japanese underwent one of those puzzling changes of mind for which they were renowned and pulled their troops out of all Mountain Province except Baguio on February 15, 1942. In this case they may have needed the troops to strengthen their forces in New Guinea or the East Indies.

Undaunted, Cushing rushed back to the coast, dynamited some previously destroyed bridges that the Japanese had subsequently repaired, and drove up and down the main highway at times and places when only Japanese military transport ordinarily used the road—all to pick a good place for another ambush. He decided on a stretch of road near Tagudin on Highway 3, well south of Candon. The site seemed ideal: along a high bank covered with tall grass that would hide men easily, between two curves in the road. There, before sunrise on February 19, Cushing placed sixty Filipinos and fifteen Americans in hiding. The men had barely settled when the lookout signaled that three cars were approaching. A murderous rain of fire destroyed the little caravan. To their elation, the guerrillas discovered that they had massacred an enemy command group headed by no less a dignitary than Major General Hara. Hara leaped out of a car during the attack and started to run across a field, where a farmer at work quickly grasped what was happening and killed him with a bolo. Cushing personally bagged two of the enemy.

Because of the eminence of some of the victims it is not surprising that some important papers were found on their bodies and in the wreckage. Other documents were merely enigmatic. Among them were U.S. fire control maps of Bataan and Corregidor, plus a detailed map of Fort Lewis, Washington, and the nearby Puget Sound! Acquisition of these strange documents was merely an introduction to a series of postvictory incongruities reminiscent of a comic opera. Exulting in his personal victory over General Hara, Cushing henceforth wore the yellow patch and silver star of a Japanese major general. Colonel Horan, comparably enthused at the feat of his newly proclaimed subordinate, recommended Cushing for a DSC for the Candon attack and promotion to major for the Tagudin ambush. Two months earlier, HQ USAFFE, then still in Manila, had offered Cushing a commission in the *Philippine* army as a reward for a minor ambush he had staged only a few days after the war began— but subject to the condition that Cushing come to Manila to get it! It was a ridiculous proposal since the Japanese controlled all of Highway 3 from Manila to Tagudin in Ilocos Sur. Now, in February 1942, Horan was insisting that Cushing had always been a member of the U.S. Army, a stance USAFFE had neither formally affirmed nor disapproved. What to do? MacArthur's headquarters did not fall between the proverbial two horses. Instead, it resolutely mounted both: It rejected a DSC for Cushing because he was a *civilian,* then made him a captain because he hadn't been in the army long enough to be a major.

Happily, Cushing's men fared better than their leader. Many

of them were barefoot and all of them were short of clothing. After the Tagudin ambush they were allowed to replenish their wardrobes by looting the vanquished and their vehicles.

The author of these spectacularly successful ambushes was the most flamboyant of all the guerrilla leaders in North Luzon in World War II and, for the first nine months of the war, the most successful.

Walter Cushing was born in 1907 in El Paso, Texas, the son of an American mining engineer. His mother was of Spanish descent. From her came his distinctively Mediterranean appearance (five-foot-five with a swarthy complexion) and his fluency in Spanish, which made it possible for him to pass for a Filipino many times early in World War II. He spent his early years with his family around mines in Mexico and Texas, then moved to Los Angeles, where he was a good high school athlete. Energetic, imaginative, adventuresome, and utterly fearless, he spent the latter part of the 1920s roaming the United States and working at such unorthodox occupations as parachute jumper for a barnstorming pilot, rivet bucker on a skyscraper, and diver on a Mississippi River pier and bridge construction project. He eventually applied for pilot training in the U.S. Army Air Corps but was washed out because he had secretly gotten married. At the bottom of the depression he worked at odd jobs around Los Angeles, even entering a boxing tournament to make a few extra dollars. In 1933 he used his last fifty dollars to bribe a steward on the SS *President Hoover* to take him on as a waiter, but jumped ship in the Philippines and joined an older brother who had earlier gone there to take part in the mining boom. Enthusiastic as ever, totally honest, and increasingly fond of drinking parties, Walter Cushing soon made a host of friends.[2]

His hyperactivity came to an abrupt halt for a time in the late 1930s when his wife divorced him. Despondent, he began to drink more heavily. One night he joined the French Foreign Legion, but the next morning he sobered up sufficiently to jump his enlistment and thereby barely avoid being shipped to Saigon. Friends soon revived his interest in mining and, in 1940, he became a partner with Maurice B. Ordun in the Rainbow Mine, a gold-mining operation in Abra. Ordun knew Cushing well, both as a mining partner and from being in the same military unit with him during the early months of the war. They went through all kinds of experiences together, and Ordun came to admire Cushing greatly.

When the Japanese in Ilocos Sur Province occupied Vigan on December 10, 1941, Walter Cushing's immediate instinctive response was to fight back. Within two days he organized some two hundred volunteers from among his mining employees, collected arms and ammunition from nearby hastily abandoned Philippine army training camps, hauled it all into his mine, and began to personally scout the coast around Vigan in an effort to detect enemy movements. At Bangued, the capital of Abra, he met two Philippine army officers in charge of the cadre there. He tried to convince them to move their arms, ammunition, and equipment into nearby mines, and also to permit him to destroy the bridges on Highway 3 south of Vigan. The officers, suspecting that Cushing might be a fifth columnist, refused to cooperate. Disgusted, he resumed his trip to the coast, intending to blow the bridges on his own. It was only with considerable difficulty that his friend and partner Ordun, who was with him, was able to dissuade Cushing by pointing out that General MacArthur might well have his own plans for dealing with the Japanese in Vigan. If these required the American army to use bridges Cushing had blown, he might well be executed by American forces, Ordun feared.

No doubt sobered somewhat by this consideration, Cushing contented himself with rescuing two American pilots who had been shot down over Abra Province and leading them over the mountains to a place where they could get transportation to Baguio. He would have been less than human, too, if he had not derived a certain rueful satisfaction from seeing the Japanese push south from Vigan on December 21. They used the bridges Cushing had wanted to destroy to roll up the right flank of Allied defenders in the Lingayen Gulf region. Meantime, back in Bengued, the Philippine officers who had denied him permission to destroy the bridges were sufficiently frightened by the sight of an advancing column of enemy troops that they hastily deserted their post, leaving men and supplies behind. Some of their cadre, having more courage and presence of mind than their superiors, managed to carry the arms and equipment into the hills, where Cushing's men eventually recovered them.

Now Cushing decided to head for the coast again. On the way he encountered Lt. Robert Arnold and thirty-two hungry, bedraggled men of the U.S. air warning unit stationed at Cape Bojeador on the northwest tip of Luzon. They too had refused to surrender, and took to the mountains and jungle in the vain hope of somehow getting to Bataan. The two groups gladly joined forces. Cushing, who had no formal military training, at once turned his men over to Arnold to give them such training.

With five Filipinos, Cushing continued to reconnoiter the Ilocos coast. He soon heard that the Japanese had murdered and raped on an appalling scale in Vigan. Enraged, he and his men set an ambush for a truck loaded with Japanese troops near Narvacan in Ilocos Sur Province. Twelve of the fourteen Japanese on board were killed. Two survived to report the ambush to their garrison commander at Vigan on New Year's Day 1942. It was his elation at the success of this operation that led Cushing to plan the more extensive Candon and Tagudin massacres.

After the Tagudin ambush, the indefatigable Cushing traveled all over northwestern Luzon to personally dynamite bridges. For good measure he terrorized the Japanese garrison in Bangued by throwing dynamite through the windows of the men's sleeping quarters, forcing them for a time to spend their nights in foxholes. The enemy never knew how many men he had at his disposal, but since he vexed them in so many places, they were sure the number must be great. In response they sent as many as seven thousand troops to comb Abra Province for him during April 1942.[3]

Cushing's ingenuity was remarkable. "When . . . [he] heard that the Japanese had stored a lot of captured arms and ammunition in an Ilocos Norte warehouse, he had several Igorot tribesmen . . . crawl thru the line of Japanese guards, get under the warehouse, cut thru the bamboo floor with their bolos and lower 124 cases of ammunition thru the hole. Others would put the cases on their chests, lie on their backs and crawl back thru the line of guards. Others would then place the cases on their heads and carry them back into the mountains. About 150,000 rounds of Cal. 30 amm." were thus secured.[4]

One of Cushing's most spectacular coups took place on April 17, 1942, when he ambushed a company of the Japanese 122nd Infantry near Balbalasang in Kalinga Province. Although the regular guerrillas who operated near Balbalasang were off gathering supplies in the lowlands, some rifles were available. These were given to mere boys of twelve to fourteen. Cushing did not want to use them but the local strongman, "Captain" Puyao, insisted that by tribal standards they were fighting men and promised they would perform well. Each of them had about ten rounds of ammunition, mostly Japanese. The ambush was laid at night. The enemy, overconfident and unheeding, as they often were early in the war, marched into a defile in a column of fours. The ambushers opened fire, inflicting substantial casualties on the leading elements. Meanwhile, a Japanese company in the rear tried to outflank the guerrillas but became confused in the dark and opened fire on its own advance guard instead. Cushing then had his "men" withdraw. When Cpl. Louis G. Heuser, who played a prominent role in the operation, ordered the boys in his squad to pull out, one of them objected stoutly that he still had two rounds of ammunition left. The intramural battle among the Japanese continued until an estimated 160 of the enemy were killed. If the whole engagement demonstrated anything, it was the accuracy of an observation by Lt. Robert Arnold that half the casualties in war are due to mere blundering.[5] The aftermath also illustrated the psychological gulf between Japanese and Occidentals. Their propaganda section promptly issued a warning that all persons involved in the Balbalasang ambush would be executed—not because they had fought the Japanese but because they "were cowards who had run away," thereby causing the Japanese to fight among themselves![6]

After the fall of Corregidor Cushing realized the futility of further hit-and-run operations for the time being, so he scattered his officers among several camps in the mountains of Abra, Ilocos Sur, and La Union Provinces and turned to propaganda warfare. Cushing had three radio sets salvaged from mines. These he used to pick up news daily from San Francisco, which he then published in a daily typewritten newspaper, The Echo of the Free North. The paper circulated widely, served to keep his now scattered followers in touch with his headquarters in Abra, and counteracted much enemy propaganda for the rest of 1942.

By June, a combination of restlessness and ambition set him off, alone, on his travels once more. This time he intended to go all over central and southern Luzon, contact other guerrilla outfits of whose existence he had only recently heard, and promote cooperation among them. His bravado in travel was equaled only by his resourcefulness. He crossed Lingayen Gulf in a small sailboat at night, hitched a ride on an alcohol tank truck across Tarlac Province because the vehicle was seldom checked at sentry posts, hid under a truckload of mangos as it passed several sentry posts in Pampanga, and everywhere employed his knowledge of Spanish to smooth his way with Spanish speakers, who were dependably pro-American. Once, while he was having tea in the house of a friendly Spaniard, the latter had a sudden unexpected visit from four Japanese officers. Cushing hastily hid in a bedroom. News that there was an American nearby had already gotten onto "the world's fastest means of communication, the Philippine bamboo telegraph." Soon twelve little girls arrived to sing "God Bless America" for him in front of the house. Fortunately, the Japanese did not know English. Assuming that the serenade was for them, they applauded heartily.

When he at length reached Manila, Cushing procured three sets of identification papers that showed him to be—as occasion might require—a Filipino of Spanish extraction, an Italian mestizo, or a priest. Relying on these plus his generally Latin appearance, he brazenly traveled all over the Philippine capital in public conveyances, greeting people he knew and being recognized by many others. Once his hotel was raided and he escaped only by hiding for two days and nights on its rooftop in the rain. Another time he was recognized by a Japanese officer with whom he had had prewar business contacts, but he managed to weave a story sufficiently plausible to get away long enough to check into a Japanese-managed hotel where no one would look for him. Another time he was involved in a minor traffic accident and was arrested and sent to Fort Santiago, where he was questioned by the Japanese for half a day but once more managed to talk his way out of trouble.

His purpose in the capital was to contact various wealthy Filipinos he knew and persuade them to give him money to buy munitions, medicines, and radios sorely needed by both bur-geoning guerrilla groups and American prisoners of war who had escaped from the Japanese and were now hidden in the Zambales Mountains or other highland fastnesses. Surprising stocks of such goods were available because Manila teemed with Japanese officers who lived like rich playboys off the money and valuables they had stolen from their various captives. As these funds ran low, they sought to continue their sybaritic life by selling every sort of military equipment seized from the defeated Allied troops. In short order Cushing was able to secure through Fili-pino intermediaries a large truck loaded with automatic rifles and ammunition, four complete radio sets, many cases of medi-cines, and twenty-two American soldiers who had been given refuge in Manila churches. Heading back northward, Cushing gradually distributed this largesse—plus four Filipino doctors—to an assortment of irregular organizations along the way, once more talking himself out of numerous tight spots with the aid of Filipino guards and sentries employed by the Japanese.

Back in Abra for the first time in three months, Captain Cushing was bursting with enthusiasm to organize all the guer-rilla bands on Luzon and make plans to assist future American landings by attacking the Japanese from the rear. His officers repeatedly reminded him that no satisfactory communication sys-tem yet existed on Luzon, that ordinary Filipino civilians were growing increasingly war weary, and that Japanese pressure was rising steadily. He impatiently brushed aside their objections and set off in September to visit Capt. Ralph Praeger's guerrilla head-quarters at Kabugao in the mountains of far northern Luzon. Cushing had heard that Praeger had a much better radio than any of his own. He was eager to gain access to it, both to learn the latest war news from Australia and to transmit to MacArthur's headquarters there all he had learned during his three-month excursion to the southern half of Luzon. On September 8, 1942, Cushing walked into Kabugao accompanied by two of his sub-ordinate officers from the 121st Infantry, Lts. W.B. Ordun and William N.L. Arthur.

To those in Kabugao who had known Walter Cushing before the war he seemed a man possessed, one of those rare individuals like Gen. George S. Patton Jr. and Marine air ace Gregory "Pappy" Boyington who are positively exhilarated by war. If proof was needed, was it not evident that in his anxiety to contact Praeger he had outwalked all his companions in his trek over the mountains from Abra to Kabugao? Moreover, Cushing seemed to care nothing for his own life. Still, he was no monomaniac. He might appear impulsive, but he planned his actions and did them for a purpose. When Corregidor fell he had dispersed his troops because he saw nothing to gain in the near future by fighting. When he did plan ambushes, he always took into account his men's limitations. Most of them were young—often *very* young—and inexperienced. Few had ever fired a rifle save in battle. Hence he planned ambushes in places where his rifle-men would be within point-blank range of the enemy when they fired their first volley. At that distance even the most inexperienced man could hardly miss—or, if his nerve failed, pull out before he had at least tried to kill the last enemy soldier in front of him. A frustrated Japanese officer once complained to a German missionary in Abra that Cushing was unfathomable, invisible, and that attempts to kill or catch him had produced only Japanese casualties. It seemed that no matter what tactics the Japanese tried, the phantom Cushing and his "bandits" always escaped.[7]

Ten days before Cushing arrived in Kabugao he slipped into a Japanese cantonment at Laganglang in Ilocos Sur Province, virtually under their noses. He had gone there to visit Colonel Horan, who was being held by the Japanese to read Lt. Gen. Jonathan M. Wainwright's surrender order to a forced assembly. Cushing wanted to discuss with Horan his own plans for uniting all the guerrillas on Luzon, and to make plans with Horan for the latter's escape. Horan was unreceptive, saying that he was bound to obey Wainwright's orders. Cushing said *he* refused to surrender, then left with only a message from Horan to send to MacArthur, and proceeded to Kabugao. Cushing was not acting on an impulsive desire to see Praeger. He wanted to use Praeger's radio to establish regular contacts with Australia before proceeding to the headquarters of Guillermo Nakar, then the most important guerrilla leader in Isabela Province. Cushing had heard that there existed in a lighthouse on the Isabela coast a powerful radio transmitter that he hoped to get for himself. Whether he got it or not, he would then go to Pampanga to meet Col. Claude Thorp, sent out by General MacArthur in January 1942 to be titular chief of all the Luzon guerrillas. Together they would set up an intelligence and communications net among all the irregular groups.[8]

Cushing left Kabugao on September 14 or 15 accompanied by three Filipino soldiers. He knew that near his destination of Jones in Isabela Province, a Japanese regiment was embroiled in a duel with Nakar's forces. He was also warned that much pro-Japanese sentiment existed among Filipinos in that sector, but he considered his mission too important to cancel. There are several versions of what happened to Cushing in Isabela. According to Capt. Albert Hendrickson, an area commander in Robert Lapham's LGAF,[9] and Capt. Thomas Jones,[10] Praeger's executive officer, Cushing and his companions were ambushed by a Japanese patrol and died without ever seeing the men who fired at them—just as five hundred to a thousand Japanese had perished in Cushing's many ambushes. Other accounts say Cushing and his guerrillas were invited into a farmhouse for dinner near the town of Jones and died dramatically on the house's veranda in a gun battle with enemy soldiers who had quietly surrounded it, Cushing saving his last bullet for himself.[11] An interesting variation on the last point is provided by Colonel Horan. He says that when Cushing saw that he was surrounded and doomed he played dead until several Japanese approached him. Then he killed six of them, saving the last bullet for himself.[12]

There is also disagreement about what happened immediately after Cushing's death. One of his three bodyguards escaped. One version is that the man then persuaded enough local loyal Filipinos to kill every Filipino involved in the betrayal of Cushing plus every member of their families, and then to burn down all their houses for good measure.[13] One has to view this claim with some skepticism if only because a virtually identical story was circulated about the fate of those who allegedly betrayed Praeger and his companions a year later. Captain Jones says that the bodyguard who escaped did not rouse the countryside at all but was so overcome by guilt at having lived when the man he was supposed to protect had been killed that his mind was affected, that many months passed before he was even able to give a coherent account of what had happened on that fatal day.[14]

Walter Cushing's military career lasted only nine months, but his fiery personality, reckless courage, and unfailing panache made an indelible impression on friend and foe alike. Many ordinary Filipinos refused to accept that he was dead, and a year later there were still some Japanese who could hardly believe that the seemingly invulnerable little man who had foiled them so many times and killed so many of them had been slain by a small patrol of their own. They were so impressed by the manner of his life and death, so like their own code of Bushido, that they gave him a formal military funeral and an honorable burial in the churchyard of Jones, Isabela. So ended the career of the most extravagantly admired guerrilla in North Luzon. It was a heavy psychological blow to all the guerrillas there.

Early in the war many other aspiring guerrilla chieftains were similarly active in several parts of northern Luzon. They ran the gamut from patriot-heroes to conniving scoundrels.

Perhaps the most attractive of these leaders was Roque B. Ablan, the young governor of Ilocos Norte Province in extreme northwestern Luzon. Like Walter Cushing, he began to resist the Japanese from the first day of the war. When the enemy landed on December 10, 1941, they occupied an airfield near Laoag, Ablan's capital, and called on the governor to surrender. Ablan replied by seizing arms and ammunition from Camp Juan near Laoag at 4:00 A.M. December 12 when the Japanese were only a mile and a half away.[15] He then withdrew some fifteen to twenty miles into the mountains near Solsona, where he established a provisional government and cached his arms. As soon as his government was operating, Ablan traveled from town to town urging people to resist the invaders. He also collected a melange of USAFFE stragglers whom he hoped to organize and train for guerrilla warfare. In January 1942 he met Feliciano Madamba, a lieutenant in the Philippine army whose unit had been cut off while attempting to withdraw into Bataan. Ablan was impressed with Madamba and on January 27 gave him all the cached arms and put him in charge of forming a military unit from the stragglers. Madamba struck the very next day. The Japanese had sent truckloads of troops off onto mountain roads all over Ilocos Norte in an effort to find Ablan, an action that left them open to ambush. Madamba caught a Japanese column of fifty men driving down the road toward Solsona. The attack was a stunning success: the enemy was virtually wiped out.[16] Enraged, the local Japanese commandant, Major Kamatsu, the highest ranking Japanese officer in Ilocos Norte, personally led another force to retaliate. It too was ambushed, near Banna. Kamatsu, two junior officers, and most of the Japanese private soldiers were killed. The guerrillas then rubbed in their triumph by stripping Kamatsu's corpse and tying it to a post to simultaneously mock and avenge the sexual abuse heaped on Filipino women by Japanese soldiers. This time the Japanese responded by bombing and strafing several mountain villages, executing twenty civilians at Banna, and taking others hostage. They barely missed capturing Mrs. Ablan. She saved herself and a small party by fleeing into the jungle and leaving behind a basket of eggs along a mountain trail. As she had doubtless hoped, the enemy took the bait. The Japanese soldiers stopped to eat the eggs, and the governor's wife got away.

This savagery merely caused other USAFFE nomads and many civilians to join the guerrillas and unite nearly all the people of Ilocos Norte behind their governor. Though unpaid since the war began, all the provincial officials from the highest to the most humble loyally stayed at their posts.[17]

Early in March Ablan learned that Captain Praeger had a radio transmitter somewhere in Apayao. He at once hiked over the mountains to Kabugao and on March 10 sent a message to Philippine president Manuel L. Quezon, then on Panay awaiting evacuation to Australia. It breathed defiance of the Japanese, described their atrocities, claimed that Ablan's and other guerrillas had already killed six hundred of the enemy, and urgently requested arms, ammunition, supplies, medicines, and a hundred thousand pesos in small bills so faithful public employees could be paid. Quezon replied regretfully that it was impossible to send either money or medicine, but praised Ablan's actions, urged him to continue his resistance, and authorized him to print his own money.[18]

Never one to waste time, Ablan immediately notified his people of Quezon's instructions. The information spread rapidly. Unquestionably its most important result was to cause many small, independent guerrilla groups composed of Filipino men and American officers to join Ablan's organization. This made it possible for one overall commander, Ablan himself, to deal effectively with one of the worst problems that bedeviled guerrilla resistance in the Philippines in the first half of 1942: The existence of scores of small bands of irregulars, often little better than bandits, who badgered the Japanese occasionally but spent more of their time robbing, raping, or murdering hapless Filipino civilians. When such groups joined his own force, the governor was able to impose uniform discipline on all of them. The merger also increased the size of his following and made him a more serious threat to the Japanese.

Ablan then went back over the mountains and called a conference of his main government officials and guerrilla followers to map out a plan for future systematic resistance and build an organization to maintain it. This task was less difficult than might be supposed. Like Marcelo Adduru, his colleague in Cagayan, Ablan had been unusually sensitive to the war clouds gathering in 1940-1941 and had begun to make detailed plans to defend his people if war came. Among many preparatory actions he had made up mobilization orders and, in August 1941, had actually begun to train guerrillas.[19] Thus, with war indubitably underway, Ablan was able to act quickly. He assumed formal command of the guerrillas with Lieutenant Madamba as his executive officer. He then divided the province into sectors, each with its own guerrilla unit, printed emergency currency to pay back salaries and present expenses, established a Relief Committee to look after the destitute, set up a system of relay runners to transmit news from village to village where there were no roads, and worked up one network to collect intelligence and another to disseminate news that would counteract Japanese propaganda. A flood of directives to implement these and many other similar decisions went out to provincial officials in the spring of 1942.[20] One wonders what success the energetic and resourceful Ablan might have enjoyed had he been located in a richer and more populous part of Luzon—and had he had better luck.

When Corregidor fell in May 1942 and Lieutenant General Wainwright ordered all USAFFE forces in the Philippines to surrender, the Japanese launched an intensive propaganda campaign to induce guerrillas to surrender as well. Various prominent persons were brought in to make public speeches urging that course. Among them were the collaborator Emilio Medina, later a puppet governor of Ilocos Norte; Gen. Artemio Ricarte, a lifelong friend of Japan and the only Filipino officer who had refused to surrender to the Americans in 1903; and even Colonel Horan, who had surrendered on orders from Wainwright. Realizing Ablan's popularity with his people, the Japanese promised to let him remain as governor of Ilocos Norte if he would surrender.

Ablan remained adamant. He scorned all overtures and continued to defy the conquerors. The enemy then changed tactics. They made it a crime punishable by torture or death to possess any of Ablan's paper money, and offered a huge reward to anyone who would betray Ablan or Madamba to them. They also brought in hundreds of troops to systematically hunt down the governor. Ablan replied by withdrawing farther back into the interior, from where he pointed out that his war notes had been authorized by Quezon, numbered serially, and signed by provincial officials, whereas the invasion currency being forced onto people by the Japanese would soon be worthless because it had neither signatures nor serial numbers. He urged everyone to continue to resist.

Hit-and-run raids and ambushes went on sporadically in the mountains for many months. The Japanese were repeatedly bloodied at Badoc, Batac (ironically, the home town of Artemio Ricarte), Pasquin, Laoag, Bacarra, and the aforementioned Banna. These successes were supplemented by guerrilla destruction of enemy telephone lines, gasoline dumps, warehouses, bridges, and other militarily useful installations or supplies. The enemy replied everywhere with fire and sword, torture and rape.

By October 1942 Ablan had regained control of all the towns in Ilocos Norte save Laoag and San Nicolas. The Japanese then imported a thousand troops to force a showdown. Ablan learned of it, established a strong defensive position at Pananniki, and in a subsequent battle slaughtered 150 Nipponese at a cost of only two of his own men.[21] Clearly, his careful prewar planning was paying handsome dividends. Exultant, Ablan delivered an impassioned call for increased resistance to an enthusiastic crowd at Sanchez Mira on Rizal Day (a national holiday),[22] and at nearby Claveria on Christmas Day.[23]

Unhappily, these triumphs proved illusory. Japanese strength was simply too great. Ablan's forces were chronically short of food, arms, ammunition, and supplies of every sort, and savage Japanese reprisals were sapping civilian morale. The troops were also growing exhausted from the constant fighting, and their numbers dwindled steadily from the eight hundred of midsummer 1942. In January 1943, Ablan's wife and son were captured. Soon after, Madamba—by far Ablan's ablest field commander— succumbed to the blandishments of Quintin Paredes, a prewar neighbor of Madamba's and member of the puppet Japanese Philippine Republic, and surrendered to the Japanese.[24] Soon the enemy were retaking town after town. They burned Ablan's guerrilla capital and wreaked a terrible vengeance on the families of his men. Ablan himself managed to escape into Abra Province, where he organized a new guerrilla band. But, by the end of January 1943, spies and collaborators revealed his hideout at Vinter. The Japanese promptly raided it. Once more Ablan managed to escape but he was never officially heard of again.[25] Perhaps he was killed by a Japanese patrol. Perhaps a collaborator turned him in for the reward money and the enemy disposed of him quietly soon after. Possibly headhunters got him. One of his followers thought he had been kidnapped by an unknown party of Filipinos.[26] There were rumors that Jose Laurel, president of the Japanese-supported Philippine Republic, personally went to Ilocos Norte early in 1943 to try to persuade Ablan to lay down his arms. But he had vanished—utterly—and by the end of April 1943 the last remnants of his government had vanished with him. An able, brave, and honorable man, Roque Ablan is the only early guerrilla leader whose fate remains unknown.[27]

After Ablan's disappearance, his widow and Pedro Alviar, who had been his intelligence and propaganda chief, tried to maintain resistance against the invaders. Their efforts consisted mainly of printing a clandestine newspaper of world events obtained from shortwave radio, an endeavor of some utility though American officers investigating guerrilla claims after the war did not think it sufficiently important to warrant recognition of Ablan's command as an official guerrilla organization, particularly since many of Ablan's followers subsequently joined Col. Russell Volckmann's USAFIP NL farther south, and were so recognized in that organization. Moreover, the investigators became convinced that Mrs. Ablan's strenuous efforts to secure such recognition were motivated largely by her own postwar political ambitions. As for Pedro Alviar, the Japanese eventually caught him—as they caught so many. He was executed December 13, 1944.[28] Thus did Roque Ablan and all his works pass out of history.

2

The Philippines in 1941

Of all the guerrilla organizations that operated in the far north of Luzon, the one that lasted longest was Troop C, 26th Cavalry—which was subsequently expanded and renamed the Cagayan-Apayao Forces (CAF). The CAF did not become a true guerrilla force as early as did the irregular bands of either Walter Cushing or Roque Ablan, but its achievements were more impressive. Most of this narrative is devoted to it. To render its deeds and its eventual failure more understandable, something should be said of the state of the Philippines in 1941, of American unpreparedness for war in the Pacific, and of the character and personality of the leader of the CAF, Capt. Ralph Praeger.

Luzon is the largest, richest, most populous, and most advanced of the seven thousand islands that compose the Philippine Archipelago. By early December 1941 the Japanese had made detailed plans for its conquest. They would launch surprise air attacks on all the major airfields on Luzon, and on U.S. naval forces in the region. Almost simultaneously they would land thousands of ground troops at Aparri, the major port city at the mouth of the Cagayan River on the north coast of Luzon, and at Gonzaga, another port thirty-five miles east; at Vigan, the capital of Ilocos Sur Province on the northwest coast; and on the Legaspi Peninsula in extreme southern Luzon. Each of these contingents would seize U.S. airfields, destroy any naval forces that had escaped the air attacks, and then move rapidly toward Manila from the north and south. In about ten days they would be reinforced by a much larger force that would be landed at Lingayen Gulf midway down Luzon's west coast and then fight its way down Luzon's central plain. Two to three weeks after the initial air assaults, the Japanese envisioned that a decisive battle would be fought near Manila. It would end in overwhelming Japanese victory, with Manila being taken and only mopping up remaining.

For about three weeks after December 8 everything went much as the Japanese had planned. Just why has never been adequately explained and probably never will be. In the first week of December the American high command expected a Japanese attack at any time, and even had an accurate idea of where it would fall. On December 3 General Douglas MacArthur appointed Maj. Gen. Jonathan Wainwright commander of the newly organized North Luzon Force, with orders to resist any invasion of the island.[1] Yet on the morning of December 8 most of the U.S. Far East Air Force was destroyed on the ground at Clark and Iba Fields, and the barracks at Camp John Hay was bombed. How was that possible when authorities in all three places had known for hours that Pearl Harbor had been bombed? Efforts to establish who should be blamed, and in what degree, have long since proved fruitless—mired in a swamp of accusations, recriminations, conflicting testimony, and missing records, as highly placed people in both Washington and the Philippines sought to exonerate themselves or others.

A bare description of the state of radar, radio, and lesser communications equipment when the war began goes far to explain why everything went so badly for the Allies early in the war. Radar was a new device in 1941. The first few sets to arrive in the Philippines in October-November were large, heavy, and complicated. Often they had been inadequately packed or protected from sea water. They were subject to tropical moisture and rot, and they lacked spare parts. Operators were scarce and required much training to become effective. When Japanese planes began to appear on December 8, radar signals bounced off mountains, causing the plotting of early flights to become hopelessly muddled with subsequent flights.

This state of affairs was merely a local reflection of the chaos that engulfed the entire communications industry right before the war and in its early weeks. Hordes of manufacturers descended on Washington seeking contracts to build communications equipment—at a time when the whole Signal Corps was in the throes of a vast and rapid expansion. The result was a plethora of incompletely filled orders, substandard equipment, missing parts, and outraged troops in the field. Great numbers of men were drafted into the Signal Corps. Many of them had neither interest in nor aptitude for highly skilled technical work, so the Corps was soon replete with misfits and incompetents. On the other hand, the most skilled people were being sought simultaneously by the army as instructors of newcomers, as administrators, and to serve in the most important war areas; by the U.S. government as inspectors to try to assure high quality in production; and by private industry. Amateur radio operators wanted choice assignments and Hollywood movie companies vied for reserve commissions for their executives and technicians so they could one day help the film industry. Factories had to be built, workers trained, raw materials acquired, priorities established, revisions of needs made, and authority allocated among the dozens of federal committees and commissions that had to examine and approve everything. It is a wonder that even a pair of field glasses ever actually got to the Philippines.[2]

General MacArthur's critics, enthusiastically supported by his ideological enemies, have long blamed him for everything that went wrong in the Philippines before the war and for the succession of debacles that preceded the fall of Bataan and Corregidor.[3] The general's aides and admirers have responded by emphasizing the hopeless unpreparedness of U.S. and Philippine forces in the islands. They have pointed out that U.S. forces of all sorts were far too few, and even those were armed with obsolete weapons; that Corregidor's defenses were inadequate; that defense plans everywhere were outdated; that Philippine army troops had been so hastily raised and poorly trained that they knew little beyond close order drill; that these troops were commanded by native officers who were far too often political appointees; that the Philippine navy was composed entirely of patrol boats manufactured in England and so were unavailable for further supply once the European war began in 1939; and, more broadly, that a consequence of the strong isolationist spirit in the United States between the wars had been general indifference to the Philippines expressed by niggardly congressional appropriations for their defense. A Philippine Scout who joined the 26th Cavalry at Fort Stotsenburg in January 1941 remarked that anyone who had been in the Philippines for any length of time sat down as much as possible. Any needless expenditure of energy was frowned upon.[4]

MacArthur, his defenders point out, was aware of all these (and many other) ruinous shortcomings, was vigorously attacking them in 1941, and would have set them right eventually, but the Nipponese hurricane swept over before he was able to do more than make a start. What is incontestable is that all U.S. defense plans were rendered obsolete by the destruction of the U.S. Pacific Fleet at Pearl Harbor, for now no substantial U.S. aid could reach the islands in the foreseeable future.

North of its rich rice- and sugar-producing central plain, Luzon is forbidding country. Along the east coast the Sierra Madre mountain range stretches up to the north coast. Virtually roadless and thinly populated, in the 1940s portions of it were still unexplored. Except for a strip of lowland a mere ten miles wide along the coast, the whole western half of North Luzon consists of the Cordillera Central, a wilderness of crisscrossing mountain ranges whose highest peaks reach nearly ten thousand feet. All are separated from others by turbulent streams at the bottoms of canyons hundreds, sometimes even thousands, of feet deep. Many of these are extremely steep, with sidewall slopes of sixty degrees or more. In the 1940s many scattered barrios in this primeval wilderness could be reached only by obscure mountain trails. Between the two mountain masses lies the Cagayan Valley, 120 miles long and forty miles wide, down which the Cagayan River flows north to the sea at Aparri. This valley is the principal food-producing area of North Luzon.

The island of Luzon north of Manila is a bit smaller than Indiana. Available to defend it were three Philippine army divisions—the 11th, 21st, and 31st—a battalion of the 45th Infantry, two batteries of 155mm artillery, one battery of 2.95-inch mountain guns, and the 26th Cavalry.[5] Of these forces, only the 26th Cavalry and 45th Infantry, composed of Philippine Scouts, were both formidable and reliable—but they were not numerous.

Before the war General MacArthur had anticipated a major enemy landing at Lingayen Gulf, and had devised a plan to confront it. Due to the skimpiness of his forces, no serious defense of Luzon north of the Gulf was contemplated. Instead, the focus was on fighting a delaying action by slowly falling back to five successive defensive positions between the Gulf and the Bataan Peninsula.

Given this general situation, what happened after the initial enemy landings in the far north is not hard to understand. The Cagayan Valley contained a single Philippine army infantry battalion headquartered at Tuguegarao, the capital of Cagayan Province. One of its three companies was fifty miles downriver at Aparri, under the command of a young reserve officer, Lt. Alvin G. Hadley. When the Japanese landed two companies at Aparri, Hadley simply retreated upriver without firing a shot. The enemy, unmolested, reached Tuguegarao on his heels two days later, December 10.[6] Meanwhile, at Vigan—located in Ilocos Sur Province on the west coast, where there were no American or Philippine ground troops at all—the Japanese encountered considerable trouble with a rough sea and suffered some damage when harassed by a few U.S. planes but otherwise disembarked two thousand men without incident on December 10. Some of the invaders promptly began to march north along the coast road (Highway 3) to link up with a small party they had put ashore unopposed at Laoag. Others started southward down the same highway toward Lingayen Gulf, where they expected to meet a major invasion force some eleven to twelve days later.

That main Japanese landing—forty-three thousand men of Gen. Masaharu Homma's Fourteenth Army, with equipment and supplies—began along the northeast shore of Lingayen Gulf on December 22. The invaders *should have* suffered devastating casualties when a U.S. submarine managed to get in among eighty-five troop transports. Although rumors circulated that the submarine's captain was reluctant to draw attention to himself by firing his torpedoes, it likely would have made little difference had he recklessly fired them all. Early in the war, U.S. submarines that did fire their torpedoes discovered that most of them had defective fuzes and would either dive under their targets or fail to detonate on contact. Such were the fruits of congressional attempts at "saving" on pre-war military expenditures, a cost-cutting effort so diligent that many submarine commanders were not even allowed to fire torpedoes in training.[7] Col. Ernest B. Miller, commander of the 194th Tank Battalion, enraged by the gross unpreparedness of Americans and Filipinos for war and all the blundering that followed, fumed that all those Americans who had kept the nation weak between the wars by parroting "there must never be another war . . . are morally guilty of murder."[8]

Though the Filamericans were not caught by surprise, the invaders encountered more trouble from bad weather and the foul-ups inseparable from war than they did from the defenders. The poorly trained Philippine army units broke and ran in the face of the Japanese onslaught. According to one disgusted American officer, each man (regardless of rank) fleeing from the battlefront told the same story: He had been fighting bravely against terrible odds but had been deserted by his leaders and left to face enemy bombs or tanks alone. Then he was either taken prisoner and escaped, or managed to hide in the dark. At last, tired and hungry, he reported in and asked for a transfer to the Motor Transport Corps to drive a truck.[9] In fairness to these Filipino troops, that officer should have added that they were hardly encouraged when most of their .30-caliber machine gun firing mechanisms were clogged by faulty ammunition.

Neither should it be concluded from these farcical performances that Filipinos are cowards, incapable of becoming good soldiers. The truth was that most Philippine army troops were short-term conscripts commanded by inexperienced Filipino reserve officers. Officers and men alike had received so little training that they were hardly more than civilians in uniform.

They bore no resemblance to the Philippine Scouts, an elite group of volunteers made up of high school graduates who spoke and wrote English well. Moreover, the Scouts had been training seriously for years in the U.S. Army. Alert, courteous, neat in appearance, and skilled with weapons, they were the bravest and best-disciplined troops on the island of Luzon. But even among the Philippine army greenhorns who fled in panic in December 1941 were many who later became guerrillas. They soon became accustomed to considerable practical (as distinguished from formal) military training, learned to handle and take care of weapons, and became habituated to danger and violence. When the regular U.S. Army at length returned to Luzon in January 1945, many of those who had fled in fright three years before had transformed. They rejoined the American forces and fought courageously in the reconquest of Luzon.

When the Japanese came ashore at Lingayen Gulf, one of their objectives was to seize the Philippine summer capital of Baguio, some thirty miles distant and five thousand feet up in the mountains. Two paved highways linked Baguio to the coast, Naguilian Road to the northwest and Kennon Road to the southwest. To block these roads was the obvious first task of Lt. Col. John P. Horan, commandant of Camp John Hay at Baguio. Horan was an amiable man of routine competence in the peacetime army but not one who would have reminded an observer of Hannibal or Napoleon. Many Filipinos are keen satirists. Among them a common name for Horan was "The Colonel Who Ran." On December 22, Horan headed a motley array of American and Filipino troops from eight different outfits, none of which had enjoyed any success at stemming the Japanese tide on or near the beaches. Much more impressive was Troop C, 26th Cavalry, some sixty Philippine Scouts led by Capt. Ralph Praeger. They cooperated with Horan—when they could find him.

As noted earlier, the real reason for the crushing defeats suffered by Americans and Filipinos alike early in the war was not overwhelming Japanese superiority but USAFFE weaknesses: far too many raw trainees, uninspiring leadership, lax discipline, lack of coordination at all levels which caused endless confusion and poor timing, much black marketeering and hijacking of rations, and a greater will to fight hard and accept losses among the Japanese.[11] All these deficiencies were painfully evident in the first serious battles on Luzon. The 26th Cavalry's Scouts fought bravely, whereas many other units broke and ran.[12] As a result, the 26th Cavalry was badly shot up in the first weeks of the war and many of its members were scattered all over central Luzon while other Philippine units worked their way to Bataan.[13] Among them were such varied persons as Maj. Claude Thorp, MacArthur's guerrilla commander, who was holed up in the north Zambales Mountains until his capture in October 1942; Sgt. Federico Estipona, who joined Lt. Robert Lapham in his trek across the Luzon plain in May 1942; and Lt. Edwin Ramsey, who ranged all over central Luzon throughout the war and aspired to unify all Luzon guerrillas under his own command. Another was Captain Praeger, who would soon establish his guerrilla head-quarters in the nearly inaccessible mountains and jungle of Apayao Subprovince more than two hundred miles north of Bataan.

When Praeger was given command of Troop C, 26th Cal-

Postcard sent home by William Bowen in April 1941 showing a view from Camp John Hay, where he was stationed. (Courtesy of Bill Bowen.)

View from the overlook in front of the officers' quarters at Camp John Hay, near Baguio. (Courtesy of Bill Bowen and Frank Thoburn.)

vary, in November 1941, he grumbled to his wife that it was "a bastard organization" without barracks or mess or morale, just the sort of rundown outfit it had always seemed his fate to inherit.[14] It indicates much about both the commanding officer and his men that just two months later he would not have written such words and they would not have deserved them.

On December 19 Praeger and sixty-eight men, then down on the sweltering plains of Pangasinan Province,[15] were ordered off north to Mountain Province. Major General Wainwright wanted them to keep him informed of developments there and, if possible, to prevent the Japanese from significantly penetrating the Cordillera Central.[16] The first small elements of Troop C, under Lt. Thomas S. Jones, arrived in Baguio about noon on December 23. The city had been abandoned by the troops stationed at Camp John Hay, and the two roads from the lowlands left undefended. Jones at once posted four men to guard the Naguilian Road, which had been blasted in many places, and eleven men to hold the Kennon Road—where only one bridge had been destroyed.

The terrain seen here near Baguio is the mountainous ground of the Cordillera Central, looking east and northeast. (Courtesy of Bill Bowen and Frank Thoburn.)

Captain Praeger arrived later in the day with the bulk of his troops. By nightfall he had found Col. Horan in the radio room of the post office. The colonel, always keenly aware of the shortcomings of others, complained to Praeger that while he had in his hands orders from General MacArthur to occupy defensive positions, he did not know where his soldiers were. Meanwhile, some thirty Philippine army soldiers who had gotten separated from their units in the fighting along the beaches the day before asked to join Troop C and were permitted to do so.

Ralph Praeger was a paradoxical figure. Although he considered himself an ordinary man, he became for the first twenty months of the war the most generally successful American guerrilla leader in northern Luzon. (Walter Cushing was the most spectacularly successful, but his career lasted only nine months.) Though both a brave man and a 1938 West Point graduate, Praeger was not a born soldier. He had even been an isolationist for a time in the

The mountains of North Luzon were both lush and treacherous. (Courtesy of Ralph B. Praeger Jr.)

1930s. Born on a Kansas farm where he had toiled long and hard from early youth,[17] he had applied to West Point mostly because he wanted to try another kind of life.[18] He was pleased to discover that though The Point was regarded by most as a "tough" place, life there was much easier than dawn-to-dusk farm labor in the summer plus farm work before and after school the rest of the year. Never impulsive or passionate, Ralph Praeger did not seek adventure and had no special hatred for the Japanese. Indeed, he had no particular feelings at all about war as such. As a soldier, he was the antithesis of stern disciplinarians like Maj. James Devereux, the defender of Wake Island.[19] He did not think there was anything special about being an army officer. To him it was merely a job—like being a master mechanic, a schoolteacher, or a lawyer—but one that should be done faithfully and well, just as a person of worth would try to do any job well. He had detested the "spit and polish" aspects of life at West Point and swore that he would never make any man under his command waste his time on such nonsense. Though he had his men do calisthenics to keep themselves in good physical condition, he never required them to practice close-order drill. Precise and rapid maneuver on the battlefield had been essential given the weapons available and the way wars were fought between the late sixteenth and mid-nineteenth centuries, yet drill persisted in the twentieth century—either from sheer inertia or from the belief (by officers) that it promoted unit solidarity among enlisted men. Praeger frankly regarded it as useless for either regular military operations or guerrilla activities.

Physically, Ralph Praeger was impressive. Six-foot-four-inches tall and strongly built, he towered over every other man in his outfit, especially the diminutive Filipinos. Prematurely bald, with a furrowed forehead and scraggly red beard, he looked more like a man in his forties than his actual twenty-eight. In personality and character he typified the best qualities of the German farmers from whom he was descended. (His mother's ancestors were English but the German strain clearly predominated in Ralph's makeup.) Though he had disliked the drudgery of his youth, the habit of hard, methodical work and devotion

Ralph Praeger, commander of Troop C, 26th Cavalry, in 1939. (Courtesy of Ralph B. Praeger Jr.)

At over six feet tall, Ralph Praeger towered over his command. He and members of his Philippine Scouts, along with two officers' children, are shown here during a trip to Mt. Pinatubo sometime between 1939 and 1941. (Courtesy of Ralph B. Praeger Jr.)

to duty remained with him always. Unimaginative and phleg-matic, he preferred facts to speculation, tinkering with machines to concerning himself about matters beyond his control. He had been regimental motor officer at Fort Stotsenburg—exactly the right man for the position. In correspondence with his wife, back home in Kansas while he remained in the Philippines in the last half of 1941, he repeatedly adverted to the long but satisfying hours he spent in the motor pool doing somebody else's work because of the shortage of trained people. He said he longed for some good American mechanics to help his Filipinos, who generally knew little about motors, but he expressed satisfaction when he at last got all the aged military equipment in running order.[20]

The same practical approach to problems suffused other portions of his letters to his wife as well. Like many big, strong men, Ralph Praeger loved sports. In his four years at West Point he had played on the football team every year and one year had gone out for track as well. At Fort Stotsenburg in 1941 he spent every spare moment bowling or playing golf, tennis, or softball.[21] Yet nearly every letter to his wife in those months also displayed Praeger's frugality and overall financial good sense. He carefully mentioned how inexpensive it was to play golf on the post course, how few balls he had lost, and what a good buy he had gotten on a new set of irons.[22] He described in detail how much of his monthly pay he was able to save for their future life together, and outlined his strategy for selling his car in the Philippines before his anticipated return to the United States. The denouement was tragic. In one of those grim ironies that abound in war, his orders to go back to the states arrived at 8:00 A.M., December 8, 1941—about four hours before Japanese bombs began to fall on Philippine airfields. Typically, he never complained about having had to stay in the Philippines. He advised Mrs. Praeger to buy a new car before prices rose, but to take his father along to do the actual dickering and not to borrow the necessary money from a finance company.[23] The same spirit appeared even in reference to their personal relations. His wife had been with him in the Philippines in the early months of 1941 and was pregnant when she was sent back to the states in May. That Praeger valued his wife highly and looked forward to the birth of their child was obvious from many of his letters, but the concern was always phrased pragmatically rather than in romantic effusions. There were no extravagant protestations of undying love but, rather promises to pray that she would have an easy delivery, assurances that he would be proud to become a father, an admonition that if she had trouble in delivery she must prefer her own life to that of the baby, and a recommendation that if the child was male she should give him a short name in case he should have to sign it frequently when he grew up![24]

The same direct, unpretentious approach to problems was equally evident when he became a guerrilla out in the mountains months later. Humid tropical weather notoriously rots leather quickly. Thus the shoes of Captain Praeger and his men were soon in tatters, and their replacement was always uncertain. It mattered little to Praeger. The thing to do was obvious: revert to the habit of youth—walk barefoot, toughen one's feet, and do without shoes. Within six months he could walk thirty-five miles a day, barefoot, over rough mountain trails. Because he had grown up on a farm, he knew a good deal about many of life's basic necessities that most officers raised in a city did not. For instance, he knew that for a considerable time humans can do without almost anything except water and salt. Hence, in the early weeks of the war before Troop C's headquarters were established at Kabugao, Captain Praeger talked about salt almost every day, regularly investigated how much was on hand, and made arrangements to assure a dependable supply. He had learned a good deal about home medical remedies, too. If a man came down with some routine illness, nobody looked for a doctor because Captain Praeger would treat the patient himself. More than one member of Troop C experienced an enema delivered personally by his commanding officer!

Ralph Praeger was, above all, a *simple* man—not simple in the sense of lack of intelligence but in the sense of being open, uncomplicated, and unsophisticated. He was not naturally aggressive or personally ambitious but he was conscientious, painstaking, and attentive to duty. His attitude always was "This needs to be done, and it is our duty to do it, so let's get at it." This virtue was also perhaps his number one weakness: he took it for granted that everybody else was like him. He took people at face value, assumed that they were trustworthy, and expected that they would do their duty. Only slowly and reluctantly, from hard experience, did he come to realize that there were plenty of men who would shrink from service to their country in defeat. "How in the world can a man do things like that?" he would sometimes burst out incredulously. Deliberate, patient, unworried, prone to remark casually that one should not make mountains out of molehills, he could never fathom the mental processes of nervous, high-strung people. After Corregidor fell he was in no hurry to rebuild the troop radio, saying that it would not be possible to send Washington any important information for a year or two anyway. He knew his men disliked guard duty, so if he thought there was no danger of a surprise attack he would not bother to set out a guard. It was a proclivity that caused chronic worriers many a sleepless night—and not a few of them a fretful personal tour of the camp's borders.

Praeger had an ambivalent attitude toward people. He liked human company and disliked solitude, but he was also uncomfortable with the unpredictable and irresponsible behavior of so much of humanity. He possessed in full measure the stubbornness alleged to be distinctively German, and he would argue at length with almost anyone on a near infinitude of subjects. However, on a matter where his own knowledge was extensive, such as motors, he would usually be content to listen and let others dogmatize. Not surprisingly, he preferred the company of children and of childlike people to that of temperamental grownups. He liked the little Igorot mountain tribesmen best of all. They were straightforward, truthful people, and they liked him in return for the same qualities. In Kabugao, many months after the war began, his favorite recreational companion was a nine-year-old Filipino boy with whom he spent many hours playing checkers. Each played as if engaged in a world championship event, and the house seemed to shake when the winner pounded on the table at the conclusion of a game. On meeting Captain Praeger for the first time, many people were struck by his size and middle-aged appearance and took him to be a man of great dignity and seriousness. After watching him grapple with his foe at the checkerboard they often changed their evaluation to, "Why, he's just a big boy at heart."

The judgment was true but misleading. War soon sorts out the able from the ordinary, and personality quirks seldom have much to do with it. Of the original commanders in North Luzon, Praeger lasted the longest and kept his troop together to the end. He kept something of the prewar regular Philippine government alive to the end, too—after it had collapsed nearly everywhere else. Nobody can ever know how many Filipino civilians owed their lives to his ability to maintain at least some order in the wild mountains of the northern cordillera. For much of 1942-1943 his was the only radio link between Luzon and the outside world. Captain Jones, who served under Praeger from the earliest days of the war, respected him profoundly as a man who cared nothing for promotions, personal honors, or even comfort, who was always considerate of his officers and men but spared himself nothing, and who always did his duty as he saw it. Ralph Praeger was precisely the sort of officer most enlisted men revered and would follow anywhere.[25]

Following Praeger's example, Colonel Horan hastily placed Capt. L.H. Giitter, C.O. of Company A, 43rd Infantry, in what seemed an ideal defensive position along the Naguilian Road with orders to hold it at all costs. Next morning Company A was back in the center of the city of Baguio. Captain Giitter explained that he had withdrawn because he feared that the Japanese would outflank him. He did not mention that he had been situated astride the highway on top of a mountain ridge that had jungle-covered flanks sloping at a 60 degree grade onto canyon floors two thousand feet below. It was only one of many times in the next few weeks that Giitter would fail in some important assignment.[26]

Before proceeding further it is necessary to say something about sources. John Horan wrote two diaries. They are quite different in content and tone. The first was composed on a day-to-day basis while the war was actually going on. The first entry in it is dated December 25, 1941; the last, May 1, 1942. It is twenty-four pages long. A photocopy of it is in Box 258, Philippine Archives Collection, National Archives II, College Park, Maryland. This diary is quite impressionistic: it is not judgmental about others, it contains several references to fine dinners Horan enjoyed at various places, it notes with pleasure that a new cook "worth his weight in gold" had been found, and it seems to be simply a running account of events composed hastily while those events were taking place. It will be referred to henceforth as the "1942 Diary."

The second diary this author was able to obtain is entitled "First Five Months of Guerrilla Warfare In Northern Luzon: Diary of Col. John P. Horan." It is fifty-three pages long and is written in narrative form rather than as a day-by-day summary of events. It is full of opinions—usually unfavorable—about many others, a number of whom are said to have failed Colonel Horan in various ways. A reader has the impression that Horan was "dressing himself up for history."

A note accompanying this "diary," signed simply "Bohannan," adds the following:

> Reportedly the manuscript of which this is a transcription was prepared by Col. Horan sometime after his surrender or possibly after his release from POW camp. A copy, very likely the original, was in the files of the Historical Section AFP. Mr. C.M. Nielsen of Salt Lake City found it there and xeroxed it. The AFP copy has since disappeared but Mr. Nielsen kindly furnished me [presumably "Bohannan"] a xerox of his xerox.
>
> This is a typed transcript of the latter xerox. The hand-writing is often difficult to read. . . .
>
> Based on other sources, both published and oral, many of the statements made are to be taken with salt.

The warning speaks for itself. The warning is also in error about the date of this diary's composition. On page thirty Horan describes blowing up a bridge in the mountains, then concludes the paragraph thus, "But it is so long ago (18 years) that this is only dimly remembered." This would indicate unequivocally that Horan composed parts—perhaps all—of the diary not in prison camp or soon after the war, but about 1960—and *then* from memory. This diary will be referred to henceforth as the "1960 Diary."

In his "1960 Diary" Horan tried halfheartedly to excuse the excessively timid Captain Giitter by pointing out that a few days before, during the initial enemy bombing of Baguio, a bomb landed so close to Giitter that it smashed his desk back against him and pinned him to a wall. Horan added that Giitter had been a model peacetime officer, remarkably conversant with infantry tactics and techniques, a master of paperwork, and an authority on army regulations.[27] Therein doubtless lay the real explanation of Giitter's shortcomings. In peacetime an army is much like other bureau-cracies. A significant proportion of those who move upward in rank are reasonably intelligent, industrious men who are not necessarily warlike but who observe the rules and regulations, do the expected things, gain the attention of their superiors, and avoid making enemies. Whether they will prove cool, brave, and imaginative in actual war, whether they can inspire and lead men in combat, nobody can know until the time comes. The usual result is that in the early stages of a major war shoals of high-ranking officers are abruptly retired "for reasons of health" or transferred to rear-area desk jobs and replaced by middle- or lower-level officers who leap several ranks in a few months when they demonstrate that they can lead men under fire.

Unhappily, heroism among the civilians in Baguio was no more plentiful than among the soldiers. The Americans there were bitterly critical of Colonel Horan and his troops. They sprinkled their conversations liberally with such words as cow-ardice, incompetence, and inefficiency. By contrast, they were much cheered when Troop C took measures to defend the city. Many offered verbally to help, but deeds were a different matter. When volunteers with automobiles were asked to carry messages between outposts and troop headquarters, nearly all the Ameri-can civilians abruptly discovered family responsibilities that did not permit them to perform such services. There were exceptions to be sure. Raymond Hale Jr., an American mestizo (half-Ameri-can, half-Filipino), who had already been working as a chauffeur for Colonel Horan, volunteered to carry messages as well. An old man and his son, and a few others, also volunteered but the overall response demonstrated the truism that in most places, at most times, the majority are selfish and heroes are scarce.[28]

In sharp contrast to this civilian sideline quarterbacking were the actions of Praeger and five of his Philippine Scouts. On his own, Praeger began preparations to defend Baguio. On December 24 he sent a patrol headed by Pfc. Joaquin Pangalinan to reconnoiter of the town of Naguilian, which had been oc-cupied and then quickly abandoned by the enemy the day before. Pangalinan and his men trudged into the town, looked things over, and made it back to Baguio in a single day—a twenty-five mile hike during which they were machine-gunned three times by Japanese planes. The difference from the action of Captain Giitter the day before was pointed and obvious.

Meanwhile, the harassed Colonel Horan, keenly aware of the growing precariousness of his situation, radioed USAFFE headquarters in Manila for permission to immediately withdraw his forces south before the enemy could cut the Kennon Road. USAFFE replied that he should not be alarmed, only to soon learn his true situation and follow up later the same day (December 24) with an order to SAVE YOUR COMMAND, USE MOUNTAIN TRAILS. (By then the Kennon Road was closed.) After a hurried conference with his staff, Horan decided that the only chance for his forces to escape was to cross the roadless Cordillera Central from west to east through some of the most forbidding mountain country on Luzon and to reach Highway 5, the main road stretching through central Luzon 275 miles from Manila north to Aparri. In the southern end of Nueva Vizcaya Province the road goes through Balete Pass. If Horan's troops could beat the Japanese to the pass they could join other scattered U.S. forces on the eastern side of Luzon's central plain and perhaps fight their way to Bataan to join the Allied soldiers fleeing into that peninsula from southern and central Luzon. Highway 5 was only some thirty to forty miles distant in a straight line, but the trails did not proceed in straight lines. In several places they went up fifty- to seventy-degree grades over five thousand–foot mountains. This, plus the usual foul-ups, caused the trek to take six days.[29]

Colonel Horan initially divided his forces to reduce Japanese chances to destroy or capture all of them. Half of them, led by Col. Donald Bonnet, were to go from Baguio to Twin Rivers, the Lusod sawmill, Santa Fe, and Carranglan. The other half, led by Horan, would take a more northerly route through Bokod, Boboc, and Pampanga to Aritao. Bonnet's men found their trail blocked by either the enemy or landslides. They dealt with these difficulties by dumping all their guns into canyons and fleeing into the jungle. Some of them managed to make it through in time to join the general Filamerican retreat into Bataan.[30]

Horan's contingent fared worse. The colonel got off to a bad start by ordering the destruction of all arms and equipment that could not be carried by individuals. His reason was plausible enough: to prevent it from being captured by the Japanese. But, more ominously, it reflected the fainthearted attitude of many among the Allies—in high places and low—early in the war. After all, a rear guard might have been left behind to defend Baguio by firing all the ammunition at the enemy and *then* pushing the vehicles and *empty* guns over cliffs.[31] Perhaps it also reflected the habitual wastefulness of Americans, our national propensity to discard whatever is not immediately useful or wanted and to trust to the future to provide something better—or at least newer. One thinks, in this regard, of the armaments and vehicles thrown off cliffs or pushed into the Pacific Ocean at the end of the war instead of being hauled home.

What is certain is that the action disgusted Captain Praeger. Always matter-of-fact, he took it for granted that since the United States was at war, it was his duty to fight the enemy—not flee from him—and he had wanted to defend Baguio. He urged Horan to send all the surplus arms, ammunition, and vehicles to safe places in the mountains where they might be retrieved one day by U.S. troops in need of such supplies. Praeger was overruled but his judgement was vindicated. Very soon, one of the primary concerns of most of the early guerrillas was to recover arms and ammunition that had been lost or wasted. Many such organizations sent out scroungers to search the battlefields of western Luzon, especially the Bataan Peninsula, for any useful military materiel. Filipino civilians joined in eagerly: to prevent the Japanese from getting the arms and ammunition, to give it to friendly guerrillas, or to add to their family incomes by selling the armaments to irregulars.[32] Vernon Fassoth, the sixteen-year-old mestizo son of sugar-planter William Fassoth—who kept a refuge up in the Zambales Mountains specifically for Americans escaping from the enemy—spent much of his time scouring the battlefields of Bataan for anything of military value.[33]

In the case of the destruction ordered by Colonel Horan, the immediate result was an abrupt decline in the morale of Praeger's men. When the latter hiked off onto a steep mountain trail on the evening of December 24, 1941, each man was heavily laden with small arms, a hundred rounds of ammunition, a blanket, and a gas mask full of canned food. At midnight their leader called out "Merry Christmas—pass the word." The men were so dispirited that the message never reached the end of the column.[34]

Colonel Horan and most of his troops reached Highway 5 in six days and even made it over Balete Pass to Carranglan in Nueva Ecija Province on December 31, only to learn that a couple of days before the enemy had occupied the towns of San Jose and Munoz farther south on Highway 5. Thus a whole Japanese army stood between Horan's meager force and the U.S. troops from southern and central Luzon who were rapidly retreating into Bataan. In his "1942 Diary," Horan says he was faced with the hardest decision of his life: to withdraw or to push on eastward and try to outflank the enemy. The latter course would require climbing several parallel ridges followed, quite possibly, by having to swing much farther east and south around the huge Candaba Swamp that occupies much of the southern end of Luzon's central plain.[35] In his "1960 Diary," Horan found many to blame for his plight: Capt. Parker Calvert, who got onto a wrong Igorot trail in the mountains and cost the expedition an extra day; the aged owner of the Lusod sawmill, who put them on another wrong trail that delayed them for two more days; and USAFFE headquarters, which repeatedly sent orders that seemed absurd—at least to Horan.[36]

Whatever the substance of these complaints, there now appeared almost no possibility of getting into Bataan. Horan called his officers together and told them that he saw no alternative save to withdraw into the northern mountains and undertake guerrilla warfare. He added that he would release any of them or their men who might still want to try to outflank the Japanese from the east in hope of rejoining the retreating Filamericans. A few decided to try. Some of them were never seen again. Others changed their minds when they neared the enemy and went back north.[37] Horan himself found two trucks, hired them with his own money, and went back north over Balete Pass to Aritao, where he encountered Praeger and Troop C, 26th Cavalry. They had arrived the day before, their numbers considerably augmented by disbanded Filipino soldiers they had encountered in the mountains. The Filipinos were a forlorn lot. Following defeats in the south, their American officers had told them to discard their arms and uniforms and go back home. Some were obviously not displeased to thus resign from the war, but others were bitter at being denied an opportunity to fight on. They also told of a Filipino private who had refused to throw away his arms and had been shot on the spot by an American officer. Praeger's men thought this story incredible but the Filipinos insisted that it was true. If so, it was one more example of how demoralization so often follows defeat. In any event, some forty-five of the stray Filipinos asked to join Troop C and were accepted.[38]

Praeger's men were hungry, weary, and had little left of the gear they had carried from Baguio save their M-1 rifles and ammunition. Worse, being cavalry rather than infantry, they were unused to hiking in the mountains—especially when wearing cavalry boots, which were now in tatters. Consequently, their feet were sore to the bone. Nonetheless, Praeger was as anxious as ever to fight the Japanese somewhere, and to operate wholly apart from Colonel Horan, whom he by then regarded as ineffectual. Specifically, he wanted to go north down the Cagayan Valley—partly to try to cut enemy supply lines there, partly to simply get his men, who were mostly lowland Filipinos, away from the tribes of headhunters who inhabited parts of the highlands in nearby Isabela and Mountain Provinces. Since Horan had no objection to Praeger's purposes, and Praeger was not officially under his command anyway, he agreed to let Troop C go.[39]

3

The Road to Tuguegarao

Since both Praeger and many of his men were apprehensive about living among Philippine mountain tribes—or even passing through regions populated by these reputed headhunters—something should be said about the dozens of different peoples who lived in the Philippines. Over the whole archipelago they fell into three major groups. The largest, the Christians (overwhelmingly Catholic), comprised about nine-tenths of the population in the 1940s. The Moros, concentrated in southern Mindanao and the Sulu Islands, were Moslems and constituted about 4 percent. Their civilization and culture stems directly from mainland Asia and sets them off from other Filipinos as distinctly as Turks differ from Italians or Greeks. An assortment of Malay tribes—most but not all pagan—often referred to generically as Igorots even though they differed markedly among themselves, were concentrated in the mountains of northern Luzon. Collectively, they were about as numerous as the Moros. The remaining 2 percent consisted of various small groups, of whom the Negritos were the most notable. These last were primitive black pygmies, more like central Africans than Asians, and they are thought to have been the original inhabitants of the Philippines. Some Americans disdained them as mere treacherous barbarians—as little concerned about what they ate as they were about sanitation—but those American guerrillas who came to know them well thought them both brave and loyal, as well as expert hunters and trackers.[1]

All of the three major groups of Filipinos are subdivided into tribes, each with its own dialect. Some dialects are closer to each other than, say, Italian and Spanish, whereas others differ as much as English and German. Likewise, the characteristics of these tribes differ substantially. The Tagalogs of mid-Luzon and the Visayans of the central Philippine Islands were prominent in politics and law, whereas the Ilocanos, who inhabited the narrow coastal plain of northern Luzon, were regarded as the most industrious and frugal farmers and traders in the islands. The dominating facts in the lives of Ilocanos were that they were too numerous for the land available and that their soil was less rich than that of the Cagayan Valley or Luzon's central plain. Consequently, their farms were small and, well before 1940, many of them had emigrated to more promising parts of the island. As with the Negritos, American opinions of the Ilocanos varied widely. Maj. Robert Lapham, commander of the LGAF, the most important and successful irregular organization on the north central Luzon plain, thought them brave, tough, and intelligent.[2] However, Lt. Donald Blackburn, one of Col. Russell Volckmann's area commanders in the USAFIP NL, disdained them as undisciplined, indifferent, and undependable and therefore useless as soldiers.[3]

Such strikingly contrasting estimates of Ilocanos (or of Filipinos generally) demonstrate more about some Americans than about any Filipinos. More than Americans, Filipinos tend to take life as it comes; they also tend to be more impulsive, impressionable, and susceptible to emotional appeals. Many American officers, failing to recognize this psychological gulf, were unable to achieve results that could have been obtained if more attention had been paid to the Filipino temperament. A sensible man would not deal with a group of seventeen-year-old boys in the same way he would handle an assembly of men of forty-five, yet many U.S. Army officers treated Filipino troops just as if they were Americans. They then blamed the inevitable failures on their men rather than on the real cause: their own uncomprehending leadership. Ironically, the Americans who complained the most about Filipinos during the war were those who understood them least. They had no explanation for the fact that a man like Walter Cushing, working with the same people, could achieve impressive results—much less the overwhelming response evoked among Filipinos by the theatrical appeals of Douglas MacArthur, a leader who understood his followers perfectly.

The Cagayan Valley is divided into three provinces: Cagayan, inhabited by Ibanags; Isabela, which in the 1940s contained many recent settlers—Ilocanos from the northwest and Tagalogs from the central plain; and Nueva Vizcaya, which is more hilly than the first two and whose population then included both Gaddangs (a Christian mountain people) and a variety of lowland Christians. The Sierra Madre range, which runs along the eastern side of all three provinces, was sparsely populated by Ilongots, a primitive Malay mountain people who contemplated civilization but had not yet embraced it.

In the nineteenth century the Ilongots had lived in something like the state of nature envisioned by seventeenth-century English philosopher Thomas Hobbes. They managed to subsist by a combination of hunting, fishing, and slash-and-burn agriculture. They dwelt in small, scattered settlements and devoted themselves inordinately to quarrels over women and honor, to the pursuit of ancient grudges, and to avenging recent wrongs or insults. These proclivities led to perpetual—if sporadic—vendettas, the main expression of which was beheading enemies. Male Ilongots also gained tribal status and proved their manhood by taking heads—whether of enemies or mere outsiders, males or females, adults or children.

These ingrained habits, aggravated by severe epidemics of smallpox in 1883 and 1889, kept Ilongot numbers small as they entered the twentieth century. American pacification efforts after the Spanish-American War caused the Ilongots to largely abandon head-hunting for a generation, but they resumed it after both U.S. and Philippine government tutelage slackened in the late 1920s. During World War II, when struggles among Japanese, Americans, and guerrillas replaced ordinary government, the Ilongots fell back into the interior of Isabela Province and bunched together—a development that ignited many an ancient feud. Moreover, the presence of Japanese occupation forces provided a new source of heads, so head-hunting underwent a renaissance. Thus it was understandable that in January 1942 American and Filipino troops tried to pass rapidly through Ilongot territory in southern Isabela.[4]

The Cordillera Central—the huge, largely roadless mountain mass of central and western North Luzon—is the home of numerous mountain tribes whose total population in 1940 was something over a quarter of a million. Among the more important of these peoples were the Benguets (the true Igorots, although the name Igorot was often loosely applied to all the mountain peoples), Bontocs, Ifugaos, Kalingas, Isnegs, and on its western slopes in Abra Province, the Tinggians. Of these, the Tinggians were both the most advanced and the most Christianized—due in considerable measure to their close contacts with their immediate lowland neighbors, the Ilocanos. The Benguets, Bontocs, and Ifugaos had all developed considerable cultures of their own, of which the famous Ifugao terrace system for rice farming on steep mountainsides remains one of the most remarkable engineering works in human history. In contrast, another mountain tribe, the Isnegs—noted for the careful construction and spaciousness of their dwellings, as well as for their personal cleanliness—never built terraces at all. The most unstable of the mountain tribes were the Kalingas, thought to have been imported centuries before by the Spaniards from the Sulu Islands between Zamboanga and Borneo. They were said to still display many traces of their former close contact with the Moros. The Isnegs occupied Apayao, the largest but least developed of the five subprovinces in huge, sprawling Mountain Province. They dominated an area three times the size of Bataan, and had been subdued by Americans and the Philippine Constabulary (national police force) as recently as 1912-1922. When Ralph Praeger made Kabugao the headquarters of his guerrilla organization in 1942, that capital "city" of Apayao had a mission, a couple of schools, and a few simple government buildings, but was otherwise unchanged from the way Americans found it in 1900. No roads reached it: travel was by horse trail or on a turbulent mountain river.

In 1940 the mountain peoples still clung to their ancestral

customs, with two exceptions. Head-hunting had not disappeared but it had declined, partly from the gradual advance of civilization, partly from pressure exerted by the Philippine national government. The other notable development was that education had come to be valued by the mountaineers quite as much as by lowland Filipinos. Most children, even in remote areas, attended school of some sort for two years or more.

Although the many peoples of the Philippines differ widely among themselves, they are all alike in two fundamental ways:[5] they are children of the tropics and, save for the Negritos, they are Malays. The first sets them off distinctly from the Chinese and Japanese, both nontropical peoples. In the tropics it may be difficult to sustain a high standard of living, but enough food is available and convenient that it is not difficult to *survive*. Thus Filipinos are usually more easygoing than the Chinese or Japanese, who live in a harsher climate. At the same time, the Filipinos's Malay heritage makes them irrevocably Oriental—no matter how much this might be overlaid by the Occidental varnish of Christianity and American education. Even so, the Cordillera mountaineers—among whom the men of Troop C were to live for nineteen months—still displayed many of the characteristics of people who had recently lived in savagery. Most obviously, they were much more warlike than their Christian brethren in the lowlands. Every tribesman over twelve years of age still carried his head axe as a weapon, though he seldom had any compelling reason to do so. Most mountaineers still regarded Christian Filipinos with suspicion, and many of the latter still hesitated to travel unarmed in the mountains although the real danger was probably not great. Igorots (broadly considered) generally regarded Americans with respect but did so without the sense of inferiority encountered so often among lowlanders. An Igorot thought of his relationship to an American as being more that of son to father than servant to master.

The code of conduct of these people challenged that of most Occidentals in its emphasis on self-discipline. A sense of loyalty was especially pronounced. Mountaineers were conspicuously honest. They were so scrupulously respectful of the possessions of others that an Igorot would not take even a coconut from another without permission. Tribal law, though unwritten, was the heritage of countless generations and was so respected. Even if an offense was dealt with properly in a government court, the Philippine Constabulary never considered a case in Mountain Province closed until justice according to tribal tradition had also been taken into account. Treason and adultery were regarded as the most serious crimes. They were ordinarily punished by death, for if a case was settled short of that there might be trouble over it at some future date. Other misdeeds were ordinarily punished quickly, usually by payment of a fine by the offender to the aggrieved party.[6] Such were the peoples among whom the men of Troop C would live, fight, and die during the next nineteen months.[7]

Back in Aritao on New Year's Eve 1941, Ralph Praeger checked over his troops. Troop C's normal strength as judged by the morning reports at Fort Stotsenburg had been eighty-nine men, but there were now only fifty-nine men and three officers present. The missing thirty had either never left Stotsenburg when Troop C was sent north on December 19, or they had been lost near Baguio, or were on special duty, or had simply disappeared during the arduous six-day hike over the mountains. Some eventually made it to Bataan only to have to surrender to the Japanese. One adventurous (and phenomenally lucky) Scout, Pvt. Joe E. Tugab, who had been wounded on December 10, managed to escape to China on a Japanese ship after Corregidor fell. He then made his way to Chungking, the wartime capital of China, located hundreds of miles inland, and eventually fought in the Papuan and New Guinea campaigns.[8] Ironically, and tragically, Tugab somehow survived the war only to succumb to tuberculosis soon after it ended.

These losses were more than compensated for by the addition of four or five Philippine army officers and about forty men who had been wandering in the wilderness and who had attached themselves to Troop C during the trek over the mountains. Thus the troop's actual strength was about a hundred. Also picked up along the way were three Americans: T. Sgt. William

E. Bowen and two civilians, Francis A. Camp and a miner named Dickey. All of them soon proved extremely valuable. The three had stayed behind in Baguio on December 24 when Colonel Horan and his entourage departed. As soon as their superiors were out of sight, Bowen and his companions liberated a car, which they then drove down the Kennon Road until they saw some enemy troops crossing a bridge several hundred yards in front of them. Darkness was falling, so they stopped and looked only briefly. Then Bowen and Dickey, with supreme unconcern, went to sleep. Camp later told Captain Jones that he was too scared to sleep. The other two awakened at dawn on Christmas Day sufficiently exhilarated to fire a few shots at the startled Japanese, following which they got into their car. The Japanese sent several armored vehicles toward them, but the Americans riposted by blowing up a recently abandoned gasoline truck in the middle of the narrow road right in the face of the enemy. They then drove a few miles back toward Baguio, stopped, and sat in their car with studied insolence while an Igorot cooked them some chickens for breakfast. Three enemy bombers flew directly overhead but either did not see the impudent soldiers or feared that American reconnaissance planes might be nearby and so did not tarry. The incident, of no importance in itself, is mentioned here because it suggests much about Technical Sergeant Bowen's personality and about the fighting qualities of all those concerned. Both Bowen and Camp were consummate individualists, men who were not at all disheartened at being cut off behind enemy lines. When they arrived at Aritao they told Praeger what they had done. He found their spirit immensely refreshing—quite understandable in a man who had just finished six days of grueling hiking in the wake of "The Colonel Who Ran," and many of whose own troops had grumbled audibly about their fate. Praeger gave Bowen and Camp "jungle promotions" on the spot, making them acting second lieutenants with the responsibilities but not the pay of officers. Jones, equally impressed by the newcomers, invited them to join Troop C, which they promptly did.[9] Soon after that the troop managed to find some field corn to boil, and the men enjoyed their first square meal in some days.

William Bowen, Francis Camp, and a third American briefly held a Japanese force on the Kennon Road, shown here. (Courtesy of Bill Bowen and Frank Thoburn.)

Technical Sergeant Bowen was a natural professional soldier of the better sort. He had been in the U.S. Army for twelve years. When the war began he was in the 228th Signal Service Company at Camp John Hay, where he served Colonel Horan as communications sergeant. Slight and handsome, with black hair beginning to turn gray and a carefully trimmed mustache, he looked more like a movie actor than the guerrilla he was already becoming. Naturally charming, he had a great store of stories and songs with which he was always ready to entertain anyone around him. He also had a keen and sensitive mind and knew how to do many things well. For instance, he and Pvt. Earl J. Brazelton worked for twelve days in late January at the Batong Buhay Mine taking parts from radios in Lubuagan, hunting for and often finding other parts that had been secreted in the mine's smelter, and making still other parts themselves in the mine's machine shop. From this they gradually built a radio for Colonel Horan, who had earlier given his own radio

Perhaps William Bowen's greatest asset was his ability to get things done. Many Filipinos never tired of telling stories about his exploits. (Courtesy of Bill Bowen.)

to Capt. Manuel Enriquez at Bayombong.[10] After his return to Baguio on Christmas Day, Bowen discovered about three truck-loads of food still in the Camp Hay commissary. Without saying anything to anyone he sent it via a mine tram line to a lumber camp. It was a wise action, for none of the American or Filipino troops then scattered in the nearby mountains had much food with them.[11]

Bowen could also act decisively. The American enlisted men who served under him briefly in Baguio were already devoted to him. Perhaps the main reason was that, like Praeger, he was selfless. It was typical of him that at Aritao, when he happened to have several hundred dollars in his pocket and none of the other men had much of anything, Bowen gave Captain Praeger part of his money and divided the rest among the U.S. enlisted men, keeping only a few dollars for himself. Bowen had his faults, but he always seemed able to face the most severe tests with an airy grace, to get things done without apparent effort. Filipinos never tired of telling stories about his exploits, real or fancied. One tale concerns an incident that occurred many months later, in September 1942. Lieutenant Bowen was eating a late breakfast when an American soldier galloped up wildly on a horse à la Paul Revere with news that three hundred Japanese were march-ing into a village a short distance down the road. Panic stricken, he shouted at Bowen to run for his life. Bowen responded, "Tut, tut, young man," and continued to eat.[12]

Frank Camp was a different type. Although not a tall man, he had broad shoulders and a strong body. More than four years before he had been a member of the 4th Marine Regiment in Shanghai during a great battle between the Chinese and Japa-nese. He often told stories about the many bloated corpses that floated back and forth before his sentry box and which the ma-rines, with typical American irreverence, had given such nick-names as Joe, Ike, and Mike. Camp admired Bowen for the fearlessness he had shown in their brief scuffle with the Japanese on Christmas morning. Whether from this experience or some other, he had also developed a cold, settled hatred for the Japa-nese—so intense that if on patrol he would almost always open fire on the enemy regardless of orders. Since shooting up enemy patrols often created more trouble than the momentary victory was worth, Camp was subject to periodic reprimands from Captain Praeger. But Praeger himself wanted to fight the Japanese, and he appreciated Camp's spirit and overall value, so he usually tempered his admonitions. He soon learned to avoid the problem altogether by sending someone else on a patrol where Japanese *might* be encountered but should not be attacked, saving Camp for assignments where the main objective was to kill enemy troops.[13]

Late on December 31, 1941, Troop C hiked nine miles northward from Aritao to Bambang in Nueva Ecija Province. There they were quartered in the rectory of a Belgian missionary, Father Diesnick. A big, poorly clad man with a rough voice and a heavy black beard, he nonetheless exuded saintliness—at least in the opinion of Captain Jones. Certainly he displayed generosity. At his own expense he had spent the preceding several days trying to find food, clothing, salt, and shelter for several thousand disbanded and thoroughly disorganized American and Filipino soldiers headed aimlessly in every direction. The priest was saddened by the sight of these bewildered youngsters, for they brought back memories of his Belgian homeland during the German invasion of 1914.

During the night of January 1, 1942, news of the fall of Manila reached Troop C. Next morning Father Diesnick preached a sermon on the theme that a good soldier must at all times do his duty to his country, regardless of the difficulties. Later in the morning a Philippine Constabularyman arrived from Cagayan Valley with information that the enemy had established a large airfield at Tuguegarao, 125 miles north. Its value to the Japanese was obvious: From it, fighter planes or bombers would have only a short hop to any target on Luzon. To attack such a base seemed to both Captain Praeger and his men an excellent opportunity to at last *do* something specific and positive, to move toward the enemy instead of always away from him. Morale rose visibly, and the rest of the day was spent in animated discussion of when and how to attack the base.

On January 3, Troop C left Bambang for Santiago, Isabela Province, about forty-five miles to the northeast. Lieutenant Warren Minton, the junior officer in the troop, was sent on ahead with a patrol to find transportation and to repair bridges when possible. Success was meager. When transport could be found at all it usually needed repair, and every bridge but one in the whole Cagayan Valley had been demolished by Allied troops retreating southward. Occasionally motor transport or calesas (two-wheeled Philippine buggies) could be used, but for most of the men it meant more hiking on feet that were still sore. The last six miles into Santiago were particularly tough due to one of those foul-ups that seem inseparable from war. In this case a balky calesa pony flatly refused to move, thereby forcing soldiers to form fresh blisters atop the old ones caused by boots made for riding rather than hiking. Thus, even though morale had risen as memories of the preceding two weeks receded, Troop C was still not an impressive portion of the U.S. Army when its members limped into Santiago on January 5. This mattered little to the natives. A large crowd of them turned out, overjoyed to see troops at last going toward what they perceived as the main threat to themselves: the Japanese army to the north.

The next day a patrol consisting of Lieutenant Minton and acting lieutenants Camp and Bowen, plus four Scouts, left Santiago to reconnoiter Tuguegarao, still more than eighty miles north by the most direct route. The rest of the troopers spent their time repairing equipment and resting their feet. A local Chinese merchant made the munificent contribution of thirty-five pairs of canvas shoes to the sore-footed men in exchange for a receipt to be redeemed by the U.S. government at some future date—if the Allies won the war. Chinese merchants are ubiquitous in the Orient, and most of them put personal and family interest above concern for the governments or native peoples where they happen to do business. This particular man was unusually generous and trusting.[14]

All the troop's food was contributed gratis by the people, as was the case most of the time after it left Baguio. Because cash was seldom used by officers in the Philippines, few had much money with them when the war broke out. The funds contributed by Lieutenant Bowen a few days earlier were virtually all the cash available to Troop C.[15]

The long trek north, mostly along mountain trails west of the Cagayan River, was interrupted on January 8 by a sad accident with a tragicomic aftermath. Two Scouts, Antero Soriano and Constancio Ocompo were out hunting wild chickens—which are plentiful in many parts of the Philippines—when Ocompo accidentally shot Soriano, who died a few minutes later. Ocompo was at once discharged and told to go home. As is customary in the tropics, Soriano was given a quick burial. A local carpenter made a coffin in about thirty minutes, and Soriano was buried at sunset with the troop as escort. Unfortunately, the hastily dug grave was a bit too small for the coffin, whereupon the Filipino first sergeant pushed the coffin into it with his foot, exclaiming, "Get down there, Soriano, get down." It was Troop C's first Filipino funeral after leaving Fort Stotsenburg.

That same day, Troop C was reorganized. Fifteen of the older men, all Scouts, were deemed unfit for arduous field service and were left at Santiago with the outfit's first sergeant. They were subsequently attached to the newly organized 14th Infantry as instructors.[16] But their luck was bad: after Corregidor fell in May 1942, all of them were either killed or captured. At the same time, thirty more stragglers—this time from the Philippine Constabulary and various units of the 11th and 71st Philippine army divisions—led by Lieutenants DeLeone, Ramos, Diesto, and Villon, had gradually attached themselves to Troop C in the preceding few days. They were formally added to the rolls and departed with the troop on the evening of Soriano's funeral. On January 10 they reached Mallig No. 2, a Philippine government farm project for landless peasants. Isabela Province was an underdeveloped area and the government had been trying to persuade rural families from more thickly settled places to move there. There was a radio receiver at this site, so Troop C got its first outside news since December 26. The men heard that the United States intended to produce sixty thousand airplanes in 1942 and 125,000 in 1943—a message that was only moderately consoling to soldiers who themselves lacked even the most rudimentary form of *land* transport and whose shoes were falling off.

Lieutenant Minton arrived in midafternoon and reported on his reconnaissance. He spoke highly of the cooperation he had received from Gov. Marcelo Adduru of Cagayan Province and the provincial engineer, Mr. Imperial. Minton said Adduru had set up his government in Tuao, twenty-five miles west of Tuguegarao, after the enemy captured the latter town on December 16. The government of Cagayan had already established a news and propaganda section and was printing emergency money to carry on its work. This remarkable efficiency was typical of Governor Adduru until his capture by the Japanese in the spring of 1943. Anticipating the war, he had begun to make serious preparations for it well before the Japanese struck. Early in October 1941 he organized about eighty Philippine Constabularymen, Philippine army reservists, schoolteachers, and Volunteer Guards to keep order and maintain civilian morale if war came. Himself a USAFFE reserve major, the governor reported for duty as soon as war began and was formally called up on December 24.[17] A week later, cut off from all higher authority, he assumed emergency powers in Cagayan Province and formed the Cagayan Military Force. It consisted of the eighty men he had already assembled and begun to train three months earlier, augmented by various newcomers. As a USAFFE major, he was granted authority to induct all of them into U.S. service, a practice he continued until July 6, 1942.[18] Captain Thomas Jones, who saw Adduru frequently in the following year and a half, called him "the most capable person, either American or Filipino, that I met in the entire war."[19]

After a brief conference about his plans, Lieutenant Minton left for Tuao. The rest of the force moved to Mallig No. 1 the next day. There the director of the resettlement project was in serious trouble with his own people.

When a war is over much is written about the heroism of many who served in it. Far less attention is paid to the indifference or cowardice displayed by many others. Virtually all human societies contain a fair number of people who are irresponsible and lawless at heart. Unhappily, some withdrawing U.S. Army units had given hand grenades to civilians for protection against the Japanese. The scoundrels among them, rejoicing at the fact that the influence of law and order had declined steeply since the war's onset, were using the grenades to assassinate or intimidate their neighbors. The director, whose life had been devoted to improving the lot of the less fortunate, was killed a few weeks later when one of those unfortunates threw a grenade into his living room. As a disgruntled philosopher once put it, no good deed goes unpunished. The whole sorry episode caused Praeger and Jones to engage in what would be the first of many discussions about what measures to take to maintain a desirable level of civilization in their part of Luzon. That Praeger sought Jones's counsel about the matter was not accidental. Although Praeger was a straightforward man who talked freely to all his associates when he deemed it appropriate, he relied on Jones more consistently than any of the others. They were about the same age, both were captains by the end of 1941, and Jones was Praeger's executive officer until their capture in August-September 1943.

Early on January 12, Troop C bivouacked west of Enrile, across the river from Tuguegarao. Lieutenant Minton met with Praeger and the other officers there and submitted plans for the attack. With only a few minor changes, they were approved. Minton also reported that Pvt. Ramon V. Aguas, a Scout who belonged to his patrol, had breakfasted that morning with seventeen Japanese flyers who were quartered near the Tuguegarao airfield. There were only a few planes left there, some of which were to be flown south that day to Clark Field at Fort Stotsenburg. The Nipponese officers had been friendly to Aguas, who had thoughtfully brought them a chicken as a gift "to welcome them to the Philippines." They responded by tweaking his nose good naturedly and inviting him to breakfast, where he was fed pancakes. As soon as he left his new friends, Aguas prepared a sketch of the airfield for Minton.

Meanwhile, Lieutenant Camp had been busy manufacturing some sixty homemade grenades. They consisted of dynamite and scrap iron bound in bamboo tubes. He then taught selected grenadiers how to use them. The grenades had burnable fuses but, since it would not be safe to light matches in the dark on the airfield, each grenadier was told to carry a lighted cigar concealed in his hand with which to ignite them.

That evening, Troop C moved to Solana, another small town a couple of miles outside Tuguegarao. Lieutenant Bowen happened to be there. Ebullient as usual, he declared confidently that there were not more than two thousand Japanese in Tuguegarao and that most of them were air force ground troops. With any luck, he believed Troop C's 150 men could rout them and "Tomorrow lunch in Tuguegarao."[20] He was keenly disappointed when Captain Praeger reminded him that the enterprise was to be only a raid, not a full-scale attack. The people of Solana were quite as enthusiastic as Bowen. No fewer than five thousand of them were on hand to wish the Filamerican forces good luck, and midnight masses were said in the town churches to bless the coming attack. Everybody seemed certain that Japan would be defeated within a few weeks. Optimism is, of course, an essential ingredient for success in war. On this occasion there was no shortage of it.

Despite the presence of so many people, which made all hope of surprise seem impossible, Praeger was so anxious to strike at the foe that he ordered the attack to proceed anyway. The attackers crossed the Cagayan River at 10:00 P.M. and reached the airfield about an hour later. The field was L-shaped and about two miles long. Despite all the people who knew of the impending assault, the overconfident Japanese were asleep, apparently certain that no American troops were within a hundred miles. A guard had been posted but few sentinels were out, so the attackers were able to crawl onto the airfield without detection. Because there was no moon it was utterly dark, and the men had to search for several hours to find the two or three planes still on the field. Just before these were located, the enemy sounded an alert. An attempt was made to destroy the planes, but success was limited. Shortly afterward Troop C's main body came under heavy machine-gun fire—fortunately in total darkness.

Perhaps the most heartening aspect of the whole raid was the daring and effective work of several individuals and small groups. Detachments under Lieutenant Bowen and Sgt. Tomas Quiocho were trying to destroy a fuel dump when they spotted Japanese machine guns at virtual point-blank range. They hit the ground just before the enemy opened fire, and Bowen managed to crawl behind the Japanese gunners and knock out two of their machine guns with the homemade grenades. This action enabled an adjacent platoon to penetrate the gap in the enemy's defenses and inflict heavy casualties on those Japanese nearby. A lone constabularyman crossed the runway to attack an enemy guard post. Lieutenant Camp, leading a small patrol, surrounded an enemy barracks and shot it up from all sides. Due to the darkness, nobody ever knew how many Japanese soldiers were in it or how many of them perished. Camp guessed that the building housed fifty to sixty men and that most of them were killed. Corporal Andres Montiadora's patrol denied a critical road junction to the enemy for thirty minutes, then proceeded to the rallying point only to learn that the rest of Troop C was still on the airfield. Rather than sit there and wait, he hurried his men two and a half miles back to their original position and held it until dawn. It was a good example of the initiative, courage, and reliability of the well-trained Scouts in the 26th Cavalry. It also raised the hope that those raw Filipino inductees who had panicked and fled under fire could also be made capable soldiers if properly trained, supplied, and led.

The attackers retired to Solana at dawn. Lieutenant Minton carried news of their success to Maj. Everett Warner in Nueva Vizcaya, who radioed it to Corregidor, from whence it was sent off to the rest of the world. Because war news from the Philippines had been so uniformly gloomy, the importance of this "victory" was understandably exaggerated.[21] Nonetheless, the raid had been a substantial success. Many enemy radios and weapons were destroyed, mine wires around the field were torn up, the houses of Japanese officials in the city were burned or wrecked, and havoc was wrought with enemy communications from Tuguegarao all the way down the Cagayan River to Aparri.

It took the Japanese several weeks to repair all the damage. More important were the casualties inflicted. They were initially estimated at between 60 and 100, but Lieutenant Minton guessed the figure to be 110—most of whom were killed when Camp shot up the Japanese barracks. He gave the latter figure to Warner, who passed it on to General MacArthur. Later estimates, based on the number of truckloads of dead observed plus corroborating civilian reports, indicated that somewhere between 100 and 200 enemy soldiers perished. A truly reliable figure was never established.

Despite the raid's success, Praeger was disappointed. He doubted that as many casualties had been inflicted on the enemy as was being claimed, and he lamented that the raid had failed in its real purpose: to destroy Japanese planes. Most of all, he disliked the publicity the action was receiving. He had not authorized Minton to notify MacArthur, and he feared that intemperate rejoicing over the "triumph" would cause the Japanese to send more troops to North Luzon to regain face by avenging their defeat. After the war Captain Praeger and Lieutenant Bowen were posthumously awarded DSCs—Praeger's with an oak leaf cluster (signifying a second award) added—for their roles in the raid.

Whatever the true casualty figure, Troop C, to lapse into baseball parlance, had pitched a shutout. Lieutenant Bowen and Private Tumanut were momentarily missing, but both soon put in an appearance. Tumanut had merely gotten lost. Bowen had been surrounded by Japanese on the airfield but his luck held. He managed to hide in a thicket beside the runway. The next day the Japanese fired at random into bushes all around him but miraculously did not hit him. By late afternoon they had finally stopped looking for him. As soon as it was dark he slipped away, swam the Cagayan River, and made his way back to Troop C the following morning. He complained only of having been thirsty the day before. Several of his compatriots reminded him with good natured malice that neither he nor they had enjoyed the lunch in Tuguegarao he had promised.[22]

The Tuguegarao raid was the first Troop C action that could

unequivocally be called a guerrilla operation. It contained a number of valuable lessons—some drawn from the Japanese experience there, still more from that of the attackers themselves. From the Japanese:

1. Don't be blithely optimistic about anything without careful checking. More specifically, no matter how friendly the natives may seem in a partially occupied country and no matter how far away the major fighting may be, don't relax and simply assume that no hostile forces can possibly be near you. Otherwise, you are apt to be in for some nasty surprises.

2. Be sure you are properly organized. Anticipating no problems, the Japanese had sited their field guns in exposed positions and set them for long-range fire. Had they been able to fire at short ranges they surely would have inflicted considerable casualties on Troop C—even in the dark.

From the Filamerican experience:

1. Do not attack on a pitch-black night across unknown terrain. If you can't see anything you will often be afraid to fire lest you kill your own men somewhere in the stygian darkness.

2. Homemade weapons are often of dubious utility. Lieutenant Camp's improvised hand grenades proved nearly as dangerous to friend as to foe. It was hard to find protection from them on a level field because they sprayed fragments so close to the ground.

3. Guerrilla warfare requires a revolution in customary military thought. Troop C's officers were still thinking as regular soldiers and had expected to pay a considerable price for their anticipated successes. Yet in a well-planned and well-executed guerrilla operation the attackers should emerge virtually unscathed. For instance, the redoubtable Walter Cushing ambushed the Japanese many times and killed hundreds of them but seldom lost more than a couple

of his own men in any engagement. The key ingredients in guerrilla combat are surprise and leadership. Well-trained soldiers, good arms, superior numbers, and other elements usually deemed essential for success in regular warfare are nice to have for guerrilla operations but are not crucial for success. If a leader has courage and common sense, a few willing men, and a few rifles (old or new) with ten rounds of ammunition apiece, an enemy is likely to be left with little to do save bury his dead.[23] All this assumes, of course, that the enemy is not *overwhelmingly* stronger than the attacker. In that case no attack should be attempted.

It should be added here that in the latter part of the war, long after Praeger's guerrillas had ceased to exist, the above principles no longer held for guerrilla combat, and the emphasis gradually shifted to collecting information. Intensive training then proved just as necessary for run-of-the-mill guerrillas as for regular troops. The fact that the Philippine guerrillas seldom got such training made it necessary to scrutinize with special care any intelligence information they supplied. To this it might be added that the same scrutiny and studied skepticism should be accorded postwar statements by guerrillas about their own wartime activities and about each other. Rivalries among them were keen, and memories have dimmed markedly in the ensuing half century.

Finally, one must acknowledge that no matter how emotionally satisfying were such victories as the Tuguegarao raid, they had little discernible effect on the overall course of the war until the irregulars could be immensely reinforced by a regular American army in January 1945. General MacArthur was correct in urging the guerrillas to be content with collecting intelligence information that might be of great value at a later date and to avoid fighting the Japanese—which mostly wasted men and led to enemy reprisals on civilians.

4

The Road to Kabugao

Perhaps it was euphoria resulting from the raid on Tuguegarao that gave rise to a myth that has persisted for decades: that Praeger's forces repeated the raid at the port city of Aparri eleven days later, then withdrew to Tuao, destroying all the bridges and culverts along Highway 5 from Aparri to Tuguegarao and along Highway 3 from Aparri to Langangan.[1] Captain Jones insists that there was no comparable operation at Aparri at all. What happened was that *somebody,* possibly from Frank Camp's patrol, shot at a Japanese plane near Aparri and that the plane crashed. The whole nonevent is a good example of how exaggerated or even entirely fictitious successes are born in wartime when the thirst for good news of some kind is stimulated by overheated imaginations or government propagandists. The legend of Capt. Colin Kelly is a far better-known case in point. Kelly received a congressional medal of honor posthumously for sinking a large Japanese ship in a suicidal dive. While Kelly was indubitably a brave man, the importance of his exploit was exaggerated.

Another often repeated but baseless assertion is that in the immediate aftermath of Tuguegarao Lt. Warren Minton deserted Praeger's command and went to join Major Warner, then said to be in Nueva Vizcaya.[2] What happened was more prosaic, if also a bit more complex. Minton was *sent* to Isabela Province on January 15 to inspect the men left earlier at Santiago, and to obtain supplies. He returned on January 19 with a letter from Warner requesting that Minton be detached to serve as a staff officer with a regiment Warner was forming in Isabela. Those Philippine Scouts who had been left in Santiago were sought as instructors. Praeger approved the request, and Minton and one Scout left for Isabela the next day. Thereafter, both Minton and the Scout-instructors were carried as attached to the 14th Infantry, Philippine army.[3]

At dawn the day after the raid, Troop C's scattered forces reassembled at Solana, two or three miles northwest of Tuguegarao. No less a dignitary than Governor Adduru of Cagayan Province was on hand to greet them. The governor was an admirable man and a true Philippine patriot. Only a few days after the war began, in anticipation of Japanese occupation of the whole Cagayan Valley, he had moved the capital of his province some twenty-five miles west to Tuao.[4] He took in stride the loss of his two largest cities, Tuguegarao and Aparri. In his view, he had lost neither his province nor the war. Fully intending to resist the invaders in any way possible, he quickly gathered his loyal officials, the police, some nearby Philippine army soldiers, some Constabularymen, and some civilians, organized them into two companies, which he named the Cagayan Military Force, and proceeded to govern from Tuao just as he had from Tuguegarao in peacetime. Adduru was disgusted to see troops who had been training in Cagayan before the war simply depart as soon as the Japanese arrived, without making any attempt to resist. When some of Troop C's officers chided Adduru mildly for risking his personal safety so close to the enemy so soon after the raid, the governor replied spiritedly that he was glad to see somebody who wanted to fight rather than run, and that the least he could do was be on hand to see that they were properly cared for.[5] Adduru and Praeger took to each other at once. Both believed it their duty to resist the invaders, and both were confident that whatever they chose to attempt toward that end would be confirmed by higher authority later.

The Japanese were not slow to take reprisals for the Tuguegarao raid. Two days later they reduced to ashes an entire barrio near the city, burned several houses in another, and killed many civilians in Tuguegarao. Governor Adduru was saddened by the massacre, as many of those slain were personal friends, but he refused to express regret on the ground that war comes with a high price and that the patriots of Cagayan must be prepared to pay it. He did not doubt that he, as leader of the resistance to the Japanese, would probably have to pay the ultimate price himself.[6]

As for the civilians, morale among those in Cagayan was considerably higher than in the as-yet-unoccupied areas to the south through which Troop C had passed. Everywhere southward civilians had been kind and helpful, but they had also been visibly glad to see troops leave their towns before their presence brought about a Japanese bombardment. Early Allied defeats in the war, the loss of Manila, and the everyday sight of Japanese planes had caused many Filipinos to feel helpless and despondent.

Actually, neither Filipinos nor most U.S. enlisted men realized the true gravity of their situation. Many who wondered if it would take as long as a month for American reinforcements to arrive were quite shocked to learn that three months was more likely. Captain Jones remarked that both he and Praeger thought they would be lucky if it was six months, and that if Singapore and the Dutch East Indies fell their prospects would be too dismal to contemplate.[7]

The day after the raid, outposts were established in Solana, Enrile, and Dungao—all near Tuguegarao; the rest of Troop C had no recourse but to withdraw to Tuao. Even if their numbers had been greater, they had insufficient ammunition left to battle the enemy. There had been no earlier fighting in that part of Luzon, so there were neither arms nor ammunition to be salvaged from battlefields. Some of the men spent hours dragging an American P-40 fighter plane out of the Cagayan River only to find that its .50-caliber machine guns were damaged beyond repair. It was still another reminder of the folly of those who ordered the destruction of arms rather than hiding them.

In Tuao, the Americans in Troop C were put up in the houses of two prominent local citizens, Captain Sanchez and Don Celestino Rodriguez, the latter a buyer for Tabacalera, a Spanish-owned Philippine tobacco company. Though Señor Rodriguez had been born in Spain, he and his wife had lived in the Philippines for more than twenty years. They had three sons and three daughters. The family was remarkably kind, generous, and warmhearted. They at once put everything they had at the disposal of the Americans billeted with them. Even their teenage daughters slept on the floor so the Americans could have their beds. The oldest boy and girl, who were about twenty, had been in Spain during the Spanish Civil War. There they had lived in the hills for more than a year before making their way to France and thence to the United States. Their experiences in Spain now stood them in good stead. Toni, the oldest girl, insisted that her parents lay in a large store of soap and matches, for she knew from her experience in Spain that these would soon be unobtainable. The family was also well stocked with canned goods, but they were all suicidally generous about sharing their bounty with everyone else; within a few months their supplies were exhausted.

Toni was a beautiful girl in a classic Spanish way, but many thought her younger sister, fifteen-year-old Nanita, would be even more alluring. Nanita was incorrigibly vivacious and full of fun. The war never weighed on her mind at all. Captain Jones said she was the only person he had ever seen who seemed to positively enjoy being bombed.[8] Whenever a bomb would explode harmlessly Nanita would shout, "Why, they can't hit a goddam thing!"—a ludicrously incongruous remark coming from one who otherwise displayed the gentle manners of a Spanish girl of proper upbringing. She had picked up the profane expression from American soldiers, and Captain Jones cautioned her that her father would surely punish her if he heard her using such language. Nanita hoped the war would be short because she wanted to get married. When their American guests reminded her that she was only fifteen, her father interposed that it was customary for Spanish girls to marry at sixteen, adding a bit wistfully that even though Toni was twenty and unmarried he was confident that her time would come soon.

Señor Rodriguez's day consisted entirely of smoking some twenty-five cigars and listening to news broadcasts from San Francisco. He completely disregarded adverse elements in the news and interpreted the obvious propaganda portions of the broadcasts as faithful reports of stirring victories. The only thing he would not tolerate from others in his house was listening to Tokyo broadcasts over his radio. Actually, it was hard to tell from either Japanese or American broadcasts just what was happening in the war. Tokyo, then in the midst of its golden shower of successes, could afford to provide more detail than the Allies, but neither side was enslaved by fidelity to the truth.[9]

Sadly, Señor Rodriguez's kindness once more bore out the melancholy adage that "No good deed goes unpunished." When the Japanese eventually discovered that Rodriguez had sheltered guerrillas, they seized his wife and children as hostages. He surrendered in December 1942 to secure their release. Then, in reprisal, they burned down his house and destroyed most of his possessions.[10]

A few days after the troop departed for Tuao, a report arrived from the Solana outpost that Japanese had entered the town and were collecting information regarding the road to Tuao. A reinforced rifle platoon led by Captain Jones was at once dispatched east from Tuao to await developments. The next morning Solana reported that the enemy had gone back to Tuguegarao. The Japanese appeared to be both somewhat confused, as they often were, and nervous. What they had actually done the day before (January 25) had been to send a Japanese-Filipino woman into Solana to make sure that no guerrillas were there. Then, after receiving a negative report, they had rushed the town. In the process they killed a civilian riding a horse. In one of those displays of Japanese psychology forever unfathomable to Occidentals they then threatened to shoot anyone on a horse because cavalry had attacked Tuguegarao. The consideration that all the "cavalry" raiders had been men crawling on their bellies in the middle of a moonless night must not have seemed significant to them.

The Solana outpost was manned by two Filipinos, Leo Tullungan and Sgt. Raymundo Camonayan, who remained hidden at their posts long after the Japanese occupied the town. Camonayan was relieved in July 1942, but Tullungan—although seriously wounded in 1942—stayed on duty for two more years before he was finally captured and executed by the enemy. Not only was this an outstanding display of both courage and loyalty on the part of the two soldiers, it was also proof of the staunch loyalty of Solana's citizens.

On January 27, a Japanese officer and patrol visited Dungao. They called on the barrio lieutenant while Ramon Aguas, then on outpost duty there, listened to the conversation from the next room—a cozy arrangement that indicates how closely Filipino officials cooperated with guerrillas on occasion. The Japanese were attempting to win the friendship of civilians while punishing people who resisted the conquerors or aided the guerrillas. It was in this spirit that the officer in charge offered five cents in Japanese invasion scrip for the cup of coffee that the barrio lieutenant gave him.

The episode, of no importance in itself, is another illustration of the notorious unpredictability of the Japanese. Whether dealing with guerrillas or with Filipino civilians, they never had a set policy to which they clung throughout the islands or throughout the war. They always had sufficient sheer numbers—force—to destroy all the guerrilla organizations in all the Philippine Islands if they had set themselves singlemindedly to that purpose. But they never did this because they were overextended strategically and so left their Philippine occupation forces undermanned because the need for troops in a dozen other places was more pressing. It was the same with their treatment of civilians. Early in the war they tried to do the sensible thing: make a genuine effort to win the friendship and support of the Filipino people. This was especially the case in the northern mountains. Thomas Jones said that where he was during the first months of the war, crimes against civilians by Japanese soldiers were punished severely. In that time he heard of only one case of rape of a Filipino woman; the offender was beheaded.[11] Other Americans in other places also reported occasional Japanese kindnesses to themselves or general good behavior toward civilians,[12] but such behavior was like so much else about the Nipponese: it was sporadic and unpredictable.

Any serious Japanese attempts to cut off civilian support for guerrillas inevitably involved mistreatment of civilians. The Japanese army, too, contained its quota of sadists, showoffs,

Bushido fanatics, psychiatric cases, and ordinary brutes—all of whom periodically insulted, humiliated, cheated, tortured, or otherwise shamefully misused Filipinos. And, inevitably, after guerrilla attacks the Japanese thought it necessary to punish somebody—oftentimes the wrong people. Much worse, after thousands of Filipino soldiers were released from Camps O'Donnell and Cabanatuan so they would die at home rather than under Japanese control, they told their families and neighbors about the horrors of the Bataan Death March and the sordid existence in the camps. Thereafter, making friends with Filipino civilians became much more difficult for the invaders. The innumerable horrible crimes committed by doomed enemy troops, especially in Manila in 1945, destroyed all faith in Japanese humanity and led Filipinos to exact a fearful vengeance in the last months of the war.

Forbes J. Monaghan, S.J., an American priest at a college in Manila during the war, attributed the notorious and unpredictable changes of mood and conduct among the Japanese to their several different and not always reconcilable religious and cultural traditions mixed, in modern times, with the comparably discordant amalgam of Christianity and rationalism they acquired from the West. The resulting melange, he thought, had produced a basic instability in the Japanese character.[13]

Whatever the accuracy of that analysis, there is no doubt that the Japanese seriously underestimated the real patriotism of perhaps 85 percent of the Filipino people and their loyalty to the United States. Filipinos are not ordinarily assertive, but they have a natural sense of dignity and love of country which, taken together, made them regard the Japanese invasion as a blow struck at themselves. Most of them came gradually to support resistance groups, even though it involved a high price to themselves in life and property, when they might have lived less dangerously if they had been content to be merely neutral and passive.

The whole situation in northwestern Luzon was convulsed briefly after January 19, 1942. On that day Walter Cushing carried out his sensational Candon ambush in which sixty-nine Japanese were killed and fourteen of their trucks were either destroyed or captured. Much to Praeger's disgust, the action was announced in a communique the next day. This attack, coming only a week after Praeger's own Tuguegarao raid, seems to have shocked the Japanese into believing that there might be some kind of organized and centralized resistance afoot in North Luzon. Within a few days they dispatched more troops to Bontoc in south-central Mountain Province. Some drove up the Cagayan Valley to Ibulao Pass in Ifugao, where they were delayed for some time by Philippine Scouts originally from Camp John Hay. Others approached Bontoc from the southwest via the Baguio-Bontoc road. They captured the Lepanto copper mine intact, then inexplicably left it unguarded and went on to Bontoc. Guerrilla forces under Capt. William G. Peryam, the mine's former manager, moved in and sabotaged it, rendering the mine unusable. This was a serious blow to the enemy, for in peacetime this mine supplied 10 percent of Japan's annual copper requirements. A third enemy force marched eastward along the Tagudin-Cervantes-Sabangan road, and got themselves ambushed again by Cushing. The Japanese were never able to catch any guerrillas, so they contented themselves with burning the whole town of Banaue in Ifugao, bombing several barrios, and destroying a few houses in Bontoc. Two weeks later they withdrew and were immediately followed into Bontoc by a patrol led by Lieutenant Bowen. He questioned some missionaries in Bontoc about Japanese behavior toward civilians and was told that despite their wanton bombing and arson they had treated individual civilians well.

Soon afterward, on January 29, another patrol under Lieutenant Camp attacked a Japanese convoy south of Gattaran on Route 5 in Cagayan Province. They destroyed three trucks and inflicted an estimated twenty casualties. The Japanese were able to encircle the patrol in a thick bamboo grove and began a search that lasted four or five hours. Fortunately for the patrol, the well-known Japanese dislike of fighting in the dark came to their rescue. The enemy called off the search when night fell, and the patrol made its escape.

The Japanese appeared to undertake a general rethinking of

their whole position in North Luzon at about this time. They reduced the Tuguegarao garrison and, after a couple of unsuccessful attempts to maintain communications between Tuguegarao and Aparri, were content to dig in and allow the road to remain closed until May. It was a passivity that surprised Troop C. The situation in Ilocos Norte and Ilocos Sur was different. Japanese army units all over Luzon were then being supplied to a considerable degree through Ilocos ports. It was essential to them that both the ports and the main highway along the west coast be kept open. Consequently, they struck back more forcefully, then and later, at the guerrillas in Ilocos than they ever did at those in Cagayan, far in the interior. In hindsight, it is possible to speculate that Troop C could have accomplished more in February, March, and April 1942 had it shifted its operations to Ilocos. This was not perceived at the time, however; main efforts then were concentrated against local enemy forces along the Cagayan-Apayao border. The Filamericans definitely overestimated Japanese strength there, and the Nipponese in turn seemed to greatly overestimate guerrilla strength.[14]

Near the end of January Captain Praeger was preoccupied with several problems. One was to distribute troops in detachments at Tuao, Manauan, and Rizal, with outposts along the Cagayan River. If a large number of guerrillas were kept together, the burden of feeding them was more than the peasant farmers of thinly populated areas could sustain. Also, Praeger himself had fallen sick with several maladies, most notable of which was hives, and was very weak. Yet he wanted to go to Kabugao, some fifty miles northwest through roadless wilderness to get a radio transmitter and investigate the desirability of making his headquarters there. Early in February he and Captain Jones set off with a patrol for Kabugao, the capital of Apayao Subprovince. Due to Praeger's illness, they went in easy stages and arrived February 11. They were quartered in the house of an old American Negro, Charles Stewart, one of those U.S. soldiers who had chosen to stay and seek his fortune in the Philippines after the repression of the Philippine Insurrection at the turn of the century. Formerly a private in Troop D, 10th Cavalry, Stewart had fought both at San Juan Hill and during the pacification of the Philippines. Like many an old soldier, he was much given to reminiscing about the past and romanticizing it. He spoke warmly of Joe Wheeler, a former Confederate major general, under whose command he had been in the attack on San Juan Hill. There Wheeler, a small man, had repeatedly exposed himself to enemy fire. When his officers and men remonstrated with him not to do this, Wheeler had allegedly replied, "Don't mind me, boys. I'm too small to be hit." Whether Wheeler had actually spoken and acted thus more than forty years before is uncertain, but Stewart was convinced that this was the way every American should feel anytime. He could not understand why American troops were currently "letting themselves be pushed around by the Japs." He listened to the radio every evening in February and March, but after Bataan fell on April 9 he never turned it on again.[15]

Meanwhile, on February 15 General MacArthur had ordered the creation of a new unit, the 14th Infantry, to be commanded by Maj. Everett Warner, who was promoted to lieutenant colonel for the purpose and charged with conducting guerrilla operations. The appointment was astounding, a clear indication that MacArthur could not have known anything about the character or proclivities of the man Filipinos had nicknamed "Major Bottle." Warner was a chronic drunkard whose professional incompetence was well known—at least in Luzon. When Colonel Horan was commandant of Camp John Hay he made Warner his provost marshal because it was "the least important job we had."[16]

Despite his unpromising reputation, the newly minted Lieutenant Colonel Warner's first order was realistic. It directed that guerrillas undertake no offensive operations, that they engage the enemy only by ambush—and then only when practically certain that they would suffer no casualties and that civilians would not be subjected to retribution. They were told to concentrate solely on gathering information, and they were given a cipher to employ when reporting the results of their efforts. Though this directive was discouraging to ardent spirits, it was simply common sense: To pick fights in order to kill a few Japanese now and then could have no serious influence on the eventual outcome of the war—and it would surely bring the wrath of the enemy down on the heads of the hapless Filipino civilians on whom all guerrillas had to depend for food, supplies, and information. By contrast, information about Japanese troop dispositions and movements, beach defenses, and air-base sites might be crucial someday when American forces grew strong enough to invade the Philippines. An additional consideration was that, after the Tuguegarao raid, Troop C had little ammunition left.

Other and much worse news soon followed. Singapore fell on February 15, and from that time on few in Troop C expected that they would be able to survive until U.S. aid arrived.

Trouble of still another sort erupted in North Luzon during the late winter of 1942. For the Americans in the area it was a fresh reminder that the various peoples of the Philippines still lived at markedly different levels of civilization.

Of all the peoples of the Philippines, those who had been most resistant to Spanish imperialism and Christian proselytization had been the scattered tribes who lived in the five subprovinces of Mountain Province (Benguet, Ifugao, Bontoc, Kalinga, and Apayao). The wildest of them, the Kalingas, had never been truly subjugated by the Spaniards. They had continued to resist any kind of orderly government in the early American years as well, and in 1942 bore a greater resemblance to the primitive Ilongots of Isabela than to any lowland Filipinos. Like the Ilongots, for a generation after the Spanish-American War they appeared to have foresworn head-hunting and to have accepted at least some of the trappings of Christianity and Western civilization. But their ancient feuds remained vivid in their imaginations. Missionaries had never been able to expunge their thirst for vengeance against enemies, and taking a head from either an outsider or a fellow tribesman still conferred prestige and influence upon the taker. Not least, a head-hunting expedition injected excitement into the otherwise hard, drab existence of the Kalingas. Tribespeople, male or female, exulted at the wild celebrations that took place after heads were secured.

When ordinary civil government lost its grip in December 1941 and was replaced for the moment by the excitement and chaos of war, the Kalingas, like the Ilongots of Isabela, could not resist the temptation to revert to past habits. In January 1942 a few cases of head-hunting were reported in southern Apayao. Thus inspired, a few weeks later a band of Kalingas descended on Enrile in Cagayan Province and took thirty-three Christian heads. Captain Praeger viewed this grisly development with great seriousness. He realized that these primitive mountain people who had been "civilized" (subdued) less than a generation before would, if left to themselves, quickly slip back into barbarism. He also believed strongly that his proper role in Apayao was to support the regular Philippine civilian government there. The main difficulty was that Milton Ayochok, the Apayao governor, while loyal, was drunk much of the time and had lost the respect of his people. Praeger and his aides considered removing the irresponsible governor but did not do so because they were unwilling to interfere in what were plainly Philippine domestic affairs. Eventually the problem was solved when the faithful Governor Adduru of Cagayan established his own headquarters alongside Praeger's at Kabugao and made himself the de facto governor of both provinces. Meanwhile, the head-hunting business was brought under control by showing everyone that the whole force of Troop C stood ready to help civil authorities do whatever was necessary to stop the practice. Interestingly, the Japanese also prohibited head-hunting in the areas they occupied, although in 1943 they encouraged the mountaineers in Apayao Subprovince to take American heads. By then, though, nearly all the natives had become pro-American and asked Praeger and his officers to let them take Japanese heads instead! It paid to make friends. . . .[17]

The whole head-hunting issue showed something more significant, too. Early in the war Walter Cushing,[18] and later on Edwin Ramsey, Russell Volckmann,[19] Ferdinand Marcos,[20] and others laid elaborate plans to unite all the guerrilla groups on Luzon. Some of them even dreamed of extending such unity to all the islands of the archipelago. Many other guerrilla leaders opposed the whole idea, Maj. Robert Lapham of the LGAF perhaps most persistently. He argued that every guerrilla leader faced problems unlike those of many of his fellows, and that communications were so poor that many different bands could never cooperate effectively anyway, hence nothing would be gained by establishing some overall unity that would never be more than a pretense.[21] The latter view was surely realistic. For instance, Lapham's most pressing problem when he began organizing in mid-1942 was to suppress gangs of bandits. Volckmann said his was to kill off pro-Japanese Filipinos. Praeger's was to stop headhunting.

In March, Praeger decided to make Kabugao his new headquarters and set about organizing his whole unit. He sent Captain Jones back to Tuao to inspect the outposts and detachments in that area. Frank Camp, who had held a "jungle commission" as a second lieutenant (later officially recognized by the Philippine army) since December 1941, was assigned to command Company B, 14th Infantry. It was a newly organized unit consisting of the Philippine army men who had become attached to Troop C. Company B would be nominally under the overall command of Major Warner, but it was attached to Troop C for tactical purposes. On one occasion the troop got a small amount of ammunition from Warner, dropped by one of the few P-40s still in existence on Bataan and sent north from there. Headquarters USAFFE promised to send money and a new cipher to further Troop C's intelligence work. This was also to be delivered by plane, but no plane ever came. It was another blow to morale, but a much lesser one than the news that the Dutch East Indies had surrendered on March 9. Very little that was encouraging came over the airwaves in early 1942.

Nevertheless, Praeger's group diligently collected intelligence. Patrols and spies were sent out regularly to seek information about the enemy, and reports were sent to USAFFE twice daily. On one occasion, Lieutenant Camp took the men at the Solana outpost, slipped into Tuguegarao after dark, captured a few pro-Japanese Filipinos, and spirited them off to Tuao for questioning. Another patrol managed to nab a Japanese soldier near Aparri. The Nipponese, perhaps emboldened by the fall of the East Indies, riposted by crossing the Cagayan River and looting some Chinese shops in Enrile. The Japanese might periodically change their attitude toward Filipinos—and were, in fact, at this time in one of their "good treatment" phases—but the animosity between Japanese and Chinese in the Far East was deep and permanent.

In March the quirky Nipponese tried a ploy that would make a good episode in a movie. The garrison commander in Tuguegarao, probably irritated by Camp sneaking into the city to kidnap the pro-Japanese Filipinos, sent a challenge to Troop C to attack Tuguegarao. He boasted that he had made his preparations and that "the mighty Japanese Army was ready" to take on all comers. His men had in fact established themselves inside the provincial penitentiary, which had high stone walls and barricaded approaches. An Allied patrol could not hope to take such a strong position, yet it would lose face if the enemy challenge was ignored. Lieutenant Camp was pondering this conundrum when he learned that some twenty Japanese soldiers were swimming in the Cagayan River. He promptly loaded several men into a sedan, drove up to the river's edge in broad daylight, slammed on the brakes, and had his men open fire, Chicago-gangster style. Nine Japanese were killed at the cost of one attacker suffering a leg wound. There were no more challenges from the enemy: only a complaint that the Americans did not fight fairly. It was an odd lament from an army whose soldiers left booby traps everywhere, who mined the dead and wounded on battlefields to kill medics who might try to attend them, who faced bunkers and foxholes "the wrong way" to mislead Allied troops and thus get a chance to shoot them in the back, and who often pretended to surrender and then tried to kill their captors.

Shortly after the end of World War II, Col. Jaime H. Manzano, executive officer of Maj. Bernard Anderson's guerrillas, penned a "History of the USAFFE Luzon Guerrilla Army Forces." In it he blistered Maj. Claude Thorp, MacArthur's choice to be commander and coordinator of all Luzon guerrillas, along with most of Thorp's associates and appointees. To him they were a sorry collection of irresponsible incompetents. The only exceptions, he thought, were Capt. Joseph Barker and Capt. Ralph Praeger.[22] Manzano, an impatient, irascible man whose judgments of others were often too harsh, was dead right about Praeger. Only three years out of West Point, totally uninstructed in guerrilla warfare, and with only three months experience of war of any kind, Praeger soon had Troop C admirably organized in its new headquarters. He separated civilian from military authority—with the latter subordinated to Governor Adduru—set up what was probably the most fair and efficient legal system in any of the guerrilla groups in the islands, established price controls, issued paper money, and stabilized the economy throughout his domain. He split his command into small groups to make it more difficult for the Japanese to strike a mortal blow at his organization. The action also lightened the burden on Filipino farmers of feeding and protecting guerrillas in any one locality. In March and April of 1942 he ambushed supply trains, captured Japanese couriers, and fended off enemy patrols. As time passed, however, he steadily reduced military activities and concentrated on gathering intelligence and transmitting it to Australia. Most remarkably, he did all this so skillfully that he was supported by virtually the whole population of Apayao Subprovince.

Captain Praeger got his first radio from the Kabugao post office when he first arrived in that village on February 8, 1942. One of the problems that immediately preoccupied him was that the radio was not reliable. It frequently broke down and reception was often poor due to atmospheric conditions or local topography. Praeger wanted especially to communicate with USAFFE headquarters, then on Corregidor. During the latter part of March he had a great stroke of luck. There came to Kabugao a handsome, clean-cut Filipino civilian named Arthur Furagganan, who had lived in the United States and studied sound engineering in California. He was inducted into Troop C as a sergeant after convincing Praeger that he could not only repair but also build radios. About thirty years old and married, Furagganan, like so many Filipinos, looked much younger than his years. He was the second son of a former mayor of Aparri, the port city on Luzon's north coast that fell to the Japanese on the third day of the war. When asked how the people in his hometown felt about the Japanese, Furagganan answered that at first they had been afraid but soon were able to laugh at their conquerors because the latter were so unintentionally comical. Many of the Japanese walked with a waddle like vaudeville comedians, oftentimes with a Filipino trailing behind, discreetly mimicking the invader and thereby causing any nearby Filipinos to break out laughing. He added that fear of the Japanese had lessened greatly also, both because they had treated civilians well thus far and because most people believed that the Allies were winning on Bataan and that American reinforcements would soon arrive.

Although Arthur Furagganan was a Filipino who was fond of his own country, he had also lived in America long enough to appreciate it and to acquire the open, breezy manner more typical of Americans than Filipinos. Yet, when asked if he would like to go back to California, he would offer an emphatic "No," adding that America was a fine place for white people but not for Filipinos—whom white Americans usually held in lower regard than Japanese or Mexicans or even Negroes. Circumstances were simply wrong there. Most Filipinos in the United States were unmarried men who had no chance to marry Filipina girls because there weren't any. Being unwilling to espouse celibacy, many gravitated to American women of undistinguished moral stature. These ladies rapidly absorbed their money and often got them into trouble as well. Furagganan added that West Coast Americans so resented Filipinos that they sometimes picked fights with them and beat them up. He concluded that only Filipino students should try to live in America. When others in Troop C tried to convince Furagganan that the experience of Americans and Filipinos fighting together for their lives on Bataan would surely reduce anti-Filipino prejudice in America, he replied that he did not think even a bloody battle would affect it much.

What Captain Praeger wanted from Furagganan, of course, was not a disquisition on Filipino-American relations but repair of the unit's radio so contact could be made with California. Furagganan was skeptical because no regular radio parts were available, but he was willing to try when Praeger assured him that he would immediately have North Luzon scoured for materials that might possibly be useful. Among those sent out to scrounge parts was Furagganan himself. On the eve of his departure Praeger urged him to move his wife, father, and mother well away from any Japanese so the enemy could not take reprisals against them once they discovered that Furagganan was aiding guerrillas. Furagganan and the others were successful in the sense that they eventually gathered materials, some actual radio parts (mostly from Manila), plus many miscellaneous pieces of metal and lots of other junk from elsewhere. Altogether, it took about five months to collect some one hundred different parts or substitutes, from which Furagganan was able to construct a workable long-range transmitter that could contact the United States.[23] It was a remarkable feat by a highly intelligent technician whose work was vital if Troop C was to contribute anything substantial to the overall Allied war effort. Other radio *operators* could be found, but only Furagganan possessed the knowledge, imagination, and brilliant intuition necessary to rebuild the transmitter entirely from such a melange of materials.

His feat was doubly remarkable in view of several nontechnical circumstances. First of all, in addition to the normal risks run by anyone who aided guerrillas, Furagganan had no official military status for a year and thus would have been automatically subject to execution if captured. (Regular military personnel had at least the hope that they would be classified as prisoners of war.) So great was his desire to aid the Allied cause that he accepted the hazards without a murmur—despite the fact that he was a brooding pessimist who was convinced the Japanese were far stronger than the Americans and would eventually prevail in the war. He was further convinced that if he stayed with Troop C he would be doomed along with it—and with American forces generally. Yet he stayed, for despite his bad personal experiences in the United States he still loved America and, despite his anger and shame at the spectacle of some of his own people serving the Japanese, he was still proud of his own country. Of course he was wrong about Japan being stronger than the United States, though it is hard to say that his overall pessimism was ill-founded since the capacity of humanity to bungle anything has always been limitless. What was truly remarkable was his stubborn bravery and refusal to weigh anything against doing his duty as he saw it. Brave optimists, after all, are at least buoyed up by the hope that their efforts will have some positive result. One who unhesitatingly risks his life for a cause he is deeply convinced will fail, and still does so because he believes one should do what is right rather than what seems inevitable, displays personal conduct of the highest order. Arthur Furagganan deserves to rank in the top tier of Philippine war heroes: With Telesforo Palaruan, the youthful guerrilla leader who chose death rather than sign pro-Japanese propaganda that would have secured him medical treatment that would have saved his life;[24] with Capt. Juan Pajota, whose courage, shrewdness, and skill under fire contributed more to the success of the raid on Cabanatuan in January 1945 and the subsequent rescue of five hundred Allied prisoners of war there than did the action of any other individual, yet who was inexplicably denied the decoration he had so obviously earned;[25] and with those numberless Philippine officials and private citizens who accepted death by torture rather than reveal information to a cruel enemy.

Arthur Furagganan died a prisoner of the Japanese—as he had expected—but he did receive posthumous vindication, at least in the eyes of one of his compatriots in Troop C. Soon after the war's end, Captain Jones was on a ship returning to the United States when an unknown American approached him and asked if he had ever known Lieutenant Furagganan of Troop C, 26th Cavalry. When Jones replied that he had, the man continued, "I saw that guy go out to die, and I never saw a man so brave in all my life—and I saw thirty-seven others die the same day. They ought to put up a monument to Arthur Furagganan in his hometown and write on it, 'Here is a Hero.'"

The speaker was Stewart Barnett, from California, where Furagganan had once been beaten up merely because he was a "gook." Human existence is suffused with pathos. Many of its most poignant examples occur in wars.[26]

On the night of April 9, 1942, Troop C headquarters was a few minutes late tuning in The Voice of Freedom, still being broadcast from Corregidor. The announcer was speaking of Bataan. Gradually the realization he was using past tense dawned on the listeners—Bataan had fallen. The announcer's voice went on, "For these men the war is over." His tone was almost one of envy. Of course the announcer could not know what lay in both the immediate and more distant future for those whose war was "over": the Death March, frightful Camp O'Donnell, the long, dreary years of loneliness and semistarvation, the foul holds of prison ships, and death in the South China Sea for thousands who would fall victim to American planes and submarines that attacked the hellish, unmarked Japanese prison ships.

After the broadcast, the members of Troop C went silently to their quarters. They were not surprised, but rather sad over the fate of the Bataan garrison and concerned about friends there—mingled with pride that the defenders had held on so long. Two days later the camp radio picked up the Japanese version of events from the Domei News Agency. It went somewhat thus:

> Troops of the Imperial Army battled their way along roads strewn with American corpses into Mariveles on the southern tip of the Bataan Peninsula. Only the small forces on the islands in Manila Bay remain. With this exception, the American army in the Philippines has been destroyed. The total liberation of the Philippines and its restoration to its rightful place as a true nation of East Asia is at hand. The Japanese people may rejoice in this great victory, which practically marks the destruction of the century-old Anglo-Saxon power that has lorded it so long in our Asiatic homeland and so unscrupulously exploited our brethren in China and the southern regions.

It would be hard to imagine a clearer demonstration that people in our nationalistic, race-conscious age often resent social discrimination and condescension more keenly and bitterly than they do common political and economic grievances.[27]

After the somber description of the fall of Bataan came the Japanese version of what Americans and Filipinos would later call the Death March. It went something like, "A long column of starved and exhausted United States troops is now being marched out of Bataan, guarded by only a few diminutive Japanese. The Americans are wholly without spirit, bedraggled and shoeless, and in a state of moral collapse."

Soon after, the Japanese began their first serious effort to crush all the guerrillas in North Luzon. For a time they enjoyed considerable success. On April 15, elements of the Japanese 65th Brigade drove down Mountain Province while another large force repulsed Major Enriquez at Balete Pass and pushed northward into the Cagayan Valley. Considerable casualties were inflicted on both sides; but, overall, the guerrillas were not able to check the Japanese regulars. Had the enemy continued this policy relentlessly he might well have smashed all the formal guerrilla organizations in North Luzon and reduced Allied resistance to tiny bands of wandering, ineffectual marauders. Such was not to be, however; the enemy, as was so often to be the case, abruptly changed tactics. The Japanese 122nd Infantry fell back to Bangued in Abra Province, regrouped, and then came back into the mountains a few days later, this time supported by air cover.

5

The Tribulations of Colonel Horan and Associates

On December 24, 1941, Col. John Horan had received an order from USAFFE to save his command. Early in January he notified General MacArthur that he was unable to join the main body of USAFFE, then in central Luzon. Since many of his units had already broken up, he simply ordered all of them disbanded. On January 16 he hiked north to the Suyoc and Lepanto mines "to get as far away from the enemy as possible."[1] Here the miners, isolated in the mountains, without hope of receiving help anytime soon, and with nothing to do, persuaded Horan to radio MacArthur for authority to organize guerrilla operations against the enemy. Horan at first opposed the idea because it was contrary to internationally accepted rules of warfare, but he soon gave in and accepted it. At least this is the version of this episode that appears in *Guerrilla Resistance Movement in Northern Luzon*,[2] and substantially that in *Guerrilla Days in North Luzon*.[3] Horan's "1960 Diary" tells a somewhat different story. It portrays the colonel as smoothing over ill feeling between personnel from two mines, then persuading them to help him organize and support a guerrilla regiment of Igorots.[4] This version is typical of the general flavor of the "1960 Diary": Horan consistently depicts himself as the pacifier of intertribal combatants,[5] the suppressor of head-hunting,[6] and the promoter of most of the positive activities that took place anywhere near him during the following three months.[7]

Whatever the case, Horan ordered all his former officers to try to reconstitute their original units, recruit new men and train them, and equip all hands with whatever arms could be secured anywhere. Left unsaid was whether he now thought about the $7 million worth of arms and supplies he had ordered destroyed since leaving Baguio three weeks before.[8] In any case, the practice did not change. Although a shortage of arms and ammunition was chronic among his guerrillas for the next three months, various bands of them either destroyed weapons and other materiel or eagerly sought to collect it—depending on the fortunes of war at different times and places.[9] Horan notified HQ USAFFE on Corregidor of what he had done and at once received congratulations from General MacArthur, as well as authorization to reorganize the 43rd Infantry (Philippine Scouts) into two battalions. On April 8, the day Bataan fell, authorization followed to organize the 121st Infantry. Both of these units consisted of a mixture of Philippine Scouts, scattered and footloose American and Philippine army soldiers from the many units shattered by the original Japanese onslaught, some Philippine Constabularymen, and civilian volunteers.

Colonel Horan got right to work assigning officers to units in the field and making elaborate plans to scatter guerrillas all over northern Luzon.[10] He also recommended to USAFFE that each mine superintendent be commissioned a major, each graduate engineer a captain, and each mine foreman a lieutenant. Headquarters USAFFE came through with the commissions, though all were a rank or two lower than Horan had requested.

In a number of ways, Colonel Horan's loosely knit organization performed creditably. In an effort to get things going, the fifty-year-old Horan hiked indefatigably all over the roughest mountain country in the Philippines—much of the time in places with no roads, or where the few bridges over raging mountain rivers had been destroyed. Most such destruction was done with dynamite because large stocks of the explosive were stored in the many mines in the mountains. It was also used to mine roads on which the enemy traveled, to blow roads off the sides of cliffs, to start avalanches on steep mountainsides that would knock Japanese trucks off into canyons hundreds of feet below, to mine buildings in towns, and the like.[11] Not only Walter Cushing, but many other guerrillas as well, became adept at setting ambushes. In his "1960 Diary," Colonel Horan describes the process explicitly:

> To ambush truck columns of troops we did not try to shoot at the people in the trucks, but at the truck drivers, thereby causing the trucks to leave the road, tumble down into gorges or irrigation ditches and cause the maximum damage with the least loss of ammunition or men. According to logistics, it takes over 100 lbs. of rifle ammunition per enemy casualty, and we didn't have it. Most of our ambushes lasted only *about 30 seconds* [emphasis in original]. It was like a constant horde of gnats instead of a rush of a herd of elephants. As one Japanese officer told me later, "You were what we might call 'A Thorn in our Flesh.' We never knew when or where you would attack. We never knew where you came from, nor where you went to." Another Japanese officer said, "Why did you not stay and fight instead of running away? A Japanese soldier fights until he dies." I told him that we tried to get the maximum results with the minimum ammunition and the minimum casualties in the minimum time. I said my orders were to "hit and run"; our motto was "He who fights and runs away will live to fight another day." He said it was a glorious honor for a Japanese soldier to die for his country. I told him it was a lot more sensible to live for his country and attack again and again, that if our small groups stayed to fight to a finish we would use up all our ammunition in our fight and would be thru for the rest of the war. He just could not understand this.[12]

Colonel Horan insisted that the 121st would have been a fine regiment if only there had been more ammunition, if Lieutenant General Wainwright had not surrendered, and if they had gotten proper support from USAFFE. The last galled him especially: "We never received one round of ammunition, one rifle, one single shoestring or bit of equipment, one ounce of food or one cent of money from higher authority."[13]

That Horan felt deserted was understandable, although it is difficult to see what MacArthur's headquarters could have done for either him or any other guerrillas at a time when the battle for Bataan was being lost for lack of food and medicines, Corregidor's situation was growing more hopeless by the day, and MacArthur himself was either planning his own escape from Corregidor or trying to get established in Australia. In truth, Horan was simply a chronic complainer. In his view, Filipino civilian officials were often demoralized and only tepidly loyal at best.[14] The courier system was no good. Filipino runners let many people along the road read their messages, which meant that soon the Japanese knew the names of all the American and Filipino resistance leaders, which barrios sheltered them, and which civilians fed them. The situation got so bad that Horan's subordinates deliberately refrained from notifying him when they planned ambushes. One could rely on American couriers, but they were posted only once in two or three weeks and carried only oral messages—hence their reports were chronically late and incomplete.[15] Half of his subordinates were undependable or worse. Warner was utterly hopeless. Captain Scholey, a former mine superintendent, raged when hundreds of tons of copper concentrate was washed into a mountain stream to prevent the Japanese from getting it, thereby showing that he valued his civilian properties and duties more than his military obligations. He was a deserter as well: "He deserted my forces and *took Lt. Nicholson,* [emphasis in original] one of his mine assistants and a very able man, with him, and went across the mountains to join Major Warner at Jones, Isabela. He never commanded any unit, never entered any engagement, went to the east coast, hired a banca to get to China, was captured and taken to Japan."[16]

Major Leo Giitter, the C.O. of the 43rd, was even worse. A

born coward, he retreated instead of fighting, deserted his troops, reported sick but proved able to hike sixty miles *away* from the enemy, then took refuge with a priest, saying he had done his share of fighting and would now stay where he was until the end of the war.[17]

As for Robert Arnold's erstwhile Air-Warning Service troops, Horan was glad to find native guides to lead them over the mountains to their old leader, who was by then a captain.

"Except for Arnao, Brazelton, and Pennington, they were all a pain in the neck, too lazy to hike the mountains as couriers, too many drunks, and too much eyeing native girls, unforgivable among the Igorots. That is the last I ever heard of them."[18] Plainly, Colonel Horan saw himself as ill-served by nearly everyone.[19]

With the unsatisfactory officers, all one can say is that it takes combat to sort out the brave and the able from those merely competent in peacetime. As for the uninspiring enlisted men, who can say for certain just how much heroism it is reasonable to expect from soldiers in circumstances for which they have had neither experience nor training, doubly so when they are commanded by an officer in whom they lack confidence?

It is interesting that in the margins of Horan's "1960 Diary" there are a number of what appear to be the colonel's admonitions to himself, one of which reads, "Cut out all adverse references to Giitter or anyone else."[20] Perhaps Horan's desire to be truthful clashed with his loyalty to the service, for few members of any organization like to display their dirty laundry in public. It is also easier to inculcate troops with pride in their units if they hear only about the heroes who have served before them rather than about the stragglers, cowards, and "eight-balls." Of the latter, there were more than a few all over the Philippines in the early days of the war. Most were killed—by somebody—before the war ended. They are not mentioned much in official literature, but many individuals who have written memoirs have been merciless in their evaluations of some of their peers.

Although Colonel Horan was disinclined to blame himself when things went badly, he was always in extremely difficult circumstances. The fall of Bataan dampened the morale of many of his officers and troops, led some to surrender, and caused many others to lose hope that General MacArthur could rescue them anytime soon. Still, on the very day that Bataan fell Horan received a radiogram from Lieutenant General Wainwright authorizing him to reconstitute the Philippine army's 121st Infantry and to regard it as a part of USAFFE. Horan went to work at once. He ordered all units—then widely scattered—to "carry on," reorganized his personal staff, assigned officers to command battalions in various of the Mountain subprovinces, instructed them to organize companies the size of an ordinary Philippine army company (104 officers and men), and to accept into their ranks initially only men with some previous military training, later adding any volunteers who were of proven loyalty and who could bring a rifle with them. On paper, the newly constituted 121st looked fairly formidable.[21]

Nonetheless, Japanese pressure was inexorable. They took Kiangan, then moved north and took Bontoc, the capital of that province. By the end of April they were pressing farther north toward Lubuagan, Horan's temporary headquarters. He then decided that he had to move still farther north into Kalinga Subprovince. He describes the Kalingas as "the most loyal and cleanest of all the Igorot natives."[22] They also possessed the virtue of hating the Japanese more than some other tribes. The area seemed an ideal retreat on other grounds too. The rainy season would begin soon and would turn all the mountain rivers into raging torrents, so the enemy would be unable to penetrate the roadless district for four to five months. Horan and his men could hide out safely in the many mountain barrios, which were well stocked with food. Months later they could all move across the Cordillera into relatively salubrious Abra Province, where Cushing had been active.

Had this plan gone to completion it is conceivable that the 121st might have seriously vexed the Japanese, but it was not to be. When Lieutenant General Wainwright surrendered Corregidor on May 6 and soon after ordered all his subordinate commanders to lay down their arms, Horan was flabbergasted. Only three weeks earlier, Wainwright had specifically ordered him "to hamper the enemy all we can whether by direct attack, by destroying transportation routes or just harassing threats."[23] His initial reaction was to refuse to surrender because his troops seemed safe and secure until at least September—when the rainy season would end, and when he still expected an American army to return to Luzon. Horan says he debated with himself for four days whether to comply with Wainwright's order but finally decided to do so when Major Giitter disbanded the 43rd Infantry on his own authority; when Walter Cushing, Horan's own choice to be his second in command, allowed his men to disband; and when he received news that Col. Nicholas Galbraith of Wainwright's staff was being sent to find him and personally deliver the surrender order. Realizing that only half a dozen of his officers and a small number of enlisted men remained untouched, he decided to obey orders.[24]

With two of his officers and a flag of truce, Horan started for Lubuagan, a four-hour hike distant. They were intercepted by Japanese and taken to see Colonel Watanabe, who proved to be a rarity, a Japanese Christian. Whether for this reason or not, Watanabe treated all of them courteously.[25] Nevertheless, other Japanese remained as mercurial and unpredictable as ever. Intelligence officers initially informed him engagingly that "he was being tried and would be executed" for beheading Japanese soldiers, disbanding his troops rather than surrendering them, heading a "band of guerrilla bandits and soldiers," and for fighting not in uniforms but in G-strings, blue overalls, or civilian clothing. Then they interrogated him for hours, subjected him to three different "trials," and repeated the threats of execution. Horan says he survived by truthfully telling his captors what he knew they already knew, telling them he did not know when such was actually the case, refusing to answer if the answer would be harmful to the American cause, and, finally, by convincing them that he understood and respected their Bushido code and that he, as an American officer, was bound by a similar code of honor.[26]

Afterward, the Japanese sent him around to many of the larger towns in North Luzon to read Wainwright's surrender order to large crowds. Then he was sent to Camp Cabanatuan, moved to Bilibid Prison in Manila on December 6, 1942, and shipped from there on December 19 to Camp Karenko on Formosa, a place reserved for generals and colonels. There, more than six months after the event, he says he received a memorable dressing down from Lieutenant General Wainwright. It went somewhat as follows: "I am surprised, Horan, that an officer of your age, grade, and experience would hesitate for a single moment to obey the orders of your Commanding General. You knew from my radio to Gen. Sharp, Col. Nakar and you, that the Japanese would not accept my surrender until you three surrendered. The lives of all prisoners of Bataan and Corregidor were at stake."[27]

Rendering a fair assessment of Colonel Horan's role in the war is difficult. It is certainly unjust to depict him as a total failure or to simply pass him off as craven. When he surrendered he was following orders from his superior officer—exactly what soldiers are supposed to do. No army can function successfully unless the great majority of individuals in it routinely follow orders nearly all the time. To maintain that there are times when soldiers have a higher moral duty to some principle—in itself religious, humanistic, or ideological—one that transcends mere obedience to orders, is not trivial but it comes most readily to ideologues. The claims of conscience are also a good deal clearer to *civilians after a war* than to *soldiers during a war*. Moreover, praise is suspect when it is bestowed after a war on enemy officers who disobeyed orders and thereby averted wanton destruction of some of civilization's monuments in the lands of those bestowing the praise. Yet who now, half a century after World War II, would say that the German general Dietrich von Choltitz, who disobeyed Adolf Hitler's order to destroy Paris, acted wrongly? But judgment also depends on how things turn out. Had Germany won World War II, it is more likely that General von Choltitz would have been executed in disgrace for disobedience to his political and military superiors than praised by his former enemies. For any soldier with a conscience and a concern for the ethical issues that are a vital part of civilization itself it is sometimes devilishly difficult to be sure exactly where his primary duty lies.

Some men in the Philippines who refused to surrender—Praeger, Nakar, Walter Cushing, and others—were subsequently, and rightly, hailed as heroes. The three named did not survive the war; others who refused to surrender *did* survive. Had they served in the old Austro-Hungarian Empire they might have been recommended for the Order of Maria Theresa, a decoration reserved for high-ranking officers who disobeyed orders and *thereby made possible a victory that otherwise would not have been gained.*

But surely Colonel Horan should not be condemned because he did not gamble on this very long shot and instead chose to follow orders. The fact that he took four days to make his decision indicates that he must have given careful consideration to the dilemma before him. Indeed, it was for this very delay that he was reprimanded by Lieutenant General Wainwright.

That Colonel Horan, while a prisoner of the Japanese, made speeches urging other American servicemen to surrender unquestionably made him look bad. But it must be recalled that he tried initially to raise up guerrilla resistance to the conquerors—with little success. Then, faced with a terrible dilemma, he obeyed orders and surrendered. This was not a heroic course but it was not cowardice, either. Failure to succeed in difficult circumstances indicates ordinary human limitations but should not brand one as an utter incompetent. Colonel Horan belonged behind a desk in a peacetime army. On Luzon in the spring of 1942 he was, as the English say, "above his ceiling"—but so were many other American and Filipino officers.

How difficult it was for many Americans and Filipinos alike to decide whether to surrender or to fight on is shown by the different decisions made by them and the varied explanations they offered for their actions. Horan, after considerable soul-searching, obeyed orders and surrendered. Colonel Guillermo Nakar insisted that, because he was a Filipino whose homeland had been invaded, he was not obliged to pay any attention to what an American officer, Wainwright, chose to do about Corregidor. Ralph Praeger refused to surrender on the technical ground that the order to surrender presented to him personally by Lt. Col. Theodore Kalakuka was addressed not to *him* but to someone else. Lt. George Barnett went into hiding to try to evade having to accept an order to surrender. Capt. Parker Calvert asked and received permission from Horan in May to delay obedience to the order to surrender. After making contact with Lieutenant Colonels Martin Moses and Arthur Noble some time afterward, Calvert decided to disobey and took part in the two colonels' guerrilla offensive against the Japanese in September.[28] Robert Arnold believed that the Japanese must have coerced Wainwright to issue the surrender order. Therefore, that order was not binding, and it was the duty of both Filipinos and Americans to continue to resist.[29] Down in Pangasinan Ray Hunt, then a fugitive, refused to surrender. He later joined Robert Lapham's LGAF, but worried about what his *legal* position would be in the eyes of the U.S. and Philippine governments at the end of the war. His guerrilla commander, Major Lapham, was in a similar situation *legally* but says he never worried about it because he could not imagine the government punishing an American for continuing to fight the Japanese. There were nearly as many different responses to Japanese overtures as there were Americans at large on Luzon.

After Horan capitulated, command of the 121st passed rapidly through the hands of Captains Cushing, Peryam, Stevens, and Abaya until its remnants were inherited by the hard, forceful Lt. George M. Barnett. Horan lists with pride the accomplishments of the 121st,[30] and adds that Barnett "made it the most outstanding organization thruout the remainder of the war in Northern Luzon." This estimate is seconded by *Guerrilla Days in Northern Luzon*,[31] but one of the major Filipino historians of the war was less impressed. He remarks that after the enemy captured Captain Abaya in January 1943, "The 121st became a mere shadow, and its effectiveness as a resistance group became practically nil."[32] The unit and its commander, Barnett, eventually became part of Col. Russell Volckmann's USAFIP NL.

Although his career was comparably short, a more heroic man than Colonel Horan was Philippine army captain Guillermo Nakar. When the Japanese landed at Lingayen Gulf in December

1941, he commanded the 1st Battalion, 71st Infantry, a unit assigned to form the rear guard that would cover the rest of the regiment's retreat from the coast. It was not an enviable assignment: Nakar's men had not only seen their brethren routed, they were themselves inexperienced, outnumbered, and inadequately armed. Yet Nakar handled them with unusual skill; they resisted bravely all the way from the coast back to Baguio, taking a considerable toll of the enemy in the process. Nakar, hoping to find refuge at Camp Hay, instead found the whole Baguio area about to fall to the enemy, so he went over mountain trails to Aritao in Nueva Vizcaya Province a few days after Colonel Horan. There he met Capt. Manuel Enriquez, an energetic Filipino officer who had spent the past two weeks busily collecting stragglers of many sorts, whom he planned to organize into a guerrilla force. Enriquez also had a radio, sent to him by Colonel Horan, who was then in Kiangan, where there was no power to operate one. Like the Americans in the north, Nakar had no hope of rejoining the main USAFFE force in Bataan once the enemy conquered Luzon's central plain, so he agreed to join forces with Enriquez and try to hit the enemy from the rear.

Had Nakar and Enriquez been alone they might have posed a formidable challenge to the Japanese, at least on the guerrilla level, for they had more than eight hundred officers and men under their joint command. Unfortunately, they had to contend with Maj. Everett L. Warner. As noted earlier, Warner's "supreme qualification was his ability to empty bottles of whiskey."[33] Back in Baguio, Warner had spent the first two weeks of the war racing around on an MP corporal's motorcycle and visiting taverns, in which he sometimes pretended to be the post commander. He had been too drunk to walk when Colonel Horan left Baguio, so he was simply left behind. Sergeants Bowen and O'Brien, also left behind with a patrol, forced him to follow Horan.[34] At Imugan, on the way to Aritao, "he promptly disappeared into the local gin mills,"[35] where he was picked up by Captain Enriquez. Days later, when they were all in Aritao, Warner pulled rank, insisted that he was C.O. of the Nakar-Enriquez forces, and commandeered Enriquez's radio. He ordered that no messages were to be sent on it without his approval—which meant that his version of events would be all that USAFFE ever heard from that sector. At that time USAFFE certainly did not comprehend the extent of Warner's unreliability. They told him to call the new unit the 1st Provisional Guerrilla Regiment, to assume command himself, and to organize his force in three companies to be commanded by Nakar, Enriquez, and Lt. Warren Minton, one of Praeger's junior officers.

Minton brought news of Praeger's raid on the Tuguegarao airfield. In an action that became typical for him, Warner sent his own version of the raid to HQ USAFFE. He placed himself in command and portrayed Minton as the leading hero in the action. Ignorant of the true course of events, HQ USAFFE responded with promotions for both men plus a DSC for Minton. When sober, Warner similarly "edited" other messages sent to him for transmission. Such habitual irresponsibility fatally undermined the Philippine army's 121st Infantry.[36]

Despite their incompetent C.O., Nakar and Enriquez accomplished a good deal in the next three months. They recruited enough men for their units to be redesignated as battalions instead of companies. Nakar's forces held several strong defensive positions between Bambang and Balete Pass in Nueva Vizcaya. For both him and Enriquez, February 16, 1942, was a landmark of sorts. In response to their radioed requests, USAFFE had two planes drop them a box of medicines, a couple of boxes of .30-caliber ammunition, and a codebook with instructions for future communication—plus a pair of shoes each for Warner and Minton! As icing on the cake, their regiment was rechristened the 14th Infantry.[37]

Soon, increased Japanese pressure compelled the new unit to withdraw from Nueva Vizcaya northward into Isabela Province. The 14th established its new command post and built an airstrip there near the town of Jones. Between them, from mid-February to April 9 when Bataan fell, Enriquez and Nakar maintained radio contact with MacArthur, trained their men, collected arms and ammunition from civilians, sent out numerous intelligence-gathering patrols, and undertook several successful raids between Santa Fe and Aritao. Ultimately, they chased the enemy back out of Nueva Vizcaya, took the capital city (Bayombong) and killed the Japanese military administrator of the province. During the same period, by contrast, Warner and Minton killed six Japanese POWs who were "trying to escape."[38]

When Bataan fell, Warner, with sublime self-assurance, sent a radio message to Lieutenant General Wainwright, then on Corregidor, requesting dispatch of a warship to Casiguran Bay on the east coast to pick up himself, Minton, and a few others of similar disposition, adding that the group would start for the coast in anticipation of a favorable reply. At that time there was no U.S. destroyer available for *any* purpose in Philippine waters, much less to rescue commissioned officers who plainly wanted to opt out of the war. Wainwright's reply was forthright, "Get the Hell back to your command."[39] A runner was sent after Warner and party but they refused to return. Soon they surrendered to the enemy at the behest of Lieutenant Colonel Kalakuka, one of Wainwright's staff officers. Nakar then assumed command of the 14th Infantry.

Captain Jaime Manzano, the Filipino executive officer in Maj. Bernard L. Anderson's guerrilla organization, wrote scathingly of the numerous Americans who, like Warner, managed for a time to evade the Japanese or escape from them but who did not want to join guerrillas or, indeed, to fight at all. They just wanted to get out of the Philippines entirely, or else to hide out with a Filipino family and be supported by them for the duration—at the risk of the torture and death of their hosts.[40] Ilif David Richardson, a guerrilla on Leyte, put the same charge more succinctly, saying all they wanted was to take a girl and some pesos into the interior and sit out the war.[41] Captain Alejo Santos, another officer in Major Anderson's organization, refers to five U.S. colonels as old, tired men just trying to sit out the war in the mountains.[42] A more equivocal case was that of Millard Hileman, who wandered for many months in the jungle, aided and fed by Filipinos. He felt increasingly remorseful about the risks they were running to help him, but refused to join a guerrilla band because he thought U.S. military forces had betrayed him by failing to come to his rescue. He also disliked what seemed to him the cool and haughty manner of Colonels Merrill and Calyer, the only two guerrilla leaders he ever met, so he resolved his dilemma by surrendering to the Japanese.[43] Major Warner's case thus was similar to many others, but it was remarkable for the sheer effrontery displayed. In addition to his expertise in emptying bottles, Warner also exhibited world-class chutzpah.

When Corregidor fell in May, Wainwright dispatched Lieutenant Colonel Kalakuka to personally contact Nakar and persuade him to surrender. Unlike colonels Horan or Warner, Nakar flatly refused. He at once holed up in a remote area in Isabela, where his situation soon appeared hopeless. The enemy was hot on his trail, with overwhelming force. If he kept his unit together so it could fight back with some chance of success, he would have to commandeer virtually all the food produced by nearby peasants. This was certain to increase the likelihood that some of them, in desperation, would betray him to the enemy. Nakar tried to evade this dilemma by scattering his men widely among the civilian population and requiring his scattered officers to make regular reports to him at his secret hideout.

In mid-May he removed his regimental staff of ten officers and seventy enlisted men, plus his radio—which he recovered from Warner when Warner decided to "retire" from the war— to the barrio of Madela in northern Nueva Vizcaya. For a month his men gathered intelligence, destroyed bridges, and badgered an enemy who had become overconfident and thus careless after the fall of Corregidor. He was able to reestablish radio contact with MacArthur's headquarters in Australia and, on June 29, received a message from the general himself, couched in the memorable phraseology so typical of MacArthur. It read, in part:

> The courageous and splendid resistance maintained by you and your command fills me with pride and satisfaction STOP It will be my privilege to see that you and your officers and men are properly rewarded at the appropriate time.
>
> MacArthur

Not long after, Nakar was promoted to lieutenant colonel and the 14th Infantry officially became part of the Army of the United States. It was, in effect, an independent command responsible only to USAFFE since Lieutenant General Wainwright had become a prisoner of the Japanese.[44] At that time its total strength was sixty-two officers and 960 enlisted men, plus three officers and 140 men of the Philippine Constabulary who were attached. Its whole situation was typical of a number of surviving organizations about that time. They still resembled the U.S. Army in some respects, but they were also in the process of becoming guerrilla outfits.

Nakar's fortunes quickly worsened. The Japanese launched furious assaults against his forces all along the Cagayan Valley. They bombed indiscriminately and tortured civilians en masse. In late July, Nakar inquired of USAFFE where and how reinforcements from outside could be sent to aid the 14th Infantry. No reply came, but he was told by others that the Japanese had located his radio station. There was nothing to do but move it at once to a new site—no easy task with the huge, cumbersome radio transmitters then in use. Japanese pressure increased steadily, much aggravated by the depredations of footloose and irresponsible American and Filipino soldiers who sometimes abused civilians, especially local women. More and more of Nakar's men grew discouraged and began to surrender to the enemy, in effect changing sides in the war. By far the most important of them was Lt. Leandro Rosario, long a confidant of Nakar. By chance, the minutes of the meeting at which Rosario announced to his men that he was changing sides survived the war. He told them he still loved his country but could not best serve it by continuing hostilities. He added, "let this act of surrender be performed with your hearts opened to imbibe the fragrance of peace with the Japanese Imperial Army and to cooperate hand in hand with them in carrying out the immence program of reconstruction."

His new Japanese friends praised him and later cited him for "outstanding service." Well they might, for Rosario joined them wholeheartedly. He cooperated with their puppet Philippine governors, led Japanese troops along with his own men, tortured Filipino civilians, raided USAFFE guerrilla headquarters, and publicly urged his erstwhile countrymen to collaborate with the Japanese because the United States would never return to the Philippines.[45]

Deserting to the Japanese along with Rosario were Lt. Antonio Castro, other Philippine army soldiers, a Constabulary-man, a village priest, the Jones chief of police, and nobody knows how many Ganaps (pro-Japanese Filipinos). Nakar, in desperation, abandoned his radio in late August and fled to Jones, where he was trapped in a cave on September 29, 1942.[46] Soon after, the Japanese found his buried records in a forest.[47] Nakar's capture was one of the heaviest blows suffered by USAFFE in its efforts to strengthen guerrilla activity in the first year of the war.

Nakar remained adamant in captivity. Despite Japanese promises of amnesty if he would sign a surrender document, he flatly refused and urged all Filipinos to continue to resist the invaders. Enraged, the Nipponese tortured him mercilessly. He remained defiant, as unwilling to join any pacification campaign as he had been to sign articles of surrender. More than a year later his captors executed him in Manila's North Cemetery.[48]

Nakar's downfall also immediately worsened the fortunes of the chronically discontented Lt. Robert Arnold. Months before, Arnold had taken his thirty-two men and abandoned Walter Cushing to join Nakar's rapidly evolving guerrilla organization. He had been rewarded by being given command of the 14th Infantry's headquarters battalion. In his book, he says that while he was glad that he had joined forces with a man (Cushing) who wanted to fight, he was also bewildered when Cushing—who outranked him (by Colonel Horan's reckoning, anyway)—took Arnold's men into his own command after they provided badly needed military training for Cushing's collection of miners and Filipino volunteers. He also resented Cushing grabbing all the credit for their several joint ambushes. Arnold says he led one of them all alone and killed an estimated two hundred Japanese. Because he was rewarded with a DSC and promotion to captain, his lament was not without substance.[49]

Nonetheless, Arnold was a contentious man, habitually critical of others. His disposition was soured further by the incompetence and irresponsibility he encountered on every side, as well as by a number of bad experiences of his own. Colonel Horan's farcical defense of Baguio so disgusted him that he wrote that it often seemed as though the best combat officers were those with the least experience in the peacetime army. He added that it was "a matter of patriotism and morale, a level head and guts,"[50] though he also groused comparably about Walter Cushing's "wild eyed impetuous schemes lacking completely in sound military tactics."[51] His disgust with Americans and Filipinos alike deepened steadily as Bataan surrendered, Lieutenant Colonel Warner tried to get a ship to take him out of the Philippines, Lieutenant General Wainwright "cracked" and surrendered Corregidor to six hundred Japanese when he still had 13,000 men on "The Rock," and as Arnold himself encountered numerous well-armed Philippine army troops in Isabela Province who acted as if they were still in the peacetime army.[52]

Nakar's capture seemed to be the last straw for Arnold. He barely managed to escape into the Sierra Madre near Pinapaggan in Isabela Province. Expecting no help from either Washington or Australia in the foreseeable future, he saw little point in trying to gather and transmit intelligence information. Within a few months he became convinced that such activity was suicidal when he pondered how quickly the Japanese had been able to locate Nakar's radio by triangulation. He stayed in the jungle for the next two years, sometimes reduced to subsisting on mountain rats and bats,[53] presiding over the sixty to seventy officers and men who were all that remained of Nakar's shattered forces. His only neighbors were Ilongot headhunters, whom he characterized as the most uncivilized, treacherous, and cowardly of all Filipino tribes.

Late in 1944, Arnold made his way back to the north coast of Luzon where three years earlier Walter Cushing had "stolen" his thirty-two men. By then, five of them were dead, twenty-six were either prisoners or missing, and one was living with an Igorot wife.[54] He eventually joined Col. Russell Volckmann's USAFIP NL and was given command of the 15th Infantry. For Capt. (eventually Col.) Robert Arnold, World War II was a distinctly unrewarding experience.

6

The Troubles Worsen

With the capture of Walter Cushing and Colonel Nakar in September 1942, the fortunes of the guerrillas of North Luzon began a general decline. Nakar was replaced as C.O. of the 14th Infantry by Maj. Manuel P. Enriquez. Nine months before, when Colonel Horan's entourage straggled into Aritao after crossing the Cordillera, one of the first people they met had been Enriquez. Handsome, smartly dressed, and energetic, he had impressed Capt. Thomas Jones quite favorably.[1] Enriquez announced that he was going to become a guerrilla, and told them he had already put soldiers to work trying to salvage arms and ammunition from the Marang River, where others had stupidly dumped them.

Estimates of Enriquez differ considerably. Albert Hendrickson, the area commander in Tarlac Province for Major Lapham's LGAF, had once been in hiding with Enriquez and thought him to be a mere playboy.[2] After the war, an American field examiner passed off Enriquez as an officer who wandered about "with no apparent objective," and whose whole unit "was bogged down in some sort of racketeering."[3] In an affidavit sworn near the end of the war, Lt. Warren Minton called Enriquez "unreliable." Minton also charged that both Nakar and Enriquez had tried to discredit the achievements of Lieutenant Colonel Warner and himself in order to gain personal fame for postwar political purposes. While either or both men might have harbored political ambitions, that was not in itself necessarily damning. Nakar was unquestionably an able man and a Filipino patriot, and Enriquez clearly had done good work training the troops in the organization he subsequently led and in harassing the enemy in the Cagayan Valley in May and June of 1942. More to the point, Minton's entire thirteen-page sworn statement is ludicrous, worth nothing as an estimate of anyone.[4]

Yet Enriquez did have deficiencies. He was too clever by half, and he lacked the "Rock of Gibraltar" qualities so evident in the makeup of Guillermo Nakar. To be sure, the brutish Japanese put him to a terrible test. They took his wife hostage and denied his ailing children medical attention unless he surrendered. Lamentably, but understandably, he eventually succumbed to his wife's entreaties and gave up in April 1943.[5] Far worse, he then made a great mistake: He assumed that he was more intelligent than his foes and that he could dupe them. Working from the fine office the Japanese gave him in Baguio, he pretended to be an active collaborator while maintaining his old connections with guerrillas and passing information to them. There were two deadly flaws in the scheme: The Japanese had thought of it, too, and the guerrillas no longer trusted Enriquez. When he sent out agents to various guerrilla units in North Luzon asking for their rosters so he, the commander of all guerrilla forces there, could coordinate them, the unit commanders detained his agents instead. Meanwhile, the *Kempeitai* (Japanese secret police) had acquired a roster of current guerrillas on which Enriquez's name still appeared. In desperation, Enriquez tried to take advantage of one of the periodic amnesties to which the Japanese sometimes resorted and surrendered again. This time they were not impressed. He had proved to be unfaithful, so they sent him to dreaded Fort Santiago in Manila and eventually executed him.[7]

For a time, Enriquez's executive officer, Capt. Romulo Manriquez, was able to build up the 14th Infantry but—like so many fragments of so many guerrilla outfits in the north—its remnants were eventually incorporated into the USAFIP NL by Col. Russell Volckmann.

The principal event during Manriquez's tenure as C.O. of the 14th Infantry was his involvement in a scandal that was both extensive and ugly. During the winter of 1942-1943, Major Lapham, C.O. of the LGAF, learned that there existed nearby a racket that featured stripping mines of steel cables, scrap iron, and the acid used in mining, and selling these commodities to the Japanese. Many men—both members of the 14th Infantry and civilians outside it—were said to be involved, with Major Manriquez the main figure. The cables were sought with particular avidity by the enemy's navy. Lapham records that he took forty of his men, went to San Nicolas in eastern Pangasinan Province, confronted Manriquez personally, and persuaded him to abandon his confederates and help Lapham suppress the illicit activities, following which Manriquez hurriedly departed for the lower Cagayan Valley a hundred miles to the north.[8]

Sometime soon after the war, Manriquez gave his version of the affair in a long affidavit. He said that while inspecting in eastern Pangasinan in January 1943, he heard of the traffic in cables, which was managed by Capt. Rufino Baldwin and some of Charles Cushing's officers. Charles Cushing, one of Walter Cushing's brothers, had little of the latter's energy, enthusiasm, or zeal to combat the enemy. He led a band of guerrillas for about a year but was plainly unsuited for the life and eventually surrendered to the Japanese. Nonetheless, he does not appear to have been *personally* involved in selling war materials to the enemy. In his postwar deposition, Major Manriquez alleged that he had ordered those involved in these illicit operations to cease, and had sent thirty-seven of his own men to the site to cooperate with Lapham in stopping it. He would have stopped it alone, he insisted, save that his small force was badly outnumbered by the thieves and their allies, some of whom, he had also learned, were members of his own command. Moreover, all the guerrilla groups were so chronically quarrelsome that he feared to act decisively lest he start an internecine war among the guerrillas. He and Lapham instead joined forces and settled the matter "by diplomacy."[9]

Manriquez added a number of interesting details in his deposition. He insisted that the traffic was carried on not for the personal enrichment of those involved but so as to "watch" the enemy and finance his own guerrilla operations, particularly to purchase sorely needed clothing and medicines for his men. He regretted that he did not know for sure just who was really involved save that most of the thievery had been the work of civilians rather than guerrillas. He concluded by saying Lapham apologized to him for disarming his men as soon as Lapham learned that Manriquez sought only to settle the whole business diplomatically.[10]

Considering the whole episode shortly after war's end, an American officer in the Guerrilla Affairs Section scorned Manriquez's deposition thus: "What a farce! . . . one of the sorriest and least excusable statements that could be made by any commissioned officer regardless of affiliation."[11] During a follow-up in 1949-1950, John H. Miller, a U.S. Army field examiner, took about a hundred pages of depositions from Filipino guerrillas concerned with the transactions in which Manriquez was involved. Collectively, they told an appalling tale. Most of them claimed they were not personally involved in the affair in any way, adding that they did not actually know any of the men involved; or, if they did know a few said to be involved, they were not sure if those men actually *were* involved; or they couldn't remember; or that they were sure that nearly all the thievery had been done by civilians anyway. Some, though, had better memories. They described the whole operation in detail and listed by name thirty-four guerrillas and twenty-three civilians who were involved. Major Manriquez's name was at the top of the list. They insisted that all those concerned had made a great deal of money out of it. One of the outstanding profiteers, they said, had been Tomas Chengay, a captain in Lapham's LGAF whose troops presided over the actual destruction of the cables after the ring of thieves was broken up.[12]

Miller's investigations ranged far beyond the affair of Manriquez, his associates, and the mine cables. He took affidavits from dozens of individuals. They testified to wholesale thefts by both guerrillas and civilians—not only of mining cables, but of sawmill machinery and other miscellaneous hardware, which was then sold to the Japanese. The affidavits included the names of thieves, middlemen, sellers, and buyers, and described land purchases made by profiteers from the operations. Several observers reported actually seeing many of the transactions take place. For good measure, they described competitive extortion of civilians by various guerrilla groups, and of civilians by other civilians—all punctuated by torture and executions.[13] Altogether, it is a sad tale of scoundrels posing as patriots. Captain Chengay, whose immediate commanding officer, Capt. Ray Hunt, praised him highly,[14] appears in these affidavits as an avid profiteer and cruel oppressor of civilians. Overall, it was a disheartening commentary on the dark side of human nature.

Still another American officer who organized his own band of guerrillas and operated fitfully for some months was Capt. Parker Calvert. When the war began he was at Camp John Hay with the 43rd Infantry (Philippine Scouts). In late December 1941 he accompanied Colonel Horan over the Cordillera to Aritao. There he, Lt. Arthur Murphy, Pvt. Grafton Spencer, and a Latvian civilian named Tom Jargoe left Horan and tried to go southward into Bataan. Like others, they were blocked and so turned back north, reaching Lusod in March 1942. They secured permission from Horan to undertake guerrilla activities in the high mountain areas northeast of Baguio, and gradually accumulated a retinue of stragglers from many sources, but especially from Calvert's old 43rd Infantry Scouts.[15] From there, they moved about periodically to Bontoc and Benguet.

In June 1942 there trickled into Benguet an assortment of footloose Filipinos and Americans, the most notable of whom were Russell Volckmann, Donald Blackburn, and Lieutenant Colonels Martin Moses and Arthur Noble. Calvert welcomed them all, fed them, and let them rest, nurse their wounds, and recuperate. During that same period, several other guerrilla bands headed by Emilion Vasquez, Rufino Baldwin, Dennis Molintas, Bado Dangwa, Lieutenant Colonel Bonnet, Major Enriquez, and Major Nakar came and went, laying conflicting claims to portions of the area and quarreling interminably among themselves. Most of them, along with several of Horan's abler subordinates, were eventually killed or captured by the enemy.

One of the ironic, sometimes tragic, but hardly surprising

facts of guerrilla life was that upright, truthful, honest, law-abiding Filipinos were sometimes poor fighters as irregulars whereas tough outlaw types, if they could be persuaded to become guerrillas, proved to be aggressive and capable. Thus the demise of one such man, Capt. Rufino Baldwin, was tragic but hardly unlikely. Baldwin performed spectacularly during the October 1942 guerrilla offensive unwisely ordered by Lieutenant Colonel Moses. His followers blocked the Kennon Road to Baguio, destroyed all the nearby Japanese garrisons, recaptured several mines near Baguio and Itogon, and killed about a hundred Japanese near Balotoc, as well as a larger number of pro-Japanese Filipinos. But Baldwin was betrayed to the Japanese by a girl he was supposed to have married but did not. Whether she acted out of pique at this affront or out of avarice for the impressive bounty on his head is uncertain.[16]

Calvert and Murphy were more fortunate. They eventually collected about forty followers, took them to Colonels Moses and Noble, the two highest-ranking officers left in North Luzon by the autumn of 1942, and asked to be absorbed into the much larger guerrilla host Moses and Noble were organizing. Late in 1943 they became subordinate commanders in Colonel Volckmann's USAFIP NL. Volkmann had succeeded to the leadership of that organization following the capture of Moses and Noble in June.[17] Calvert eventually became Volckmann's executive officer.

Of all the guerrilla leaders in North Luzon during the war, the foremost empire builder was Col. Russell Volckmann. Geographically, his realm occupied the portion of the Cordillera Central south of Praeger's domain in Apayao but north of Lapham's LGAF in Pangasinan and Nueva Ecija. Volckmann throve and survived during the period 1943-1945, but his activities lie outside the scope of this book. He describes his own purposes and deeds in *We Remained*.[18] By general consent, the ablest man he ever persuaded to join his organization was Lt. (eventually Col.) George Barnett, another of the many mining engineers who received commissions soon after the war began. Barnett had no military background, but he was energetic, systematic, determined, and tough—some would say harsh and brutal as well. Colonel Horan appreciated Barnett's work at such tasks as training troops, ambushing the Japanese, and demolishing truck convoys. He called Barnett a Rock of Gibraltar.[19] Barnett was equally impressive as Walter Cushing's aide. After the Tagudin ambush, Cushing went to Ilocos Sur Province and left La Union to Barnett. The latter assumed the reins of authority at once, quickly attracted the usual mixture of wandering soldiers and volunteers, and began preparing for guerrilla action. He also contacted provincial and municipal officials, worked out plans with them, and soon had both the civil and military government running smoothly in La Union.[20]

Both Barnett and Cushing abruptly vanished when Corregidor fell. After persuading Horan to capitulate, Lieutenant General Wainwright's emissary, Col. Nicholas Galbraith, began to look for Barnett. He soon found one of Barnett's subordinates, Lt. Sofronio Z. Concepcion, to whom he gave the equivocal advice that if Cushing and Barnett surrendered, Concepcion should continue to fight the enemy until the Americans returned. A couple of days later Galbraith found Barnett's hideout in the mountains of La Union Province, but Barnett flatly refused to surrender. Three years afterward Barnett claimed that neither he nor Cushing ever received a surrender order from Horan, and that Horan had told him he was surrendering only himself to the enemy and that his officers should continue to resist. Whatever the truth of this allegation, Colonel Galbraith returned empty-handed to San Fernando in La Union Province and reported lamely that he had been unable to find Barnett.[21]

The latter then began to organize a special unit, the La Union Regiment. Enough arms had been stored by Lieutenant Concepcion in Bacnoton, by Lieutenant Perez in Caba, and by Capt. Felipe L. Rodriguez in Balaoan to supply the new regiment. Barnett also began to put together a medical company to protect the men's health and attend to the casualties that would surely follow the action against the Japanese that he was anticipating. Barnett later insisted that he planned a general attack on the Japanese because they had intensified their raids on his forces in August 1942, claiming that his only alternatives were to fight back or give up altogether.[22] Moses and Noble would offer the same justification a month later when they undertook their calamitous offensive.[23] In both cases the Japanese undertook savage reprisals, predictably justifying their actions as retaliation for USAFFE guerrilla aggression.

Unfortunately, the Japanese soon learned what was transpiring. On September 12, 1942, they raided the regimental headquarters and captured valuable records that had been buried near the camp. They found the names therein of all the government officials who had any connection with the La Union Regiment. These unfortunates were promptly rounded up, and the Japanese made plans for all-out war. Fearful of the horrible reprisals the Nipponese were likely to inflict on those who had given him so much support, Barnett sent a letter to the Japanese commander in San Fernando, Colonel Watanabe, offering to surrender if he would spare the civilians. Watanabe offered to discuss it if Barnett would meet with him.

Meanwhile, several of Barnett's staff officers and battalion commanders had planned a major attack. They started promptly on September 19—before Barnett could reply to the enemy's proposal. There followed three weeks of raids, ambushes, and small-scale battles in which the enemy suffered heavy casualties and the destruction of many vehicles, some supplies, and a couple of ammunition dumps.[24] But the price was high. The enraged Japanese undertook a major mop-up operation supported by tanks and planes. They killed more than two hundred civilians suspected of aiding guerrillas, burned five hundred houses, and recaptured their lost ammunition. For good measure, Colonel Watanabe announced that every guerrilla would be wiped out. The various 121st Infantry units in La Union were so scattered by the debacle that Captain Peryam, their C.O., lost all contact with Barnett. The defeat also discouraged large numbers of Barnett's men and produced a wave of surrenders.[25]

It was typical of the confusion all over Luzon in 1942 that the 121st Infantry and the La Union Regiment were overlapping organizations. Many of the personnel of the latter came from units of the 121st in the Ilocos Provinces that had refused to obey

Wainwright's surrender order. In the last half of 1942 the 121st was commanded successively by Captains Peryam and Abaya. Neither was as forceful as Barnett, so a general impression prevailed that Barnett was the real C.O. of the 121st—which he became in early 1943 when the Japanese captured both Peryam and Abaya.

Barnett set about his new job with his customary zeal. Many Filipinos wanted to join the 121st, but Barnett would accept them only if they brought weapons with them. Some spent months tracking down a rifle so they could enlist. The medical company set up in the La Union Regiment was expanded, and a nursing corps made up of female volunteers was added. Some of these women brought medical supplies with them, while still more were secured from compliant pharmacists or donated by civilians. Medical officers lectured hospital personnel on hygiene, sanitation, and first aid. Combat casualties and civilians alike were cared for at a first-aid station. A runner system was established to facilitate communication. A unit consisting of men armed only with bolos was organized as an auxiliary of the 121st. Intelligence gathering was made more systematic, and the 121st began the practice of keeping at least some of the men in camps where they could be trained and disciplined like regular troops. Others conducted raids and ambushes. Afterward, Barnett claimed in his own defense that he undertook such attacks in order to accustom his men to actual combat. He denied that he had deliberately disobeyed orders from either MacArthur or Cushing to merely lie low and collect intelligence information. He was technically correct on this point for, like most Luzon guerrillas, he had no radio contact with Australia from May 1942 to mid-1944. Rather more disingenuously, he claimed that he had acted as he believed Cushing himself would have acted in similar circumstances. Although Barnett's spirit and courage were admirable, and while raids and ambushes continued to be employed after he joined the USAFIP NL, the disasters that began in the fall of 1942 and continued until most of the North Luzon guerrillas were wiped out by the enemy in August 1943 demonstrate conclusively that MacArthur had been right to urge guerrillas to restrain their bellicosity until American support became available.

Nonetheless, Barnett's overzealous activities did bear some fruit. The 121st became the best-organized and best-armed unit in North Luzon, thereby whetting the desire of Col. Russell Volckmann to gain control of it, an objective he finally attained in 1944. The merger with his larger USAFIP NL in turn made the 121st more attractive to Filipinos desirous of offering their services.[26]

The anonymous writers who produced *Guerrilla Days in North Luzon* (which was published by Volckmann's organization) remark that the 3rd Battalion, 121st Infantry, commanded by Lt. John O'Day, an ex-Brooklyn policeman, "did a fine job in cleaning the area of enemy spies."[27] Therein lies a tale. Volckmann himself said his number-one priority was to kill all the Filipinos who collaborated with or spied for the Japanese.[28] Many of his subordinates united word to deed with great enthusiasm. One such subordinate was George Barnett. He once hanged a pro-Japanese mayor of San Fernando, La Union Province, right next door to a Japanese garrison.[29] This act in itself was remarkable only for its bravado, for guerrilla leaders all over the islands killed known and suspected pro-Japanese Filipinos without mercy. All considered such action absolutely essential because they had to have the support of civilians to exist, and they could not secure it unless they made it safe for ordinary Filipinos to extend such support. What is noteworthy is that some Filipino writers have charged that many guerrillas in North Luzon, particularly in Volckmann's USAFIP NL, pursued this policy far beyond the bounds of all reason and humanity.

Ernesto Rodriguez Jr., who spent the last year of the war with the 121st Infantry in Abra Province and adjoining areas, published a grim book in which he describes numberless horrifying murders and atrocities visited on Filipino civilians by those whom he calls savage and depraved American and Filipino officers. He singles out for special opprobrium George Barnett; John O'Day, who allegedly did such things as line up all the males in a village and then publicly behead them; Lt. Julio Acosta, whom Rodriguez says he personally saw torture several victims atrociously before bayoneting them to death; and Emilio Escobar, nicknamed "Sagad" (Broom), who openly boasted of having killed four thousand of his countrymen before he was himself killed on the order of another of Volckmann's subordinates. Rodriguez acknowledges that Volckmann's guerrillas fought valiantly in the last months of the war in 1945 and that most did not mistreat civilians. He also concedes that many Filipinos are vengeful, and that a lot of the worst atrocities were the work of small, stray bands of irregulars who fought each other and pursued personal vendettas under the cover of rooting out Japanese agents or informers. He does not accuse Colonel Volckmann of ordering such crimes, and he admits that Volckmann sometimes expressed his disapproval of them. However, he does charge that Volckmann was insufficiently vigilant to prevent such atrocities, and never punished anyone for committing them. The result was that many of his lieutenants became drunk with power—and often suffused with blood lust as well—and so struck down anyone they suspected, or merely disliked, or who stood in the way of something they wanted—all on the pretext that they were exterminating Japanese sympathizers. The USAFIP NL was the worst guerrilla group in the whole Philippines in this respect, Rodriguez alleges, and those Americans who were prominent offenders were not only never punished, but went back to the United States as heroes when the war was over.[30]

It is difficult to evaluate this indictment. Rodriguez includes many pages of correspondence with prominent Filipinos that bolster his allegations.[31] Teodoro Agoncillo, a respected Filipino historian, tells much the same story but more briefly.[32] There is no question that most guerrilla outfits in the Philippines were hard, even cruel at times, because they thought it necessary for survival. Many were savage in their conflicts with each other. Most American officers who have written memoirs or been the subjects of biographies have acknowledged that some of their subordinates, both Filipino and American, at times did things on their own that their superiors would never have countenanced. Oftentimes there was little that the commander could do afterward save swallow hard and hope some atrocity would not be repeated. What they do not admit, at least in print, is that they often would tell a Filipino subordinate to "take care of" some vexatious situation or troublesome individual, and make no inquiries afterward. Such an instance was the revoltingly barbarous execution of the father of Ferdinand Marcos (who later became president of the Philippines) on the pretext that he was a known collaborator. The atrocious deed was done by Filipinos under the command of George Barnett, although Barnett was not present at the execution. Those who carried it out were clearly motivated at least as much by a long-standing political and family vendetta as by indignation over the elder Marcos's alleged collaboration.[33]

A much more complex case in which Barnett was also a central figure emerges from an analysis of archival materials. It illustrates not merely the periodic callousness of many guerrillas but the difficulty of knowing just *what* to do with ambiguous cases in extremely trying circumstances—not to mention the likelihood that superior officers often did not *want* to know what was being done. It all began on March 2, 1942, when Barnett met Felipe Rodriguez, the former mayor of Balaoan in La Union Province. Barnett had just been appointed C.O. of La Union by Colonel Horan, and was there to muster anew and reorganize troops formerly stationed there. During the first months of the war, as mayor, Rodriguez had aided local guerrillas. Shortly before encountering Barnett he resigned as mayor and joined Walter Cushing's guerrilla force as a civilian volunteer. His uncle, who was probably a Japanese collaborator, replaced him as mayor. Rodriguez also had a brother who was later executed as a collaborator.

Before long, Rodriguez became commander of Company A, 121st Infantry. He saw action against the Japanese but accomplished little beyond shooting up a great deal of ammunition. Soon after that he was pressed hard by the Japanese, who threatened to kill all his men and their families and burn down their houses unless Rodriguez surrendered. On November 14, 1942, Rodriguez, still the C.O. of Company A, succumbed to the pressure. He capitulated along with several of his Filipino officers. More damning, he compelled a number of his unwilling enlisted men to surrender as well. Worst of all, at least in the eyes of the U.S. Army, he turned over sixty or seventy rifles and three thousand to four thousand rounds of ammunition (a great deal at that time and place) to the enemy. All American and Filipino officers knew that surrendering arms and ammunition to a foe was punishable by death.

The Japanese kept Rodriguez for four and a half months, then released him. He went back home, began to farm a bit, and remained as inconspicuous as possible, seldom stirring from his house. Meanwhile, his wife began to give covert aid to guerrillas, likely with quiet encouragement from her spouse. A year and a half later, in the fall of 1944, Captain Rodriguez resumed guerrilla activity. By then all the major Luzon guerrillas were in regular contact with MacArthur's headquarters in Australia and were aware that an American invasion of Luzon was not far off. Not only Barnett, but Volckmann, O'Day, and many other guerrilla leaders—both in Volckmann's organization and elsewhere—decided that a necessary prelude to all-out guerrilla aid to the anticipated Allied invaders must be the elimination of all spies and collaborators. Many hundreds, even thousands, of Ganaps or suspected Ganaps perished during the next few weeks. It was in those circumstances that Barnett learned Felipe Rodriguez, newly returned to guerrilla action, was having second thoughts and had begun negotiating with the Japanese to surrender again. Barnett seized him at once and had him executed. His zealous subordinates killed Rodriguez by hitting him over the head with a crowbar five times and burying him on the spot in December 1944.

In a deposition soon after, Barnett said he merely ordered Rodriguez's execution. He said he did not personally witness it, did not know how or where it was carried out, or what was done with the corpse. He had simply given an order to eliminate spies and collaborators and left the implementation thereof to underlings.[34]

What took place elsewhere in northern Luzon at the same

time is no less interesting than the demise of Felipe Rodriguez. Ilocos Norte Province was notoriously rife with pro-Japanese elements at that time. Colonel Volckmann sent O'Day, Barnett, and others to lead guerrillas drawn mainly from Mountain Province—illiterate "bandits by nature"[35]—into Ilocos, where they "smeared a bloody path."[36] More specifically, they tortured, raped, murdered, and burned the houses of other guerrillas and civilians alike on a mass scale.[37] Volckmann arranged transfers stateside for O'Day and Barnett[38] before they could be called to account by local military authorities, and replaced them with Robert Arnold (then a colonel) and Capt. Harley F. Hieb. There followed an immediate change for the better in the conduct of the 15th Infantry, USAFIP NL.

It should be noted that these charges of despicable conduct by Volckmann's subordinates, about whom there is general agreement that John O'Day was the worst, were not made by Ernesto Rodriguez but by Vincente Erieta, one of Roque Ablan's most able and trusted officers, and by *five different American* officers charged to investigate allegations that U.S. guerrillas on Luzon had been guilty of atrocities.[39]

There is no question that Russell Volckmann, a stern disciplinarian generally, bore down harder on known and suspected collaborators than did many other guerrilla leaders. But Volckmann survived the war, whereas many of his more lenient peers were betrayed by Japanese spies or Ganaps. Moreover, if one considers what was happening to guerrillas during the spring and summer of 1943, it is not hard to imagine what Volckmann's state of mind must have been. In March his friend and supporter Donald Blackburn records that they learned that Herb Swick had been captured by the enemy; that Charles Cushing, Walter's brother, had surrendered; that Enoch French had disbanded his unit; that a helpful Filipino doctor's wife had been raped and bayoneted to death by the Japanese; and that Parker Calvert, Arthur Murphy, and E.M.G. Spencer had taken flight for parts unknown. In mid-April an informer told Blackburn that the Japanese knew where both he and Volckmann were staying, thereby causing them to abandon five months of planning to expand their guerrilla organization and flee for their lives to new locales. Ten days later he heard that Rufino Baldwin had been betrayed to the enemy by an ex-fiancee and that Enriquez had surrendered so his children could receive needed medical treatment. Then, in accelerating succession throughout the summer, he learned that Moses and Noble and all their records had been captured; that one of his own emissaries named—with tragic appropriateness—Fish had been taken by the Japanese while drunk, after which he and his wife had been tortured to death; that French had been killed by a disgruntled subordinate; that Baldwin had been tortured every day for two weeks at Baguio, then sent on to grim Fort Santiago in Manila, from whence few returned; that Major Lapham had barely escaped capture near Umingan; and that nobody had heard anything from or about Captain Praeger for many weeks.[40] Viewed against such a background, the harshness of Volckmann and those under him toward anyone even suspected of being pro-Japanese cannot be totally justified, but it is not hard to understand, either. George Barnett once remarked offhandedly to Thomas Jones that all of the guerrillas should have killed more of the collaborators than they did.

Overall, it is difficult to accept Rodriguez's indictment of Barnett without question. Jones, who knew Barnett fairly well during the war and corresponded with him for three decades afterward, insists that Barnett was quite unlike the person portrayed by Rodriguez. Jones thought him an efficient, practical man who could be tough when he needed to be but who was ordinarily modest and in no way the ogre of legend. When the Philippine Commonwealth brought charges against Barnett after the war, he passed off the action as the work of collaborators who had become part of the postwar Philippine government—a stance adopted by many other Americans and Filipinos accused of wartime atrocities. Jones adds that in 1946 at Fort Riley, Kansas, he urged Barnett to stay in the U.S. Army but says that Barnett objected that he did not know anything about military affairs and wanted to return to the life of a mining engineer.[41]

The allegations against Barnett resemble those about Harry

Fenton, an American guerrilla on Cebu who has been depicted by many writers as a monster of cruelty and depravity. His crimes and general savagery, they claim, destroyed the morale of Maj. James Cushing's (a third Cushing brother) entire guerrilla organization and led to Fenton's own execution by his fellow guerrillas. Yet Fenton kept a diary, which has survived. It is replete with accounts of the ideas and plans of the leaders of the group, as well as their everyday problems and difficulties. It also contains many references to his own wife and child and other prosaic matters. All are described in commonplace language and bear no hint that there was anything unusual about the character or predilections of their author.[42]

What is one to conclude? Unhappily, that many judgments about guerrilla activities in the wartime Philippines can be no better than provisional because there is so much uncertainty about not only the interpretation of facts, but what those "facts" were.

7

Interlude at Kabugao:
Summer 1942

On May 5, 1942, Troop C made its last radio contact with Corregidor. The Rock fell the next day. On May 14, Colonel Horan submitted to Wainwright's orders and surrendered himself and his staff at Lubuagan. He bestowed command of the 121st Infantry on Capt. Walter Cushing, who at once dispersed the regiment into small groups with orders not to engage in further combat.

For a short time both sides seemed carried along by sheer momentum, only to slide to a general stop that lasted for a few months. In the mountains of northern Luzon, the Japanese suspended tactical operations against guerrillas almost at once, but gradually completed such movements as they already had underway. They continued to push northward in the Cagayan Valley but did so slowly and unobtrusively. It gradually became clear that they would be content to occupy the important towns without engaging the guerrillas. Their propaganda underwent one of its periodic metamorphoses and became extremely friendly in tone. The Japanese praised "the gallant remnants still resisting," but declared that with Corregidor's fall, further combat was purposeless. Filipino guerrillas were told to turn in their arms to local police chiefs and return to their homes. Americans were advised to report to the nearest Japanese garrison commander for instructions. This new enemy policy was not in itself unreasonable, and it is quite possible that the unhappy experiences of

the Japanese with guerrilla warfare in China in the 1930s motivated it. Yet it did not work out as they had hoped.

On the Allied side, reception of Japanese overtures varied
widely. As noted earlier in this account, some obeyed orders and
surrendered, others continued to fight on, still others fled into
the mountains, and some changed their minds more than once.
In Troop C, Privates Leo Tullungan and Raymundo Camonayan,
both Filipinos on outpost duty in Solana, made their decisions
on May 24. Although armed only with Lieutenant Camp's homemade hand grenades, they undertook a hit-and-run attack on a
patrol of forty Japanese. The result was as inconclusive as guerrilla policy itself in these weeks. Tullungan was gravely wounded
and fell unconscious. The enemy, thinking him dead, took his
pistol and left him. Camonayan then rescued him, and Tullungan
eventually recovered. A few days later, Lieutenant Camp, Private
Garcia, and a few others attacked a convoy of Japanese barges
in the Cagayan River. The commander and a few of his soldiers
were killed but the patrol was driven off by fire from enemy
75mm guns, the ammunition for which had been captured from
Americans. Thereafter, only desultory action took place until the
end of August.[1]

Both the Japanese and guerrilla patrols continued to set
occasional ambushes. Sometimes they even sought each other
out to provoke a fight. In the case of the Japanese, the purpose
was usually to season green troops who had not yet experienced
combat. With guerrillas, the motive often was simply to allow
bored Filipinos to let off steam, hopefully at the enemy's expense.
But, more often than not, if a dust-up occurred it was accidental.

The slackening of activity had other repercussions as well.
Sharp-eyed individuals from the lower levels of human society
observed long ago that whenever an organization—be it government, business, education, military, or some other—suffers reverses, goes broke, wishes to change policy, or is compelled to
do so by outside forces, it usually throws out a great smoke screen
of reassuring words and feverish activity to demonstrate that its
members are still in business, are as industrious and "dedicated"
as ever, are still determinedly optimistic, and are as well supplied

with brilliant ideas as they have always been. Often the result is an orgy of reorganization, which takes such forms as bestowing new titles on leaders or groups, redecorating executive offices, energizing official statements of group objectives and, in armies, painting convenient inanimate objects and requiring enlisted men to practice close-order drill.

In Captain Praeger's case, although he had always disliked the "spit-and-polish" aspects of army life, it seemed to him that the troops needed to be reminded that they were still soldiers. Thus, to their ill-disguised disgust, it became the fate of men in Troop C to once more practice the old "Hut, two, three, four." It must be acknowledged, however, that nobody in the outfit, officers or men, had borne much resemblance to Fort Stotsenburg soldiers for a long time. In fact, the commander himself had been notorious for his personal laxity in this sphere. Praeger usually covered his large body with an abbreviated pair of white tennis shorts, a faded khaki shirt, and a Stetson campaign hat. He cut the tops off his cavalry boots and, being a frugal soul with foresight, saved the soles for emergencies. Meanwhile, he usually went barefooted.[2]

Lieutenant Bowen, an inspired scavenger, gave Captain Jones a pair of tennis shoes, which Jones treasured and guarded thereafter. Most men in the troop had Stetson campaign hats, which Jones describes as "the one article of uniform we could never improve on."[3] Otherwise, neither they nor anyone else in North Luzon wore trousers when they could get shorts. The latter were far more comfortable, which a cynic would no doubt say was the reason the army never adopted shorts for garrison wear. When traveling through the jungle, the men usually wore long-sleeved shirts to protect their arms from the sharp cogon grass. Why skin on the legs seemed to suffer less from the abominable grass nobody knew exactly, but it was so, and it was also true that many streams had to be negotiated when traveling cross-country. There, trousers were much more a hindrance and a source of discomfort than a help.

Although it was not implausible to claim that the unit needed shaping up, administrative reorganization was more impressive than the resurrection of close-order drill or picayune uniform alterations. A new unit, the Apayao Company of the Philippine Constabulary, was added to both Troop C and Company B, 14th Infantry, Philippine army. The whole lot was then rechristened as the Apayao Force, U.S. Army, with Capt. Ralph Praeger commanding.

Unquestionably, the greatest service Captain Praeger rendered to his command in those dark days was his personal example. He did not panic at news of Corregidor's fall but accepted it stoically, kept others busy at accustomed activities, and remained resolutely untroubled by events either local or distant. During the summer of 1942, Japanese planes would fly over Kabugao periodically, and even occasionally drop a few bombs. On such occasions Praeger would walk out into the open unconcernedly and gaze at the planes because their changing designs interested him. Now and then he would remark that the Japanese were poor pilots, not even as proficient as the air cadets at Randolph Field, Texas, where he had once been in prewar days.

The most important net gain made by Troop C in that phase of the war, however, had nothing to do with close-order drill, changes in dress, or Praeger's ruminations. It was the acquisition of Capt. James C. Needham from the 121st Infantry. Before the war he had been general manager of the Batong Buhay gold mine and was considered one of the most promising young mining engineers in the Philippines. Colonel Horan had wanted to keep Needham close to him, but Needham had a low opinion of Horan's character and abilities, and so took pains to occupy himself with efforts to raise troops elsewhere.

Physically, Needham looked more like the popular conception of a guerrilla than any of the other Americans. He was tall, slim, and wiry, yet had abnormally large hands and feet better suited for someone seventy to eighty pounds heavier. His oblong face was mobile, with high cheekbones and a jutting chin, topped by thick, black, wavy hair, and embellished by a heavy mustache. He had an olive complexion made darker still by the tropical sun. It was incongruously set off by his light blue eyes. Needham was an obviously intelligent man. He grasped situations quickly and acted without hesitation. He was not talkative, but what he did say was serious and sensible—and was heeded by all. A patriot in every sense, he was visibly unhappy at not yet having been able to do much for the Allied cause.

Captain Needham brought with him his wife Edda, a native of Maine. When the war began he sent her, along with other women from the mine, to Baguio so they would not be endangered or in the way if the mine was attacked. Edda had a lot of what country people used to call gumption. Infuriated by the lack of spirit among the inhabitants of Baguio, she decided that she was not going to spend the next several years in some Japanese prison camp, so she borrowed a pistol, got in her car, and started down a road in the general direction of her husband. Decades ago, before it became politically and socially unacceptable to make good-natured jokes about various categories of humanity, there was a common saying that there existed a special branch of Providence that looked after dogs, small children, and women drivers. That agency must have toiled feverishly overseeing Edda as she drove a hundred miles over heavily mined dirt roads and arrived intact at the far end.

After meeting her husband, the two of them, along with Lieutenant Bowen, started off toward Kabugao. Along the way the men were unable to resist the temptation to try to ambush a Japanese patrol. What to do with Edda? They parked her in a cornfield, with a bottle of warm carabao milk for consolation. Happily for all concerned the Japanese disappeared before the ambush could be sprung. Thus was Edda introduced to combat.

The pair were devoted to each other, but Captain Needham was one of those men for whom business and duty come first. When Edda returned to him from Baguio against orders, he told her she might stay but that he could not let her presence interfere with his duties as a U.S. military officer. Conscientious to a fault, inactivity weighed heavily on him. It was as though he had a duty to kill a certain number of Japanese to justify his rank and earn his pay, as if he was still being paid to produce certain amounts of gold from his mine. To Mrs. Needham's credit, she understood her husband's feelings perfectly and never interfered with his duties. Quite the contrary. On one occasion, when he was leaving for a fight, another officer asked her to persuade her husband to stay in the rear because the presence or absence of one officer would make no difference in the outcome of the anticipated operation, but that if he was killed, the rest of the outfit would have to look after her. She refused, picked up a volume of poetry, and read aloud the line, "I could not love thee, dear, so much, loved I not honor more."[4]

Edda Needham was small and slight, but gracious and charming. If smartly attired in some big city restaurant or theater she would have deserved the appellation "glamorous." But glamorous she was not when she and her husband rode into Kabugao in April 1942. She was clad in stained riding breeches, miner's boots, a khaki shirt, a red bandanna, and a straw sombrero from which a leather thong dangled under her chin. Hanging from her waist was a pistol. Spattered with mud and soaked with sweat, her naturally ruddy, freckled complexion burned red by the sun, she looked like a Kansas pioneer woman.

But clothes do not the woman make—any more than they make the man. Edda was both sharp and subtle. She gradually became the confidante of old neighborhood headhunters and their wives and was able to gain from them a truer picture of their real opinions than were any of the men. She was one of the first in Troop C to realize that local natives were beginning to believe that the Japanese had won the war. For a time, Captain Jones disputed the point with her. One day they called over a boy standing nearby and asked him if the people in his barrio believed that Japan had defeated the Americans everywhere. Like many Filipinos, he wanted to say whatever he thought his listeners would like to hear, but he finally acknowledged, "Yes. That is what they believe—but please, you Americans are our friends, and you can stay with us forever."[5] The remark was one more example of the remarkable loyalty of so many Filipinos. Like Arthur Furagganan, they continued to support Americans and guerrillas even after they had come to believe that the Japanese had already won the war or would eventually do so.

Edda Needham was habitually cheerful and talkative and thereby was a boon to camp morale. She was also a valuable member of the command at times, especially when someone was needed for such tasks as typing secret matters. Jim Needham was not a blind optimist but, like his wife, he was not a worrier. Both Needhams realized that their chances of coming out of the war alive were small, but the practical conclusion they came to was that they should make the most of what precious time they might have left together. Everyone respected Captain Needham for his many talents, and his gallant wife quite as much for the stoicism with which she accepted the dangers among which they habitually moved. When the war began, Needham had resigned his position at his mine and started for Manila to accept an appointment in the Army Corps of Engineers. Before he reached Baguio the enemy had isolated North Luzon. Thus he, and eventually Edda as well, returned north and ended up in Kabugao. It was typical of Captain Needham that he tried to pay for Edda's meals from the small amount of money he still possessed. When told that an officer's wife was entitled to a ration, he could hardly credit such a strange arrangement since she was "not in the Army."[6]

Captain Needham was one of those restless men who looked for things to do. He had brought several cases of dynamite with him and was soon trying to construct new grenades that would be superior to the crude specimens turned out by Lt. Frank Camp. He eventually succeeded. Needham's new model had a core of dynamite, around which was wrapped shrapnel. This was wound in cloth and covered with beeswax for protection. A blasting cap was then fixed in the head and a pin or sharp nail lightly inserted into the cap. This portion was then bound with a woven net. A rounded stick projecting from the end opposite the cap served as a handle. A feather looped to the stick added balance in flight. When the grenade was thrown and the point struck a target, it drove the pin through the cap and produced an explosion. To construct this firing mechanism required drilling a hole in each dynamite cap, a delicate and dangerous operation. Needham drilled each hole personally. Edda knew this and so was perpetually on edge for the three or four months the dynamite grenade factory was in full operation. Much testing was necessary to make the product as reliable as possible, particularly in the early phases of the enterprise, and the tests inevitably involved frequent explosions. When she heard one she would swallow and hurry to the door of her house to see if she still had a husband.

The Needhams were quartered in a small bamboo hut which they rented for five pesos a month. The American mess was located in their house, which had only three rooms, so they were left with little privacy. Drill started at dawn, so breakfast had to be early. If Edda wanted to eat, she had to get up with everybody else. This left her with much time on her hands the rest of the day. Some she spent trying to raise a garden, but her efforts met with little success because it was the wrong time of the year for planting. What little she did manage to grow was eventually harvested by the Japanese when they overran Kabugao in the summer of 1943. For exercise she rode a small stallion, complete with saddle and bridle, which she had purchased from a Chinese for fifty pesos (about $25 U.S.). The horse was a memorable member of the community. Considering his customary behavior, he had an appropriate name: Casanova. He also knew only one gait, a gallop, so he clearly got more exercise than Edda.

Having spent all her married life in the Philippines with cooks and servants, Edda knew little about cooking—a deficiency that made her the butt of many good-natured insults. The men declared that they had never known a woman who was such a sorry housekeeper, and often advised her husband to turn her in for salvage and look for a new wife. The Needhams accepted the joking with good humor on all occasions save one. One of the American officers complained at several successive meals about the difficulty of going month after month without female companionship in bed. Captain Needham finally burst out vehemently that conversation in front of his wife should be limited to more genteel subjects. The officer whose remarks brought about the outburst should have reflected on the observation long made by disgruntled enlisted men that if the U.S. Army, in its wisdom, thought a soldier needed a wife he would have been issued one.

In any case, this was the only time Edda's presence created any friction on the post.

June and July 1942 were the least eventful months of the war in northern Luzon. Save for Lieutenant Camp's raid on the Cagayan River convoy and the destruction of an enemy plane at Aparri, both in June, all was quiet. The patrols and outposts still kept in contact with the enemy, but life in Kabugao was otherwise suspended somewhere between peacetime Regular Army routine and rare guerrilla exertions. The bugler sounded reveille, retreat, and taps. Mornings were given over to drill, Saturdays to inspections. Japanese planes flew overhead occasionally, but unless they had propaganda to drop they paid no attention to Kabugao or the twin American and Philippine flags floating in front of the Constabulary barracks.

Kabugao itself was probably the smallest and least significant of the Philippine provincial capitals. It might be the administrative headquarters of Apayao, but Apayao—although large geographically—was only a subprovince, and so underdeveloped that there was not even a regular road into it. In 1942 a horse trail ran diagonally across Apayao from southern Cagayan northwestward through Kabugao to Ilocos Norte. A telephone line followed the trail. Soon after Praeger's forces arrived, arrangements were made with the provincial engineer to lay another line along the Apayao River from Kabugao to the north coast. These primitive telephone lines rendered excellent service. They permitted outposts to contact troop headquarters promptly and provided the basis for an air-warning system. While the Allied force had neither arms nor ammunition to employ against an air attack, the warning system at least insured that if an enemy plane penetrated the screen everyone in Kabugao would have time to take cover.

Peacetime Kabugao was a mere rural village of four hundred people set on a hill and encircled on three sides by streams beyond which lay low mountains. At the south end of town, on a knoll, was a small, wooden, cream-colored Catholic church that resembled many New England churches. A red clay road ran from the church to the plaza, some two hundred yards away. On either side of this "street" were a few bamboo houses in which Americans lived. Most of the native population lived around the plaza, which was itself merely a square covered with grass that cows both mowed and fertilized. Two weather-beaten frame structures, the provincial building and the municipal building, also fronted the square. North of the plaza was the Constabulary area. It consisted of two officers' quarters, rather like American single-family houses; the barracks—a long, freshly painted wooden building superior to the barracks at Fort Stotsenburg— and a few more bamboo houses for enlisted men's families. There were also basketball and tennis courts, and—alongside the barracks—a small building that doubled as a radio station and NCO quarters.

Kabugao also had two stores, a rundown schoolhouse, and a dispensary. One of the stores stocked bolts of cloth so that when troops wore out shirts or underwear it was possible to make replacements of sorts. Men's shorts made from gingham dress material seemed ridiculously effeminate at first, but everyone soon got used to the sight.

As can be readily imagined, social life in Kabugao was something less than exciting. There was drill in the morning, checkers or dominoes in the afternoon, and at dinner the opportunity to see Edda Needham dressed in her homemade housecoat. During the day she usually wore slacks, but she managed to find some brightly colored material from which she made a garment that looked like an evening dress to the men but which she insisted was a housecoat and which she unfailingly wore to dinner. The officers' mess sergeant was a dignified old Philippine Scout named Juan Miguel who felt personally shamed because "los Americanos" were reduced to eating Filipino chow and living in a style clearly beneath that of the officers at Fort Stotsenburg. Actually, the chow was quite good. Moreover, it was consumed by the light of homemade candles and washed down with basi, a Philippine wine made from sugar cane and called "Luzon port" by the Americans.[7]

Major Praeger was renowned among his officers and men

for the importance he attached to justice and fair dealing, his constant concern for practical matters rather than grand designs, and his supposedly Germanic attention to details. Nowhere was this more vividly illustrated than in his attitude toward their diets. He wanted everyone to have plenty of meat, and his directive to the two corporals whose business it was to keep camp headquarters supplied ran to sixteen articles. These specified such fine points as exactly where a cow was to be shot in the head, what kind of ammunition was to be used, how the carcass was to be butchered, who was to be paid how much to transport the meat, and how the owner of a slaughtered animal was to be compensated.

After dinner the men would sit around and converse idly while chain-smoking black cigars. These cost a mere one centavo each, wholesale. They were ordered in batches of a thousand or more and were smoked only halfway down, after which the butts were flipped out the window. Edda joined the conversations enthusiastically but disdained the cigars and openly disapproved of the casual way they were discarded. The only headway she ever made on the last score was to organize a weekly cleanup operation to pick up the half-smoked stogies.

If conversation lagged and the night was clear, those with intellectual interests often went out to study the stars. The Needhams had been enthusiastic amateur astronomers for some years and knew a great deal about the heavens, so listening to them was genuinely enjoyable for most of the Americans. Others might flex their intellectual muscles by reading American pocketbooks borrowed from the small personal library of the Belgian village priest, Fr. Gerardo Decasteker. Sometimes Captain Jones, who had been an Oxford student before the war, would read his Bible, printed in Greek, for the edification of the Scouts in his platoon.

Corporate intellectuality received a big boost in August when a Filipino from Hawaii who had brought a set of the latest edition of the *Encyclopedia Britannica* to the Philippines when he returned before the war agreed to sell it for $125 in emergency scrip. It was read avidly in the camp for a couple of months before even it began to pall. A major complaint was that articles on subjects of greatest interest to the officers and men tended to be insufficiently detailed. No doubt this was true, but articles on such subjects as the stellar system, international law, military law, soap making, tropical diseases, ciphers, radio, explosives, and anything pertaining to the Philippines retained their popularity. Maps, in particular, were of great interest and value to locate places that came increasingly into the news received on the camp radio: Buna, Gona, Milne Bay, Guadalcanal, Stalingrad, and, late in the year, El Alamein. Other highly popular articles were the ones on Japan—to help them find out more about the enemy—and Russia—so they could learn something about the European ally that was resisting the Germans so forcefully.

Those uninterested in reading could not resort to movies since none were available. Many of the Isnegs in and around Kabugao had never even heard of movies, much less seen one. Occasionally there was a dance, and these gradually increased in frequency as the population of the village swelled with growing governmental and military activity.

Each person responded in his own way to the quietness of life. Captain Praeger, phlegmatic as ever, was completely undisturbed. In his view, unless duty required action, running about the country from one town or province to another was nonsensical and merely wore out precious shoes.[8] Captain Jones sometimes grew edgy and invented reasons for undertaking reconnaissance or inspection trips, sojourns that came to an abrupt end in early June when he cut his foot on a barefoot march. Lacking a disinfectant, he soon acquired a tropical ulcer on the foot, which kept him in camp for the next two months. Lieutenant Bowen, always antsy if not busy, presented a more serious problem. Shortly after the Tuguegarao raid back in January he had returned to Colonel Horan and did not rejoin Troop C until after the fall of Bataan. A week of the somnolent life in Kabugao was all he could stand without resorting to strong drink. Captain Praeger resolved the problem by appointing Bowen commander of the north coast of Luzon. There he remained until he was captured by the Japanese in the spring of 1943. As usual, when he was busy he did

a fine job—this time relaying information to Kabugao and set-
tling disputes among Filipinos. The latter was a chore for which
he had a particular knack and which increased the already considerable esteem in which he was held by Filipinos. Captain
Needham kept busy manufacturing grenades, while Edda tended
her garden and flowers and rode her amorous horse. Once, when
she returned from a ride, Mess Sergeant Miguel remarked to her
that she should not be offended if local Isnegs stared at her while
she rode. She replied at once that she was not offended at all and,
indeed, liked the local people. Miguel said he was glad to hear
that, adding that the neighbors stared because they had never
seen a white woman before, and many of them believed she was
the Blessed Virgin Mary.

Poor Sergeant Miguel had troubles of his own far more
serious than the misidentification of Edda Needham. He learned
that his house in the lowlands, which he had built with his life's
savings, had been bombed and burned to the ground. Captain
Praeger, in a typical display of his concern for the tribulations
of others, sent Miguel on an intelligence mission to his home
neighborhood and gave him a furlough to visit his wife and
children as well. Miguel reached his hometown but was never
heard from again. Apparently the Japanese had learned that he
was a Philippine Scout—and when he was coming home.

The general tedium of life was broken only once in the
summer of 1942—by a Fourth of July celebration. For reasons
known only to themselves, the Japanese reinforced their garrisons but did not follow through with any land or air activity on
the holiday. This was still another of the many instances in which
one of their seemingly quixotic changes of mind brought a temporary respite. In this case the inhabitants of Kabugao and its
environs ignored everything save the big party centered on the
holiday. The day began with a moving speech from Governor
Adduru, which was well received by his listeners. This was
followed by roasting a couple of pigs, a cow, and two or three
deer over open fires. Much rice was then brought in to embellish
the roasted meat, and copious quantities of the best quality local
basi washed down the feast. Next to a fight, what ex-headhunters

William Bowen could not long bear mere lounging around in inactivity, and so was made C.O. of the CAF on the Luzon north coast. (Courtesy of Bill Bowen.)

seemed to enjoy most in life was a rousing party. This one was surely one of the finest in Kabugao's history, measured either by the quality of the patriotic oratory or the hangovers that followed.[9]

As noted earlier in this narrative, Gov. Marcelo Adduru was an honorable man and an exceptionally capable political leader. He also held a commission as a major in the Philippine army reserve. On June 6, 1942, he and the recently promoted Major Praeger decided to carry further the reorganization undertaken a couple of months earlier. Praeger began by formally inducting Adduru into the U.S. Army. He was careful to emphasize that Governor Adduru was now a major in the U.S. Army, not merely in U.S. *service* as was previously the case. He likewise impressed on all other members of the CAF that they, too, were in the U.S. Army, and not just the *service* of America. Captain Jones was also adamant on this point and adverted to it repeatedly in postwar correspondence with higher military authorities. To an outsider this might seem mere military pedantry, but it was administratively convenient, and Praeger was a stickler for formal and legal niceties in other matters, as was shown by his great care to devise a proper system of military law and justice for the CAF. But there were also sound *substantive* reasons for the distinction. In the event of a later surrender to the enemy a man who was unequivocally a member of the U.S. Army was likely to receive better treatment from his captors than if he was merely in USAFFE service or, worse still, only a guerrilla, a description the Japanese equated with bandit. Being in the U.S. Army also figured to improve one's chances of securing postwar remuneration for wartime service, or, in the case of Filipinos, to secure American citizenship.[10]

After his induction, Adduru assumed command of all military units in Cagayan and Apayao, an organization called the Cagayan-Apayao Force, U.S. Army (CAF). Adduru then named Praeger as his assistant commander and Captain Jones as executive officer. It was indicative of the confidence Americans had in Marcelo Adduru and the mutual respect that existed between him and Praeger that the organization that emerged from these arrangements functioned smoothly thereafter.

After the fall of Corregidor in May, and the subsequent slackening of Japanese and guerrilla actions against each other, the CAF turned its attention to gathering news and disseminating it among Filipinos as far as a hundred miles away. Radio London was depended on more than Radio San Francisco for war news. The American radio broadcasts indulged in so much undue optimism, and had been proven wrong so many times, that listeners greeted each new report with skepticism. To be sure, London did not always tell the unvarnished truth, but it did present the big picture with considerable frankness, a policy the CAF sought to emulate.

Efforts to educate readers and listeners accompanied CAF news dispatches. Many natives in Apayao had no concept of world geography. To them, Manila seemed as remote as New York, so the CAF writers emphasized the global nature of the war. At that time Radio London began its newscasts, "The United Nations fights on a battlefront that stretches around the world." This made an apt heading for guerrilla news reports. Sometimes the reports concluded with patriotic quotations from Lincoln or Thomas Paine. Readers were told that it was essential to make the chief effort against Germany because Germany was the trunk of the enemy alliance, whereas Japan and Italy were mere limbs that would be pulled down whenever Germany was defeated. Great battles were forecast in North Africa and Burma in 1942, the invasion of Europe and possible defeat of Germany in 1943, and an American return to the Philippines in late 1944. Considerable time was also spent discussing the undersea war as part of an endeavor to lead Filipinos step-by-step to understand why America had not been able to live up to their expectation of aid. Although the timing of expected events proved optimistic, the whole effort was a fairly accurate projection of how World War II would unfold.

By painting a picture of the current situation in fairly dark hues—while at the same time reemphasizing a conviction that eventual Allied triumph was inevitable—civilian confidence was

regained and present disasters were made to seem less important. Quite a few people—especially in Apayao, where many were
totally uneducated—had come to think that the Japanese had
already won the war. They had been led to this by their personal
experiences and observations, and there is no reason to suppose
that their morale would have been elevated merely by repeating
the rosy effusions from Radio San Francisco that they had come
to mistrust. It was not until February 1943 that Radio San Francisco began to speak frankly of past disasters and current set-
backs. Some Americans in the Philippines were actually cheered
when it admitted that temporary Allied reverses had taken place
in North Africa, for to them this meant that America was at last
strong enough to speak the truth. By that time, Captain Jones
notes ruefully in his narrative, the war had come to seem very
old to the beleaguered guerrillas. Peacetime, with its comforts
and security, seemed almost as remote as childhood. He regretted only that "it had taken fifteen months for American propaganda to learn that in war, as in other things, honesty is the best
policy."[11]

It is interesting to note that Maj. Robert Lapham, whose
circumstances were not unlike those of Jones, was less sure than
Jones that honesty was really the best policy. He acknowledged
that this is so abstractly, but he insisted that in war winning must
take precedence over every other consideration—that if one's
supporters are deprived of hope, victory becomes impossible. It
thus seemed to him that he had to provide hope to those whose
homeland had been invaded and ravaged by an oppressive enemy.
While he sent "truth squads" around his domain to rebut "Japanese lies," he also sometimes represented Allied successes as
having greater significance than was warranted. When questioned
about the likelihood of specific Allied actions, he took refuge in
vague talk about "after the rainy season is over." It is well to note
that governments of all types side unreservedly with Lapham in
practice—although, being Machiavellian, they would indignantly
deny this. The steady diet of good news that governments feed
their people in wartime indicates how little rulers respect those
they dominate. They plainly regard their citizens (or subjects) as

essentially grown-up children who are neither bright nor brave and who must, therefore, have their morale bolstered by a regular diet of optimistic pap.

If collecting reasonably accurate information about the general course of the war and then deciding how to present it to guerrillas and civilians alike required much labor and discussion, the collection of information about major enemy troop concentrations was more difficult still. The Japanese disrupted communications between individual guerrilla units by occupying the main cities and ports of North Luzon, forcing each irregular unit to seek information about the enemy on its own. Praeger's solution to this problem was to periodically send individuals—like his ill-fated mess sergeant, Juan Miguel—or small groups of enlisted men down into the central plain to locate their families, spend some time with them, visit Manila if possible, and all the while keep a sharp eye out for information about the enemy, living conditions among Filipinos, and the state of their morale.

Captain Jones says that maintaining morale and order in the civilian population was always a serious problem, especially down in the lowland areas controlled by the Japanese. This view was shared by Yay Panlilio, the backbone of Marking's guerrillas, and by Jesus Villamor, the Philippine air ace sent by General MacArthur in early 1943 to infiltrate the islands, travel extensively, and report on the general state of things. By contrast, Robert Lapham, C.O. of the LGAF, acknowledges that there may have been serious problems of that sort in the larger Philippine cities, especially Manila, but insists that he had no serious difficulty maintaining either order or morale where he was. The crucial difference may have been simply that Lapham's headquarters was at the north end of Luzon's central plain, where food was always plentiful, whereas in the cities and remote northern areas, where fields had to be cleared laboriously from mountainsides and jungle, there was always the threat of starvation.

Another delicate matter that troubled the CAF increasingly in late 1942 and early 1943 was what to do with a few Japanese soldiers who had been captured months before. It presented problems as old as warfare itself. POWs consume food, a drawback at all times but especially when the army holding them may be short of food for its own troops. Nobody wants to guard prisoners, yet when armies are in the field there are usually no prisons in which to deposit them. If a battle is impending a C.O. wants *all* his men ready and able to fight. If some of them have to watch prisoners, it reduces their own force's chance to gain victory. Conversely, if prisoners are released, some—if not all—will promptly flee to the enemy camp and thus improve his chance to defeat one's own forces. What to do? On the eve of the battle of Agincourt in 1415 Britain's King Henry V ordered the execution of all the French prisoners his army had taken. Mexican revolutionary leader Pancho Villa, confronted by the same question when his own troops were short of food, is supposed to have replied, "Let's shoot them for the time being."[12]

That the Japanese intended to begin the defense of their home islands against an American invasion by killing all their Allied prisoners is by now well known. To this author's knowledge there has never been an official American acknowledgment that Japanese POWs were deliberately killed in the Pacific War. Nonetheless, many such accusations have been made in the stories told by American and Filipino veterans since World War II. It is against this background that the following episode should be considered. In June 1942, six POWs were transferred from Lieutenant Bowen's coastal command to Kabugao, where they were used as laborers. They worked well and made no trouble, but Praeger decided to liberate them in March 1943 because he felt unable to take care of them according to the specifications of the Geneva Convention. It was a rare act of humanity in a war widely remembered for its exceptional brutality. It was significant also that some of the freed Japanese did not want to leave.[13]

About the end of July 1942, the Japanese-Allied "honeymoon" that had existed in North Luzon ever since the surrender of Corregidor began to disintegrate. One day Captain Praeger received a communication from Lt. Col. Theodore Kalakuka, Wainwright's official representative, to attend a conference in Tuao concerning surrender. (Kalakuka was then a Japanese prisoner.) Praeger believed that Wainwright never truly wanted all

Americans to surrender but had been coerced into ordering such action. Kalakuka had proper credentials addressed to Col. Nakar, C.O. of the 14th Infantry, but none addressed to Praeger. (Nakar had refused even to talk to Kalakuka). After an hour's discussion with Praeger, the talks broke off without agreement save to proclaim an armistice until midnight August 4-5, which Kalakuka promised the Japanese would observe. Both sides did so until the appointed hour, but immediately afterward a patrol destroyed several bridges on the Aparri-Tuguegarao road. Henceforth, the enemy did not try to secure the surrender of guerrillas through negotiation. The guerrillas, whom the Japanese had hitherto referred to as "heroic" and "gallant remnants" abruptly became "murderers, bandits, rapists, misguided elements, Communists" who would shortly be annihilated by the "mighty, victorious Imperial Army."[14]

Actually, the respite the Japanese gave the guerrillas between May and August 1942 was quite detrimental to their own cause. Many Allied officers and men dutifully obeyed Lieutenant General Wainwright's order and surrendered. If the Japanese had then treated them well, while at the same time mounting an intensive mopping-up operation throughout North Luzon against those who did not surrender, they might well have broken the back of all resistance efforts there. By suspending operations against guerrillas for three months, however, they gave the irregulars an invaluable time-out. The deterioration in morale so noticeable immediately after the fall of Corregidor was reversed by August. Moreover, many guerrilla groups reorganized under new leaders, became determined not to surrender, and acquired some useful experience in living in small, dispersed groups—leaving the Japanese with the task of hunting down each guerrilla group separately.[15]

Even when war proceeds only perfunctorily, as it did in the summer of 1942, it still exerts mental strain on its participants. One consideration the guerrillas could never forget was that time always seemed against them. They were confronted by an army that had just won a series of brilliant victories and had yet to be stopped. Patrols were in frequent contact with local enemy troops who might at any time begin to push hard. If so, how far could the guerrillas retreat? It did not seem possible to survive indefinitely, yet survival until at least 1944 was surely essential if guerrilla activities were to be of any real use to the Allies. Praeger and his CAF officers often discussed this situation, generally concluding that they might have a one-in-three chance of lasting that long. Actually, the odds against them were far greater. Nobody knows how many Filipinos died in northern Luzon during the war, but of the approximately two hundred Americans who were there in the early months of the war, fewer than ten were left when the U.S. Army returned to Luzon in January 1945. Thomas Jones was the sole survivor of the American officers with whom he had any association after May 1942 until his own capture in September 1943.[16]

Another constant concern of the guerrillas was the danger their presence posed for the civilians on whom they depended. From the first days of the war the Japanese dealt out harsher punishment to civilians who fed, sheltered, or otherwise aided guerrillas than they did to the occasional irregulars they captured. The Japanese knew that if they were hard enough on the civilians there would come a breaking point between the two, after which the guerrillas would have to use force to get supplies—an action that was sure to alienate their suppliers. When the Japanese raided an area the guerrillas could always fade away into the mountains, but poor Filipino families could not simply abandon their homes and fields. What would they eat? In Apayao, where the natives were more primitive than lowland Filipinos, evacuation of larger towns was actually carried out at times. However, it caused much suffering and some deaths from disease and malnutrition. No man of conscience could lightly contemplate the starvation and brutalization of the heroic people who were helping him and his organization.

Still another problem that was at best only partially solved was the lack of medical and hospital facilities. Omitting small conflicts that lasted only a few weeks or months, the first war in which battlefield casualties exceeded medical casualties was World War I (1914-1918)—and that is true only if one does not count the great influenza epidemic that swept over the whole earth in the fall and winter of 1918-1919. A quarter century later—in both the Japanese and Allied armies in the Pacific—at least as many men were lost or disabled because of disease, starvation, and malnutrition as ever died in combat. The fall of Bataan was more a medical disaster than a battlefield defeat because more Filamerican troops on the peninsula died of malnutrition and tropical diseases than were felled by Japanese bullets. Even the eventual Japanese victory there was delayed for two months by the ravages of malaria among General Homma's troops. In the north, the CAF had to contend with every medical hardship that had plagued both American and Japanese forces throughout the islands, and to do it without either hospitals or essential medicines. A serious wound could easily become a death sentence. Minor wounds took so long to heal and so sapped the strength of sufferers that they often became useless to their organizations. Some bolo cuts Captain Jones incurred in March 1943 ulcerated and were growing worse six months later. Captain Praeger suffered a fall in October 1942 and for months afterward drained a cup of pus from his wounds every day. The unit's malaria rate was extremely high early in 1942, and treatment was largely ineffective because the Japanese had conquered the old Dutch East Indies, then the world's main source of quinine.

Throughout the war both guerrillas and inmates of Japanese prison camps tried all sorts of home remedies for tropical maladies, especially malaria. Some prisoners in Cabanatuan learned to leach small quantities of vitamin C out of grass, which they said moderated the effects of both scurvy and beriberi; others there extracted yeast from fermented rice for the same purpose; still another shaved mold off the cheese from a Red Cross package for the penicillin he hoped it contained.[17] Russell Volckmann said that when he was in the Fassoth camp he learned from the Fassoths and some Filipinos that the bran between the rice kernel and the outer husk was a beriberi remedy, so he got some Filipinos to get him some. He boiled it and ate it. It was not tasty but it cured his beriberi.[18] Improvised treatments for malaria approached the limit of human ingenuity. Millard Hileman and

Clay Conner say they tried dita tea, a remedy used by some of the most primitive Filipino tribes. Conner, a freelance guerrilla, thought it was helpful; Hileman was noncommittal.[19] Lapham boiled some cinchona bark but found it too bitter to drink.[20] Blackburn says a Filipino doctor helped his malaria by giving him many salvarsan shots.[21] "Long Tom" Baxter, a guerrilla with Ira Wolfert, managed to get some Atabrine tablets which he "stretched" by dissolving them in water and injecting the fluid with a needle. He thereby not only overcame the malaria fever but used only a small portion of a tablet in the process.[22] The only drugs and medicines that were unarguably beneficial were those that came in occasional Red Cross packages—but none ever reached the guerrillas in the mountains of North Luzon.

In early July, when Captain Praeger and Governor Adduru reorganized their followers and created the CAF, they followed this action by composing a list of general orders for the new command. These orders were as follows:

1. Commandeering of supplies by military personnel is forbidden. Henceforth, all supplies are to be paid for in emergency currency.
2. Disbanded soldiers, such as those from Bataan, are to be put on partial pay status, and are to live at home or engage in some useful occupation unless they elect to join an authorized military unit.
3. No military units are to be raised in Cagayan or Apayao other than those included in the CAF.
4. Municipal authorities are advised, but not required, to retain their offices if their towns have fallen under enemy occupation to prevent pro-Japanese elements from obtaining the offices.
5. The civil police system is to be strengthened.
6. Provision must be made for the maintenance of medical and other services, and for producing substitutes for medicines, such as quinine, that are no longer available.
7. A cooperative merchandising system is to be established

and operated by the government in order to eliminate the black market and to make available to the people articles that have to be shipped in from other regions of Luzon.
8. A military commission is to be created to try persons charged with crimes not punishable by local magistrates.
9. No person is to be executed without proper trial or signed authorization from Major Adduru and Captain Praeger.
10. Spies and military offenders are to be tried by court-martial.

Provisions 8, 9, and 10 indicated Praeger's and Adduru's determination to govern in a regular, lawful, and humane fashion rather than emulate so many other guerrilla organizations, which executed hundreds, perhaps thousands, of persons in 1942 and 1943 on mere suspicion of fifth column activity. Nobody will ever know how many of those victims were innocent, but there must have been many.[23] No civilian was ever tried by court-martial in the CAF's domain.

A comparison with ideas, systems, and practices that prevailed elsewhere is instructive. A historian who studied guerrilla activity on the island of Leyte remarks, "We may define guerrilla law, in the last analysis, as the will of the sector commander, tempered by his private sense of right and wrong and his fear of later punishment." As an example of what this system could produce, Antonio Cinco, the judge advocate in Col. Ruperto Kangleon's Leyte guerrillas, ordered the bodies of enemy agents or collaborators to be minced but their faces left recognizable, then floated downstream or abandoned in the public squares of barrios as warnings to civilians.[24] Major Robert Lapham—whose LGAF was probably the most efficiently run guerrilla enterprise on Luzon and who was commended by the U.S. Guerrilla Affairs Division at war's end for having the best-disciplined organization on that island—tried to establish a set of recognized legal procedures but admits it was no easy task. No legal code governing guerrilla activity existed anywhere, and some offenses, trifling in peacetime, absolutely cannot be tolerated by guerrillas.

The area where he was had neither courts nor judges nor jails nor jailers, so in practice he had to do what he thought was necessary but still could be called civilized.[25] The CAF's procedures were much more formal.

The Cagayan-Apayao Military Commission got its first test a month after its formation: six cases involving murder and robbery. Captain Jones served as the president of the court. The trial judge advocate was Captain Praeger. Major Adduru reviewed the trial record and acted on the findings and sentences. The defense counsel, drawn from prominent lawyers in nearby towns, opened proceedings by challenging the legality of the commission itself. That body had been formally established under the provisions of the Philippine Articles of War, which differ little from the American articles. The commission at once began a meticulous consideration of the history of martial law in both England and the United States insofar as available documents permitted. After two days the body found itself lawfully constituted on the ground that a state of martial law existed in fact, although not by formal proclamation in the portions of the two provinces occupied by the CAF, and that under such circumstances the head of the government in the area had the power to appoint military commissions.

Although the point was decided in favor of the prosecution, Praeger joined with the defense in appealing the decision to Governor Adduru. Praeger was heartily opposed to establishing martial law in the free area; he wanted to keep intact the power of the civil government, and for this reason never declared a state of martial law. One other member of the court, Milton Ayochok, the nominal governor of Apayao, also opposed the finding because he feared that it would give the army additional power over the civil government. All of the opinions asserted and contested—of which one, the court's, alone ran to more than five thousand words—were submitted to Governor Adduru for approval before the trial continued.

Adduru rose splendidly to the occasion. He approved the court ruling, arguing that when the matter was stripped to its bare essentials the real power of the local government was based on military force and that without the army, the civil government would collapse.

Some members of the bar were of the opinion that while the governor's authority to appoint a military commission was open to question under commonwealth law, such a right did reside in the head of the de facto government. Thus, even if the commonwealth did not approve, the military commission would still have been legally established under international law.[26] That such fine points of constitutional law were debated so vigorously, and that the subsequent legal practices of the CAF were more refined and humane than those of most other guerrilla organizations, testified to the admirable character and good intentions of both Praeger and Adduru.[27] However, it also owed something to two extraneous circumstances: there were more lawyers in that part of the Philippines than almost anywhere else save Manila itself, and the CAF's headquarters happened to possess an *Encyclopedia Britannica*, which contained many fine articles on legal matters.

The court consisted of three military members, including its president; a civilian law member; seven or eight other civilians who were judges of inferior courts rather like American city or county judges; and qualified defense counsel who were always practicing lawyers. In Apayao, Praeger served as trial judge advocate. Ordinary rules of evidence were adhered to but sentencing followed guidelines in the Philippine penal code rather than the Punitive Articles of War[28]—a crucial difference. Philippine law is Spanish in origin. Its penalties are fixed by a table according to the number of mitigating and aggravating circumstances. The average sentence for killing, for instance, was only four to eight years. Rape brought the maximum punishment: sixteen years. War crimes were not tried by the military commission, but instead were reserved for court-martial. However, no such case ever came to trial in Cagayan or Apayao.

The trials proceeded with refreshing dispatch. Although the rights of the accused were scrupulously observed, neither side resorted to the nit-picking so common in peacetime civil trials and which leave the general public disgusted with both lawyers and the legal system. Neither side wasted time trying to score points, as if they were engaged in a game; both were intent that justice was served. There was great interest in the trials, and the courtroom was so packed that when Japanese planes flew over Kabugao it proved difficult to get everyone out of the courtroom and into air-raid shelters. Altogether, the trials were conducted with decorum, and the findings and sentences met the high standards of American military justice.

The commission was welcomed by the civilian population as a whole, for the people realized that law and order could not be maintained unless there was some way of punishing serious crimes that was more regular and lawful than merely shooting criminals or suspects out of hand. Late in 1942, when radio contact was established with the United States, the creation of the military commission was approved retroactively by President Quezon, thereby ending any surviving doubts about its legality.

8

Serious War Returns: Defeats and Losses Accumulate

About the middle of August the Japanese abruptly announced that they intended to wipe out all guerrillas in the vicinity of Tuao. Suiting deed to word, they dispatched a force to move westward from Tuguegarao through Solana toward Tuao. In addition to the usual assortment of rifles and grenades, the Japanese also hauled several field pieces with ample ammunition. Captain Praeger decided not to await the enemy's advance but to attack him as soon as possible in hope of capturing ammunition to supplement the CAF's depleted supply.

Because time was short, Praeger decided not to attempt an ambush along the Solana-Tuao road but to set a trap in the Tuao area. The Japanese, suspecting as much, swung north and entrenched on a hill at Piat. The CAF (minus Lieutenant Bowen's coastal command units) assembled at Tuao on August 22, 1942. The next night they crossed the Chico River to Piat and dug in, but were forced back the following day by heavy mortar fire. Then they tried to surprise the enemy by crossing the river in daylight, but some of the boats were driven off by machine-gun fire that cost Company B, 14th Infantry, some casualties. Meanwhile, the Japanese sought to catch the CAF in a pincers, rushing some forces south from Aparri via Gattaran and Dungao, and dispatching a seventy-man patrol northward from Lubuagan to

Abbut, only four miles south of Tuao, where it was checked by CAF security patrols. This proved to be one of those occasions when the guerrillas had reason to be thankful that enemy occupation troops in the Philippines were not the cream of the Japanese army. With just a little determination, this large Nipponese patrol could have driven around Tuao and joined the forces at Piat. Instead, the Japanese remained where they were while aircraft reconnoitered the whole Tuao area, contenting themselves by sporadically machine-gunning nearby barrios.

Brief skirmishes between CAF and Japanese patrols took place, but by August 28 it was apparent that the CAF attack could not achieve its objective of capturing enemy supplies and ammunition. On August 30, two Japanese planes bombed and machine-gunned Kabugao for about forty minutes and dropped many propaganda leaflets. Two guerrillas, Private Rilla and Sergeant Patayan of the Philippine Constabulary, were seriously wounded and never served again due to that constant unsolved problem, lack of medicine to treat wounds. The enemy leaflets proclaimed that within a year the Japanese would kill every guerrilla in the Philippines. Although it was a promise they were never able to fulfill, it did mark the beginning of a hard eighteen months for the guerrillas.

The CAF units fell back to Mauanan, and the next day crossed the Telefugo River. There, the rear guard under Lieutenant Flores fought a delaying action. The Japanese retaliated by burning some houses in Mauanan—including that of Don Celestino Rodriguez, which had been used as a command post. By August 31, when it was clear that substantial Japanese reinforcements were moving into Cagayan, Praeger decided to break off the action. All the CAF was able to accomplish in more than a week's fighting had been to deplete its already meager supply of ammunition. Praeger left Sergeant Arnao behind to maintain contact with the enemy and "To see what trouble you can get into." He also sent local outpost detachments back to their bases, then led those CAF units he personally controlled back west of Rizal.[1]

The military commission was scheduled to convene in the port town of Pamplona on the north coast on September 4, but the enemy seized Pamplona on September 2, so the session was postponed. Lieutenant Bowen and his command group were cut off in Numuuc, near another port town, Sanchez Mira, but suffered no casualties. Bowen, who was sick at the time, was carried in a litter by civilians to a bridge west of Numuuc, which he typically proposed to defend single-handedly. He was overruled by the barrio lieutenant, Pedro Volin, who quite sensibly ordered Bowen's bearers to physically remove him from the bridge. Nobody wanted to see Bowen killed. Bowen, however, refused to leave Numuuc, and stayed in the village while the Japanese bivouacked nearby.

Then came another of those providential, if temporary, breaks that repeatedly saved the CAF in 1942-1943. Enemy forces arrived in the Claveria-Pamplona area and at once began to collect information about various routes to approach Kabugao. Then, seemingly acting on new orders, they abruptly withdrew to Ilocos on the northwest coast. At the same time, Japanese troops in the Piat-Abbut-Tuao sector were also withdrawn. These actions, coming just when CAF troops were growing convinced that the Japanese had outwitted them and were about to encircle them, seemed flabbergasting, yet served as additional proof that the Japanese mind was unfathomable to westerners. It was learned later that this time the explanation was prosaic. A Japanese general, most likely the overall commander in the Philippines at the time, had arrived in Baguio from Manila and had decided that all occupation troops should be moved about a hundred miles south to scour the southern portions of the Cordillera before mopping up in the north. The unexpected action not only gave the CAF a respite, it also harmed the enemy in another way. After two or three such switches from being studiously friendly to civilians, to being harsh and brutal, to being friendly once more, the only people who took such changes seriously were the elderly and children.[2]

Even though CAF military operations had turned out badly, progress was made in a collateral area. Arthur Furagganan spent most of the summer repairing Praeger's transmitter, which was then moved to a hill behind Gok-Gok, about a mile from Kabugao.

Sergeant Earl Brazelton and Domi Caluen, who had been a Globe Wireless operator in Manila, volunteered to serve as operators. Furagganan became the radio engineer. Throughout September attempts were made to contact any Allied station, but all proved unsuccessful. Finally, Furagganan tore down the original transmitter and started from scratch with its essentials plus the assorted parts and junk that had been collected from everywhere north of Manila. He eventually built a new radio that would both receive and transmit on the thirty-six-meter band.

September was an eventful month in other ways, too. Early in the month a letter dated July 26 was received from Lt. Col. Claude A. Thorp in central Luzon's Pampanga Province. Thorp reported that he had assumed command of all Luzon guerrilla forces and included orders assigning Capt. Joseph R. Barker II as commander of central Luzon, including Manila; Captain Praeger as commander of northern Luzon; and Capt. George J. "Jack" Spies as commander of southern Luzon.

Most of the Americans on Luzon were in a state that might best be termed "advanced confusion."[3] The southern borderlands of northern Luzon were eventually dominated by Major Lapham's LGAF, although *his* jurisdiction in Pangasinan was constantly disputed by the Hukbalahaps (Communist guerrillas), by the Merrill-Calyer guerrillas, and, at least theoretically, by the sweeping if shadowy claims of Edwin Ramsey. In between Praeger to the north and Lapham to the south lay territory commanded by Lieutenant Colonels Moses and Noble, but eventually led by Col. Russell Volckmann, whose USAFIP NL soon contested Lapham for domination of Nueva Ecija and Nueva Vizcaya. Praeger's appointment by Lieutenant Colonel Thorp thus meant nothing at all. In true geographical northern Luzon, where Praeger was actually ensconced, the appointment was merely recognition of a de facto situation to which Thorp had never contributed anything.

Thorp's arrangements proved both tenuous and temporary in other ways as well. Spies was killed before he could ever assume his command. Barker, an unusually energetic man,[4] made a fine start in central Luzon, and assumed command of Thorp's whole evanescent domain when Thorp was captured by the Japanese in October. However, less than three months later, Barker was also taken by the enemy. Praeger thought so little of his appointment that even though Thorp directed him to send a message to General MacArthur over Thorp's signature, recommending Praeger's promotion to major, the latter tossed the letter aside. His promotion eventually came directly from GHQ SWPA rather than any source on Luzon.

Thorp's letter to Praeger included an enclosure from Barker to the effect that he had five thousand armed men divided into squadrons of a hundred each, and that he politically controlled all the towns in central Luzon save Angeles in Pampanga Province. Thorp requested that General MacArthur be informed by radio that the enemy had about a hundred thousand troops in the Philippines but contemplated reducing that number to twenty-five thousand. If and when such a reduction took place, Thorp expressed confidence that he could reconquer Luzon from within if given effective air support. Actually, the whole message was a mere collection of air castles. In the summer of 1942 neither Barker nor anyone else on Luzon had five thousand armed men save in some scheme on a piece of paper; no Allied air support would be available for more than two years; and the Japanese never reduced their occupation garrison because they neither crushed the guerrillas nor won the support of most of the Filipino people. In 1944 they even felt compelled to *increase* their occupation force. Praeger was merely being realistic when he ignored the communication entirely.

Kabugao was bombed again in that disastrous month of September 1942. By then, CAF headquarters had dug several large air-raid shelters and every civilian family in town had a private dugout. The CAF's six Japanese prisoners heartily disliked air raids and had named one of the larger shelters Corregidor-san. At the first sound of an airplane motor, which occurred almost daily, the most sensitive of the POWs would make a mad dash for Corregidor-san. Guards were instructed not to shoot at him on the ground that anyone that scared would never try to escape lest he be bombed or strafed. Some of the other Japanese, ashamed of their companion's cowardice, assumed an air of nonchalance when planes came over, but when bombs actually began to fall they took off for the shelters with as much alacrity as their compatriot.[5]

Of course being bombed was not funny, and warfare in the larger sense is never funny, either. But in most wars there are occasional episodes whose absurdity or incongruity seem funny in retrospect. One such incident occurred on the north coast at about this time. Several skirmishes took place between the Japanese and the Aparri Company of the Philippine Constabulary. A Troop C, 26th Cavalry, patrol was also involved in one of them. The patrol was surrounded and nearly captured at Ballesteros, but all members save Private Galam, who was nearly unconscious with malaria, escaped. Galam was extraordinarily young looking, even for a Filipino, and the Japanese refused to believe he was a Philippine Scout. They gave him an energetic slapping for presuming to wear khaki clothing and let him go. He was then rescued by the rest of his patrol and carried to a safe place. The patrol itself had been in Aparri in disguise buying medicine from the Japanese only a few days before. The Japanese who captured Galam promptly took from him the medicine he was carrying. Although they did not know it, they were just stealing back the bicarbonate of soda they had so recently sold to the guerrillas as quinine.[6]

On September 30, Captain Jones and Lieutenant Ordun, left on a reconnaissance patrol of Abra Province. They wanted to see if there were any Japanese there and, if so, how many, where, and what seemed to be their intentions. There was some concern that Japanese in Abra could move quickly from the town of Aximao into Apayao, especially since there were no telephone lines from Kabugao into Abra. Such lines did exist to the capitals of all the subprovinces in Mountain Province. Even though these lines were often cut, the wire remained intact and could be repaired. Jones and Ordun wanted to investigate what problems might be encountered if an effort was made to extend such a line into Abra. They crossed the Cordillera between Telefugo in Apayao and

Sapol in Abra. The rainy season had begun and the forest was alive with loathsome tropical pests. After a week in soaking jungle and mountains where few white men had ever set foot, and having suffered from both leeches and malaria during the whole trip, they emerged onto the pine-covered slopes of Abra. Looking down into the carefully terraced valleys, they felt like American pioneers must have when they first saw California, or the Mormons when they first viewed Utah's valleys from the mountain passes—or even Balboa when he beheld the Pacific from the peak of Darien. Abra is a beautiful province, and Sapol, its first stop, lies in one of its loveliest valleys. The country there was high and open, with none of the thick, unkempt, gloomy jungle and stunted growth of Apayao. The pines around Sapol were the first that the party had seen since leaving Baguio nine months before.

The people in Sapol were quite friendly and begged the Americans to base some troops in their village so they would be protected from the Japanese. The Americans tried to convince them that they would be better off without such meager protection as the CAF could afford. How dolefully wise this counsel was they discovered only a day later when they reached a 121st Infantry outpost at Guinguinaban and learned of the disastrous failure of Capt. George Barnett's rash attacks on the Japanese in the preceding three weeks. Barnett had inflicted serious injury on the enemy, but the Japanese had responded savagely by murdering numerous civilians who had aided the guerrillas and torching their houses.

Soon after, Captain Jones and Lieutenant Ordun proceeded to the 121st Infantry's command post, situated in a remote clearing on Mount Bawao. Set in a mountain fastness and covered in all directions by outposts and patrols, the place appeared to Jones to enjoy maximum security. One of the Americans declared confidently, "The Japanese will never take Bawao." The remark was overheard by Ah Yee, a Chinese soldier-cook. Ah Yee abandoned his culinary tasks, came outside, and responded, "You think Japanese soldiers no come here? That Japanese colonel in Vigan—him say to Japanese soldier 'you go to Bawao.' You think then him no go?" Ah Yee returned, cackling, to the kitchen.

Three months later the Japanese did take Bawao—in the course of which Ah Yee, two other Chinese soldiers, and four Americans were surrounded. The four Americans, believing the situation was hopeless, surrendered. Not so the Chinese. They fled in a hail of fire. Miraculously, all three escaped without a scratch.

Afterward, Captain Jones talked to one of the Chinese, Pvt. Ng Lai Soo, and asked him why they had taken such a desperate chance. The question came easily from an American whose nation was then only 150 years old and had never lost a war. But Ng Lai Soo (whom everyone called Lee) was heir to a civilization thousands of years old, one that had accumulated a great store of melancholy wisdom in two hundred generations. He answered, "It's like this, Captain. The Japanese are our long time enemy. Someday you Americans and Japanese will be friends again. We Chinese will never be friends with them, nor they with us. If you are captured maybe they'll let you live. If I am captured I know I die."[7]

Soon after, a typhoon set in, marooning Captain Jones and his patrol on Bawao for the rest of the month. The bad news piled up while the storm howled. Although no messages were getting through from Captain Barnett, sufficient reports were arriving from adjacent units for Capt. William Peryam, acting commander of the 121st Infantry, to know that the regiment was being mauled. A horrible tale came in which proved all too true. It concerned one of the 121st's most capable officers, Capt. Candonia Gaerlan, who had performed brilliantly before the fall of Corregidor and who commanded a battalion near San Fernando, La Union, the principal Japanese base in the Ilocos area. A graduate of an American college, Gaerlan had been an electrical engineer before the war. His was a striking appearance: One-eyed and a fastidious dresser, he usually topped off his attire incongruously with a large sombrero. The bizarre getup was misleading. Gaerlan was highly intelligent, logical in thought and deed, and suffused with a cold but passionate hatred of the Japanese. He had been the best of Cushing's Filipino officers, especially adept at setting ambushes. The enemy had tried in every way to induce him to surrender, even promising him an important post in the occupation government. He had steadfastly declined. On October 5, 1942, Gaerlan ambushed and practically wiped out a Japanese company near Manating in La Union Province. It was to be his last ambush. On October 16 he was betrayed, surrounded by a large enemy force, and riddled with bullets as he came riding along a trail. The Japanese cut off his head, put it in a bottle, and displayed it along the National Highway.[8]

This dismaying news reached Bawao at about the same time as other news about Barnett's disasters, and about the death of Cushing and the capture of Nakar. No one said much. Cushing, Nakar, Gaerlan—all gone within a month; Barnett driven back into the hills. At that rate the guerrillas would soon be wiped out. October 1942 seemed even more terrible than September. Elsewhere, Americans had just landed in North Africa, but it would be two more years before MacArthur's army would land on Leyte and twenty-seven months before landings on Luzon.

The senior officer in Bawao at that time was Capt. William Peryam. Before the war he had struggled to get an engineering degree, and then to become manager of the Lepanto copper mine. He considered himself to be a hard, tough man, but the war changed him. He formerly had regarded Filipinos as a labor supply to be exploited, but he soon found himself indebted to Filipinos who risked their lives to feed him and other Americans. He felt ashamed and resolved that if he lived through the war he would accept Filipinos as equals and change the whole spirit of operations at Lepanto. Thus can acts of heroism change the historical reputation of whole peoples, at least in the minds of the beneficiaries of such heroism. Alas, Peryam's chance never came. He was captured by the Japanese after a stint as leader of guerrillas in Kalinga Subprovince. He died on an enemy prison ship, the *Oryoko Maru*, sunk by American gunfire while en route to Japan in December 1944.[9]

The typhoon slackened at last and, on November 1, Captain Jones and his patrol left Bawao for Kabugao. En route he had further opportunity to study the inhabitants of Abra. The main native people there were the Tinggians, more advanced in civilization than their neighbors, the Isnegs of Apayao. A major reason was that in Abra manual labor was considered honorable for men, whereas in Apayao, with just a few tasks excepted, it was regarded as women's work. Abra thus had a far more productive labor force than did Apayao. The Tinggians had also been influenced heavily by the Christian Ilocanos, themselves one of the most progressive and industrious of Philippine peoples. In recent years they had adopted the most advanced methods of agriculture in use by lowland Christians and by their mountain neighbors in Ifugao. Abra's terraced farms contrasted strikingly with the cleared patches on which rice grew in dry soil in Apayao. The Abra people were also much less warlike than other mountain tribes, and welcomed strangers as readily as did lowland Christians. They made great efforts in 1942 to see that the command post and organizations of the 121st Infantry were well supplied. Some people even made a three-day march every two weeks to carry their rice donations to the regimental headquarters on Mount Bawao.

But such are the idiosyncrasies of humanity that Tinggian villages were neither so clean nor their homes so spacious as those of the otherwise inferior Isnegs. Isnegs like long, wide houses, and think nothing of spending ten years carving out boards that will go into them. Their barrios were extremely clean thanks to the women who swept the ground beneath and around the houses every morning. Rivers were ordinarily used as toilets, and excrement was never left on the ground. In Abra, by contrast, an area close to the barrio was assigned as a community lavatory and the excrement deposited there consumed by pigs—a practice disgusting to most westerners but not uncommon in many parts of the world. Tinggian houses, usually made of bamboo, were huddled together and badly lighted. Isnegs would not deign to live in such buildings. In far northern Abra, around Naglibacan and Anayan, the land is poor and most people depended heavily on trading pine wood for rice. They often carried pine timbers for many miles over rough mountain trails. There, and among northern mountain peoples generally, wild fruits and plants were still a significant portion of peoples' diets in contrast to the yams and camotes that constituted so much of the subsistence of people in the southern tier of the Mountain subprovinces.[10]

After leaving Bawao, Captain Jones and his patrol spent the following night in Aximao, the nearest village. There they had a heartening experience. They encountered one of those exceedingly rare individuals who are entirely unselfish and idealistic: a rather delicate looking schoolteacher of about thirty named Felipe. Although his job was to teach the first two grades in the village school, Felipe had revolutionized the entire system of agriculture in the Aximao area in the ten years that had passed since his graduation from Laganglang Agricultural High School. The principal there was a Filipino graduate of the New York State Agricultural College at Cornell University. He described Felipe as the most brilliant boy ever to pass through his school. The principal had wanted him to go to the commonwealth agricultural college at Los Baños, but Felipe said his family responsibilities and life's work required him to return to Aximao immediately upon graduation. There he lived alone with his mother. Meanwhile, slowly, patiently, and good-humoredly, he had persuaded the old people there to give up their ancient agricultural methods and adopt the terrace system of Ifugao, to rotate their corps, and to use only the best seed. In addition to the staples, rice and corn, a great variety of vegetables were being raised. Animal production had risen steadily as surplus grain was fed to pigs. After ten years of Felipe's endeavors the harvest had almost doubled, and Axiamo's standard of living had risen far higher than in similar barrios in Apayao. All this had been accomplished purely on his own initiative; his teaching job had nothing to do with improving agricultural production.[11]

The village had also been the home, for the preceding four months, of another memorable individual, Cpl. Louis Heuser. He was known throughout northern Luzon as "Apple," perhaps because he had been born in an apple growing region—the mountains of southwestern Virginia. He had all the prejudices and limitations of an uneducated Appalachian farm boy, but he was simple, true, and had a heart of gold. Of German descent, he was a tall, slender, dark-haired young man with burning eyes and fierce loyalties. He was loyal to his native Virginia, to his mother, to his cause, and to his friends. Above all, he was loyal to God. A deeply religious man whose constant companion was his Bible, he read from it first thing every morning and again each afternoon before dark. He knew scores of passages by heart. Oddly, Corporal Heuser feared that he lacked courage, although Captain Jones, who was close to him for the next six months and saw him in many crises, thought him one of the bravest Americans he had ever known.

Apple's good qualities far outweighed his faults, but he did have a weakness: he loved liquor. Most days he disciplined himself and did not drink at all. But when he slipped, it took only one drink to start a binge—and when on one, he got completely drunk and became uncontrollable. Heuser was with Lt. Robert Arnold's air-warning unit at the northwest tip of Luzon when the war began. There, chafing at what he regarded as Arnold's inactivity, he abruptly left. With a Bible in his pocket and a canteen of basi on his belt, Apple had roamed North Luzon, a one-man expeditionary force dedicated to shooting Japanese. He took part in Cushing's raid on Candon in January 1942, and ever after viewed Cushing as the greatest human being who ever trod the earth.

Here a distinction must be made. In January 1942 Lt. Edwin Ramsey lay in a makeshift hospital at Mariveles on the southern tip of the Bataan Peninsula, suffering grievously from jaundice. He recorded that Capt. Arthur Wermuth, a patient there recovering from a serious wound, would get up from his bed at night, take a tommy gun, and go off into the jungle to hunt Japanese and shoot up their command posts. He always went alone and he seemed a true monomaniac—obsessed with hunting and killing, and brave to the point of madness. Corporal Heuser's greatest desire was also to kill the enemy, but, as noted, he was also a deeply religious man—and a sociable one who enjoyed the company of others. He was not one *totally* overborne by hatred of the foe, as was Wermuth.[12]

On one occasion Apple was the inadvertent cause of a remark by a prominent American military commentator that produced much laughter among the guerrillas. He had taken part in a skirmish with the Japanese in a valley in Abra Province. The outcome was indecisive, but afterward the Japanese had with-drawn. When Apple reported to his regimental headquarters, the C.O., an old colonel, asked him what he had been doing. Apple answered that his patrol had just driven the Japanese out of the Abra valley. He had made the remark facetiously, but the colonel missed the intent and reported that the valley had been cleared of enemy troops. Major George Fielding Eliot picked up the news release and commented that this clearing of large areas of North Luzon demonstrated that the enemy had only a tenu-ous hold on the conquered territory. Apple thereupon became famous as the man who had exposed Japan's weakness. The whole episode indicates the difficulties under which commen-tators labor when offering "penetrating judgments" based on fragmentary information.

When Captain Jones and his party arrived in Aximao they at once encountered Corporal Heuser and, soon after, two shy and blushing girls of about sixteen who bore with them a plate of rice cakes and honey. Heuser explained that the two had cooked for Sergeant Brazelton and himself ever since they had come to Aximao. The girls, both economics students when at school, had the side job of cooking for all soldiers who stopped in the barrio.

They were an attractive pair, and one of them—named Juanita—was positively beautiful, with slender limbs and firm breasts. In Abra their clothing consisted only of a skirt and head kerchief. They and Apple were obviously friends. The girls were timid and shy around the strange visiting Americans, but quite the opposite with Corporal Heuser, who teased them good-naturedly every day and whom they thought very funny. Juanita was engaged to be married the following spring to one of Apple's orderlies. This afforded him the opportunity to repeatedly warn her that if she didn't marry her boyfriend promptly, somebody else would hook him. The girls had their own sense of humor, too. Knowing that Apple was quite religious, they would some-times embarrass him when he was bathing by coming down to the river, dropping their skirts, and diving in naked. Heuser, red faced, would grab his soap and scurry off. He was also interested in learning the Tinggian language, which allowed the girls to even scores with him in another way. They taught him all the bad words, which he then used innocently—to everyone's merriment—until Felipe overheard him and enlightened him.

It was all lighthearted and innocent. Aximao was one of the happiest little towns in northern Luzon in the autumn of 1942, and everyone there was hospitable to the newcomers. Juanita's grandfather, an old man of about eighty, personally assured Heuser that no matter what happened or how long the war went on, all the Americans were welcome to stay and that the natives would die before they would reveal their guests' presence to the Japanese.

When Captain Jones and his men arrived in Aximao on November 1, 1942, they were promptly put in the finest house in town—one with three good-sized rooms and a galvanized iron roof. In the Philippines, such a roof indicated at least modest wealth, and in the mountains it marked the fortunate owner as one of the elite. In all of Apayao there was hardly a native whose house had such a roof, so it was not only a surprise for the party to see several metal roofs in Aximao but indicative of the relative prosperity of the place as well.

The troopers dumped their packs in the living room of their new quarters and were quickly served some roasted ears of corn and a bamboo tube of basi. Both food and drink were particularly welcome after the long, arduous march from Bawao. Progress had been slow due to the rainy season swelling the mountain rivers. Just before reaching Aximao they had forded a river where the current was so strong that only the vigilance of husky Tinggian guides had saved them from being swept over a falls. Traveling through the mountains of northern Luzon during the typhoon season would have been impossible without these guides, who were constantly alert for any danger an unwary American might get into. The only accomplished mountaineer among them was Corporal Heuser, and even he was handicapped by a crucial disability: he couldn't swim.

The visitors stayed an extra day in Aximao, hoping that the

weather might break. The sojourn was by no means unpleasant. The local people were both intelligent and friendly, there was plenty to eat and drink, Felipe and the girls were good company, and everyone got caught up on sleep. Nobody was really anxious to get back to Apayao save Sergeant Nank, who said he was sick of Abra's standard fare—boiled corn three times a day—and anxious to eat rice again. Duty called as well, and as much as Captain Jones would have liked to have stayed in Aximao, he and the patrol departed the next day.

They forded the Tineg River without too much difficulty and reached Naglibacan by early afternoon. The following day they made Anayan, the most remote barrio in northern Abra. Very few Americans had ever been there. A few old people recalled Americans in blue shirts coming there in the aftermath of the Philippine Insurrection and planting the American flag. What they probably remembered was a reconnaissance party led by Maj. Robert Howze, which had passed through Abra and Apayao in 1910. That party had raised the stars and stripes in the village of Anayan. A few other Americans had come twenty-five to thirty years later to prospect for gold. Since then there had been no more—until Captain Jones and his entourage arrived. Perhaps this would not have created a stir had not Jones, speaking through an interpreter, announced that he would take the same bed that Captain Cushing had slept in. The U.S. Army might regard the redoubtable Cushing as only another mining engineer who had been given a commission because he happened to be in the Philippines when war broke out, but to these people Cushing was one of the foremost warriors in all of history. They welcomed the new American visitors tumultuously.[13]

The next day the party crossed the divide into Apayao. The very atmosphere soon grew somber. Gone were Abra's open, grassy mountains, the mere sight of which raised one's spirits. They were exchanged for the gloomy jungle and rocky waste-lands of Apayao. The guide, Sgt. Edward Barcelona, a native of Aximao, was discouraged when he saw the condition of the Dagarra River. Perhaps it was indicative of the malignant char-acter of this vagrant stream that its name changed by the time it reached Kabugao, where it was called the Apayao River. Whatever the case, it was a wild, swollen stream that roared down a deep, narrow valley. Worst of all, it had to be crossed and recrossed seventy-eight times before the troop arrived in Kabugao, with the stream growing larger, though not necessarily more dangerous, each mile of the way.

Barcelona had one especially admirable quality as a guide: he never underestimated the time it would take to reach the next barrio. With him in the lead, one usually got there a little before the expected time, invariably a pleasant surprise. Most guides try to encourage hikers by assuring them that the destination is "only a little farther," while hours pass, tempers shorten, and the goal remains evanescent. (One thinks of that legendary platoon sergeant who tried to inspire his exhausted men by calling out cheerily, "Only sixteen more miles, men, and we'll be halfway there.") Sergeant Barcelona was also exceptionally patient and considerate. The Americans were quite unused to navigating mountain torrents and so had to be helped constantly. Every one of the dozens of times the river had to be crossed, Barcelona and his assistants had to cross and recross several times to get all the Americans' baggage over. If the crossing was bad, they practically had to drag the Americans themselves across. Although most would dive in well above the anticipated landing point on the opposite shore and then swim madly, some of the Americans would misjudge and have to be rescued by Tinggian boys. No American could swim well enough to make headway against the river.

Jones's group reached Barrio Dagarra the night after leaving Anayan. There they were welcomed by an outpost of the Apayao Force. A cow was slaughtered and a feast followed—the first good steaks in many weeks, rice with honey, and basi, which they drank far into the night. There followed two more days of virtually constant crossing and recrossing of the hellish Dagarra River before the exhausted patrol made it into Kabugao. What they found did not send their spirits soaring. Major Praeger had fallen through a rotten bridge into a gulch some time before. His injuries, which had not been serious and would have healed quickly with proper medical attention, had become seriously infected. This was not the fault of the Apayao surgeon, Dr. Irenio Reyes, who had almost no medicine. Praeger, although weak and in great pain, remained strongheaded as ever and refused to leave his radio to be treated. He was off at the radio station, as usual, when Captain Jones arrived. Most of the men were out on patrol. The Needhams had gone to the north coast. The skeleton garrison on hand was living on peanuts since all other food had been destroyed by the typhoon. Sergeant Arnao capped the mournful litany by presenting an information report indicating that the Japanese intended to launch a mop-up operation in Apayao Province in December. Arnao added that only the day before an enemy plane had reconnoitered the Kabugao district.

9

Civil Government in Cagayan-Apayao: Late 1942

With a heavy heart, Captain Jones cleaned up, put on a fresh uniform, and called on Governor and Mrs. Adduru to pay his respects and report on his trip to Abra. Besides the military subjects to be discussed, there were pressing civil matters as well. Due to the transfer of the Cagayan government headquarters to Kabugao, the town's population had almost doubled in the past three months. Now, just after the typhoon and at the height of the rainy season, feeding all these extra people had become a grave problem. Several cargo boats laden with supplies had started from the coast up the swollen Apayao River only to be upset in the turbulent stream, losing everything. To make matters worse, inflation was rampant thanks to an unusually large amount of money having been put into circulation in the Kabuago district due to the influx of government personnel. The price of rice, for example, had risen 400 percent. An executive order fixed the prices of basic commodities, and an Emergency Food Administration was created with orders to buy up rice in the lowlands and ship it to Kabugao without delay so as to break an emerging black market. The rice was to be sold at thirty-four cents for five pounds, only slightly above the prewar price.

The question of the shortage of prewar currency to finance intelligence operations was also pressing. Adduru addressed this by publishing a bulletin over his signature as governor, rather than as an army officer. In it he pointed out that a large percentage of prewar Philippine currency had fallen into enemy hands and so might never be redeemed. He directed that after a certain date no prewar money was to be accepted by provincial treasurers in payment of taxes and that only scrip issued by the wartime Cagayan-Apayao government could be used for this purpose. The order had the desired effect. Many persons rushed to treasurers' offices to exchange their prewar currency for scrip. Although he of course never said so, Adduru had an ulterior motive for his action. The prewar currency provided him with a supply of money that was everywhere familiar and recognized as official. It could be used to pay intelligence gathering operatives and to meet ordinary government expenses, as well as to lessen a possible postwar burden. Good money notoriously drives out bad: hence the money printed *during* the war was unlikely to be redeemed by anyone after the war, whereas there was at least a chance that prewar currency *might* be redeemed by the Philippine government. If it should be, the less of it there was in circulation, the less the postwar government would have to buy back. Most CAF personnel parted company with Governor Adduru on this issue. They believed that Apayao's wartime currency would eventually be redeemed by the Philippine government, as indeed it was after the war.

The root of many administrative difficulties for all parties in the wartime Philippines lay in a gigantic official pretense: that the Japanese occupation forces ruled the whole archipelago. In fact, they dominated only those towns in which they had garrisons. In Cagayan and Apayao Provinces, this meant the cities of Aparri and Tuguegarao, as well as some small towns on the main highway along the Cagayan River. Real authority in the villages and countryside of far northern Luzon was exercised by either USAFFE (American-led) guerrillas or Filipino-led independent guerrillas, all of whom influenced in varying degrees regular prewar Philippine local government officials. In the late fall of 1942, Governor Adduru reported to Pres. Manuel Quezon that of the twenty-six municipalities in Cagayan, three were governed completely by the Japanese, twelve by the CAF, and eleven were shared. Of provincial administrators, only three mayors and a few minor officials were clearly pro-Japanese.[1] In Cagayan-Apayao, the functions of the exiled Philippine national government were directed by Governor Adduru. His administration operated openly at certain times and places, clandestinely at others, and always in close association with Praeger's military forces—in all areas save education. By the autumn of 1942 it was clearly necessary to energize existing emergency departments or create new ones in such areas as relief administration, propaganda, and the issuance of money. Some of the most capable men in both provinces were drafted to administer these agencies. Generally, they did an excellent job.

The activities of all these agencies were closely intertwined but, for the sake of clarity, they will be described separately here. Much the most complicated of the problems was the issuance and management of wartime currency. What follows is a *general* description of how that task was handled by the provincial governors and/or guerrilla leaders of North Luzon in 1942. Details differed from one area to another and from one individual guerrilla commander to another.

Within a month after the war began, several provincial governments were cut off from all outside help. They quickly ran out of money to pay the back salaries of provincial and municipal officials, pensions, other entitlements, and everyday operating expenses. Provincial boards met and created currency committees. These then secured authorization from President Quezon to issue money up to the amount each province had on deposit in the national treasury, plus a small additional amount for emergency relief measures. The banknotes to be manufactured were to be used to carry on normal local governmental functions, not to finance guerrilla operations. This injunction was obeyed, for the most part. Guerrillas did get a little of the money periodically, but they got their main support throughout the war from the contributions of civilians, either given freely, purchased with IOUs, or commandeered. Most guerrillas served without pay.

Most of the notes were printed on different shades of white

or brown paper, ranging in degree of quality from fine, watermarked bond to ordinary shopping-bag paper. Paper of other colors was also used occasionally, and oftentimes the color of the paper indicated the value of the note. Many different kinds and colors of ink were employed in dozens of combinations with different shades of paper—again often varying with the value of the notes. Frequently, too, the *size* of the note indicated its denomination. Some of the money was mimeographed; some was stamped from carved wooden blocks not unlike the block-printed books of the late Middle Ages before the invention of movable type. Notes came in many denominations from one-tenth of a peso to two hundred pesos, with one-half to ten pesos most common. Some were dated, many were not. Some had serial numbers, others did not. Those with serial numbers were marked by a numbering machine, if one could be found. If not, they might be numbered manually with pen and ink. Sometimes two notes, each printed on one side, would be glued together so the bill would be the same on both sides. Occasionally, colored threads would be inserted between the sheets to complicate the endeavors of aspiring counterfeiters. Despite this and other precautions there was a good deal of crude counterfeiting. In Bontoc, some of the notes sported the embossed seal of the provincial governor, while others were signed by individual members of the currency commission. Also in Bontoc, late in the war much guerrilla currency was redeemed and then sent to the Philippine National Bank in Manila to be destroyed. Unluckily, an American bombing raid on March 10, 1945, caused the building housing much of the currency to be abandoned long enough for looters to break in and steal many different kinds of wartime currency, much of which was then circulated anew.[2] Some Cagayan money had internal revenue tax stamps affixed to it.[3] In Apayao, banknotes were notarized by the nominal governor, Milton Ayochok. In both provinces, and in Nueva Vizcaya as well, the Japanese eventually seized and destroyed all records relating to currency manufacture and distribution. Discussions of financial management there are thus based on memories, the study of surviving banknotes, references in accounts of other wartime events, and the like. In

all parts of North Luzon the issuance of scrip had been authorized by President Quezon, save in the elastic and short-lived
domain of Walter Cushing. He issued money entirely on his own,
as he did so much else. Little of it survived the war, probably
because many who got it destroyed it for fear of what the Japanese might do to them if it was discovered in their possession.[4]

Each province in North Luzon appears to have issued somewhere between two hundred thousand and a million pesos in
homemade currency, although not all of it was put into circulation. In Isabela Province, where less is known about the whole
subject than anywhere else, it is thought that the money was split
about evenly between civil government and guerrilla groups,[5]
even though the original intention was *not* to finance guerrillas.
In Nueva Vizcaya, by contrast, it is believed that guerrillas received only about forty-five hundred pesos, most of it going to
Nakar and Enriquez. Nobody can be sure, however, because the
Japanese burned the building that contained all the records there.[6]
Maybe 70 percent of the estimated 880,000 pesos printed in
Cagayan went to the civil government and 30 percent to guerrillas. Some of the latter probably went to Praeger. It is unlikely
that more than this went to guerrillas because the irregular bands
were small and the few ordinary soldiers in them received only
six pesos per month. How much went for other guerrilla expenses is unknown. Cagayan notes also circulated widely in
Apayao, although it is known that there were two separate issues
there: Legal Tender and Emergency Scrip Series A. However, the
whole matter is extremely uncertain because the Japanese destroyed all the records, so nobody knows for sure even which
issue came first.[7] In all areas, most of the money given to guerrillas was used to pay intelligence gatherers.

The Japanese quashed the whole enterprise of privately
printing money before the end of 1943. After the war, the Philippine government redeemed some of it, although far less was
submitted for redemption than had been printed.[8] Most had long
since been spent, lost, destroyed by the enemy, or squirreled away
by collectors. The U.S. government never redeemed any of it,[9]
despite the fact that a million Filipinos had died alongside

Americans resisting their common enemy. America also spent untold billions resuscitating the economies of former enemies after the war—conduct that eventually gave rise to mordant remarks that "the United States treats enemies like friends, neutrals like enemies, and friends like neutrals."

In Kabugao, Captain Praeger considered that once President Quezon's permission had been secured it was not only justifiable but necessary to manufacture money promptly to run the provincial government. Unhappily, there was no printing press, ink, or proper paper for the million pesos in small bills Praeger had in mind. Proverbial Yankee ingenuity came to the rescue. Ink can be made from many substances. Paper of some sort can be secured in most parts of the earth. Nobody could get a printing press, but a number of carpenters' vises were secured. Lead was melted down into plates, engravings were then made on them by trade school instructors, and the vises were used to clamp the paper firmly against the plates. Five plates were required to print bills of one peso or larger, but only two were needed for the simpler ten centavo notes. Each note bore the provincial seal. So far as is known, nobody tried to counterfeit the money made in Kabugao. By the end of 1942 the exchange value of new money to old was four to five. This was deemed excellent, especially since the Japanese would not honor emergency money in territory they occupied,[10] although they did allow prewar money to circulate there.[11] An effort was made to prevent inflation by carefully regulating the amount of money in circulation and by fixing prices. A bond campaign was also contemplated, but it never got off the ground because intensified Japanese military action soon claimed the attention and effort of everyone.[12]

A variety of other social and economic problems were as pressing as the shortage of money. One of them was dire poverty. Many ordinary people lived on the edge of destitution in normal times. However, the war meant they also had to feed guerrillas, submit to periodic Japanese demands, and occasionally evade Japanese raids by deserting their houses, possessions, and gardens to flee into the mountains. It was partly to deal with this problem that Governor Adduru sought permission from President Quezon to issue wartime currency.[13] Having secured the permission and printed the currency, Adduru was then able to establish an emergency relief administration to combat widespread poverty. This body collected clothing, medicines, and other goods chronically in short supply but occasionally available, and provided for their public sale.

Less publicly evident but probably more important was finding some way to employ the many Filipinos who had lost their white-collar jobs when the Japanese closed schools and offices. With no income and nothing to do, some of these unemployed had begun to grumble that provincial and municipal governments had no right to exist. Others, from jealousy or personal grudges, tried to undermine the authority of those lucky enough to still have public jobs. Since the disgruntled were among the best educated and most intelligent members of the community, they were potential leaders of either resistance to the invaders or, if they grew disillusioned, collaborationist movements. The last had, somehow, to be prevented. President Quezon had ordered all schools closed when the war began. Opening them again was considered but rejected because many school buildings had been used by guerrillas as barracks and so were often bombed or machine-gunned by the Japanese.

The problem posed by the unemployed was finally attacked by creating several bodies to compose propaganda, issue currency, establish fixed prices and rules for merchandising, staff justice-of-the-peace courts, and establish military commissions. All these activities required fairly large numbers of educated people, especially lawyers. They thus provided work for those who had been hit hardest economically by the war, and eliminated most of them as potential collaborators. Much of the new work was genuinely useful and not simply make-work. Probably the most was achieved by stocking the propaganda service with jobless schoolteachers. This branch of the CAF did much useful work disseminating information to the civilian population about the war's progress. Special attention was given to explaining why it was necessary to wait patiently for help to arrive in the Philippines and thereby, hopefully, overcoming the pervasive feeling that America had abandoned the Filipinos. War news was released and explained honestly, and morale rose visibly.[14]

Meanwhile, the ordinary activities of local government were carried on as routinely as resources and conditions permitted. The few roads were kept in repair, as were the government trails in Apayao. The police and engineers were kept up. The telephone lines in Apayao were maintained and a new line was laid from Kabugao to the north coast of Cagayan.

Although GHQ SWPA in Australia had tried by every means possible throughout the war to impress upon guerrillas in the Philippines that *gathering* as much information as possible about the enemy should take precedence over all other activities, this proved to be a much harder task than merely circulating war news among Filipino civilians. On October 20, Troop C radio operators Domi Caluen and Sgt. Earl Brazelton had a stroke of luck. They managed to contact station KFS in San Francisco, a War Department monitoring station. It has been repeatedly emphasized earlier in this narrative that much of the information circulating in the wartime Philippines was unreliable. A fair amount of it eventually made its way into published books and semiofficial records. One example, drawn from a biography of General MacArthur by Willoughby and Chamberlain, gives November 4 as the date KFS intercepted the call from Praeger's station WYY.[15] The error is noteworthy only because it was so typical. The number of radio contacts between GHQ SWPA and the Philippine guerrillas increased steadily in 1943 and 1944 but never entirely clarified the blurred picture MacArthur's headquarters had of what was going on in the islands, especially in faraway northern Luzon. It was hardly surprising that guerrillas often received mystifying advice, requests, and orders from GHQ SWPA.

Initially, Caluen and Brazelton were so startled that they stopped sending and telephoned Praeger in Kabugao for instructions. A cipher was soon worked out, after which the War Department began to bombard the CAF with requests for every sort of detailed information about the size and location of Japanese forces, their offensive and defensive capabilities, their relationship with Philippine civilian officials, and many other subsidiary matters. Agents were sent promptly from CAF headquarters on all sorts of specific missions to places as far distant as Manila, but concentrating on the area around Lingayen Gulf. These efforts were only partially successful. Lack of money that could be passed in areas controlled by the Japanese prevented agents from traveling as legitimate businessmen, and limited to some degree what *any* sort of agent could accomplish. Even more limiting was the language barrier. Nobody in the CAF, American or Filipino, knew Japanese. Agents thus were able to report accurately only what could be ascertained by sight, such as the approximate size of enemy garrisons, or that could be learned from talking to knowledgeable Filipinos. Identification of Japanese units, by contrast, was virtually impossible—partly because the enemy was secretive about military matters and partly because they often mixed troops from several different units, but mainly because CAF agents could neither speak nor read their language. When patrols occasionally captured Japanese documents, nobody could translate them. Not even the insignia of troops could be deciphered. The only enemy units ever clearly identified were the 16th Division and 122nd Infantry. The situation grew even worse in late 1942 when Japanese mop-up operations intensified and caused CAF agents to lose much of the raw information they *had* secured.

In October 1942, Governor Adduru and Captain Praeger drew up an elaborate plan for an intelligence system that would encompass the whole island of Luzon. Under it, Lt. Col. Claude Thorp and Capt. Joseph Barker would head the enterprise in central and southern Luzon, Capt. William Peryam along the whole Ilocos and Lingayen northwest coasts, Lieutenant Colonels Martin Moses and Arthur Noble the southern portions of Mountain Province and the upper Cagayan Valley, and Adduru and Praeger the Cagayan and Apayao provinces.[16] Considering their isolation in the far north and their general lack of resources, this wildcat scheme seems in retrospect even more madly optimistic than the similar designs of Thorp, Cushing, Edwin Ramsey, Ferdinand Marcos, Moses and Noble, Colonels Gyles Merrill and Peter Calyer, and others. It seems doubly chimerical that it was proposed at the same time Thorp was sending out news of his similar scheme. Finally, it was quite out of character for Ralph Praeger to build air castles of any kind. Why then was it even contemplated? Probably merely to give a plausible positive response to the repeated requests of GHQ SWPA for more information.[17]

Whatever the motivation, a start was made on the project. Early in November, Frank Camp and Pvt. Lino Puddoc were sent from Kabugao to begin establishment of this intelligence net. They were to go first to Isabela to contact Colonel Nakar, and from there to somewhere south of Lingayen Gulf, where they hoped to find Thorp. It was almost exactly the same scheme Walter Cushing had pursued two months earlier and that had ended in his death. The new expedition did not begin auspiciously. Lieutenant Camp was cautioned that he must proceed to Isabela in extreme secrecy and avoid contact with the enemy. So what did he do? He went straight to Solana, on the outskirts of Tuguegarao, under the very noses of the Japanese. While having lunch there he sent them a message, through the mayor, to come and get him. Fortunately, the Nipponese delayed to make sure they were not being drawn into an ambush. Camp later explained that he had not intended to fight the Japanese; he had merely wanted to send them a message via the mayor so they wouldn't blame the mayor for keeping Camp's presence a secret! Only when he and Puddoc eventually reached Isabela did they learn that both Nakar and Thorp had been captured and that their subordinates had been driven into the jungle to escape Japanese mop-up operations. It was one more reminder of how ignorant guerrilla organizations were of each other's activities.

CAF legal affairs proceeded more expeditiously in late autumn of 1942 than did amassing intelligence. The military commission headed by Captain Jones traveled a great deal to administer justice. Between November 24 and December 6 it convened in the north coast town of Pamplona. The whole town was guarded by outposts during the time the court was sitting. Because Japanese pressure intensified every day, the commissioners were shown the appropriate exit in case an abrupt departure became

Thomas Jones served as president of the Cagayan-Apayao Military Commission and was the only American CAF guerrilla to survive the war. (Courtesy of Thomas Jones.)

necessary. The precaution proved needless; a number of trials were conducted routinely. Nevertheless, strict legal procedure did suffer occasional interruptions due to extraneous incidents. One day, Jones ordered a recess until the next day for no apparent reason. His motive was personal. Sitting in the front row, immediately before him, was the niece of Pamplona's mayor. Jones later described her as "a dark-skinned edition of Hedy Lamarr." She had adopted a provocative pose, which made it impossible for him to fix his attention on the detailed evidence in the murder case being tried.[18]

On another occasion, the other American member of the court, Lieutenant Bowen, a man not celebrated for his patience, grew restless during the protracted examination of an evasive witness. He pulled out his pistol and laid it on the table in front of him. He had no malign, or even irregular, intention: he was merely bored. The effect on the reluctant witness was nonetheless electric. He was immediately transformed into a highly voluble lover of truth.

Such incidents were aberrations, though. The trials were conducted on a high plane throughout, and no accused who was found guilty ever complained about the verdict. In fact when Captain Jones left Pamplona, the man who carried his pack down to the boat shook Jones's hand warmly and said he prayed that the Japanese would never kill or capture him. Jones had just sentenced him to five years in jail.[19]

10

The Disastrous Enterprises of Lieutenant Colonels Moses and Noble

"The road to hell is paved with good intentions." That ancient adage may be trite and musty, but that does not lessen its truth. The eventual destruction of most of the guerrilla forces in North Luzon followed hard upon the decision of two American officers to strike heavy blows at the Japanese occupation forces in that area. Lieutenant Colonels Martin Moses and Arthur Noble had been with the Philippine army's 11th Infantry in La Union Province when the Japanese landed in the Lingayen Gulf in December 1941. Their troops, who had been in training for only ten days, gave way quickly in the face of an enemy assault, barely escaped a trap, and fled to Baguio. The two lieutenant colonels then withdrew and managed to join USAFFE forces retreating into Bataan. There they secured commands in regiments of the 11th Division. As the struggle for Bataan neared its end, Moses and Noble, weary and sick like so many others, destroyed their arms and prepared to surrender. But the enemy disregarded their white flags and continued to attack their headquarters mercilessly. Desperate, they fled into the jungle. For nine terrible days they wandered, half-starved, through the mountains and tropical forest of north Bataan onto the central Luzon plain. There they rested for a few days and regained their strength somewhat; then they resumed a forty-night trek across the northern part of the plain into the mountainous north. Along the way they made several stops, one of them at Maj. Robert Lapham's LGAF headquarters near Umingan in extreme eastern Pangasinan Province. Lapham, then close to death himself from malaria and dysentery, was not impressed by his visitors.[1] They did not seem to him to be in either the physical or psychological state necessary to undertake the guerrilla activity they talked about so freely. He also remained skeptical about their later claims to have assembled six thousand armed guerrillas in the north. This proved to be a serious underestimate— at least of the capacity of Moses and Noble to make trouble. They soon collected a melange of escapees from Horan's forces, survivors of Nakar's downfall, scattered elements of the 14th Infantry, Philippine Scouts, and small units formed by Capt. Parker Calvert, Lt. Arthur Murphy, Lt. Rufino Baldwin, and others. Most important, they acquired the 11th Division's intelligence and signal officers, Capt. Russell Volckmann and Lt. Donald Blackburn.

On October 1 Moses, after conferring with several guerrilla groups, announced that he, as the senior officer in North Luzon, was assuming command of all units there. This included the followers of Ablan, Praeger, Enriquez, Barnett, Lapham, Charles Cushing (a brother of Walter Cushing), and Dennis Molintas of Benguet. Moses assumed that all these men and their organizations recognized his authority. He thereupon proclaimed his new organization to be the USAFIP NL, and proceeded to assign the leaders of its component parts to a variety of specific tasks.[2] The C.O. of one of the most important of them, the LGAF, finessed these proceedings adroitly. Robert Lapham, always unsympathetic to centralizers, replied to Moses with the bland observation that he was still under the authority of Lieutenant Colonel Thorp but that he desired good relations with Moses's forces and was willing to cooperate fully with their activities.[3]

Undaunted by such tepid enthusiasm for his designs, Lieutenant Colonel Moses made plans to unleash all the guerrillas in lower North Luzon in simultaneous coordinated attacks and ambushes against the Japanese, beginning October 15. Unfortunately, due to the rash assaults by Capt. George Barnett's forces in La Union Province, Moses was forced to begin his attacks well ahead of schedule. But perhaps it mattered little. Communications among separated groups in Moses's new domain were so poor that the attacks could not be coordinated and so lost much of their effectiveness.

Just what motivated Moses and Noble is not altogether certain. Moses himself said it was necessary to "beat the Japs to the punch."[4] Capt. Thomas Jones did not always agree with the judgments of the "two old colonels," but he did admire their spirit. Thinking, perhaps, of Lt. Col. Claude Thorp and Colonel Horan, he expressed regret that such brave and patriotic officers as Moses and Noble had not been available to lead guerrillas in North Luzon from the beginning. Jones thought the pair were actuated by nothing more complicated than consuming hatred of the Japanese combined with the wildly mistaken belief that U.S. forces would return to the Philippines by December 1942.[5]

Here it must be recalled that throughout the war guerrilla leaders and their followers all over the Philippines were suspicious and jealous of each other, and that bickering among them was endemic—to the point of sometimes descending to actual battles between rival groups. They squabbled over jurisdiction, objectives, tactics, rank, and a dozen other matters. Major Bernard Anderson, C.O. of a large guerrilla band centered in the Sierra Madres, in Tayabas Province northeast of Manila, agreed with Lapham that Moses and Noble were just a couple of empire builders.[6] Donald Blackburn, who was skeptical about the depth of Moses's and Noble's zeal to battle the Japanese, thought the two officers undertook extensive operations against the enemy mostly so they would not lose control of their own loose organization to Volckmann and himself.[7] Volckmann, by contrast, says Moses and Noble were two of the finest officers he ever served under,[8] but he neglects to add that he had largely assumed control of their organization three months before they were captured by the enemy.

Such sharply differing views indicate that the testimony of guerrillas about each other, and especially about each other's designs and motives, must always be viewed with caution. Many American escapees who became guerrillas had been compelled by circumstances to do things they did not wish to remember, much less publicize. Most knew things about others that caused them to mistrust their character, intentions, or capabilities.[9] Finally, who among us is always sure of his own motives, especially when attempting to recall them decades after some event?

A further complication in this particular case is that Volckmann's and Blackburn's relations with each other, and of both of them with Moses and Noble, were equivocal. Of the four men, subsequent events indicate that Volckmann was the ablest, the most ambitious, and, many would add, the least scrupulous. Yet the two "old colonels," the most senior officers then on Luzon, retained Volckmann and Blackburn in their command throughout, even though the latter pair established their own separate headquarters, did much as they pleased, and even lived apart from each other for more than a year.[10]

Whatever the intentions of Moses and Noble might have been, their action proved to be dreadfully mistaken. The Japanese were enraged. They rushed in thousands of troops and undertook fierce and indiscriminate retaliation. Within the next nine months most of the guerrilla outfits in North Luzon were crushed; most of their leaders were killed or captured; civilian supporters of the guerrillas were robbed, tortured, and massacred; and their towns and barrios were destroyed. The overall effect was to cow civilians, making them more receptive to Japanese propaganda, and scaring thousands of them into becoming Japanese agents and informers. This, in turn, speeded the decimation of the guerrilla bands.[11]

The Japanese ultimately crushed the CAF, as they had Cushing's, Nakar's, and Ablan's organizations before it. However, they managed to commit some spectacular blunders along the way. One such blunder took place on November 14 when Lieutenant Camp passed through Solana on his way to Isabela. By mere coincidence, Lieutenant Bowen made a reconnaissance of Aparri, some forty to fifty miles away on the same day. The day following was Commonwealth Day, a national holiday in the Philippines. The Japanese put these three events together in their minds and concluded that a major attack was imminent. To forestall it, they spent the night of November 14-15 firing artillery shells across the Cagayan Valley when actually the only Allied troops in the vicinity were a few routine guerrilla patrols. Then they announced expansively that they had broken up an important guerrilla offensive. At the same time, their regular propaganda people in Manila were proclaiming that Filipino guerrilla units had been completely subdued and that the errant ex-warriors were working cordially with the benevolent occupation forces to build that shining hope for the future, the Greater East Asia Co-Prosperity Sphere.[12] It was just this sort of thing that negated the effect of much Japanese propaganda: two branches of the Nipponese armed forces or government making flatly contradictory claims at the same time, or their propagandists insisting that something was true when most Filipino civilians knew from common observation or personal experience that it was not.[13] Surprisingly, the Japanese never seemed to learn from their own experience. A Tokyo broadcast of March 20, 1943, proclaimed that "In central Luzon 1300 'bandits' surrendered in February and were now 'cooperating whole-heartedly with Japan.' 'American and Filipino bandits, who were active in Northern Luzon are almost wiped out, and the rest—about a hundred—have fled to the mountains, where they will starve to death.' Peace prevails in Mindanao, where the majority of the Moro race are cooperating with Japan. 'It has become clear that the day is not far away when the whole Philippines will cooperate wholeheartedly with Japan.'"[14]

How ridiculously remote from the truth such a statement was is indicated by the consideration that the best estimate of the total number of active guerrillas in the Philippines in the spring of 1945 was around 240,000, with at least 33,000 of them on Mindanao where "peace prevailed," and something like 80,000-90,000 on Luzon. The latter numbered around 22,000 in Volckmann's USFIP NL, 13,000-14,000 each in Lapham's LGAF and Edwin Ramsey's ECLGA, 12,000 in Marking's irregulars, 7,000 in Anderson's BMA,[15] and lesser thousands in the Merrill-Calyer USPIF, The Hunters, John Boone's organization, Clay Conner's Negrito followers, and many still smaller groups. Tens of thousands of them fought alongside Allied regular troops throughout the last eight months of the war and took a heavy toll of the enemy. The Japanese were always much closer to victory in the Philippines in assertion than in reality.

Phenomena of the sort described above sometimes made it appear, at least to Americans, that the Japanese were truly inscrutable, or that they simply lacked good sense. How could they plan the Pacific War with such meticulous skill that most of the Far East and many Pacific islands fell to them in rapid succession in the first months of the war, and then prove such abominable administrators that they alienated most of the people they had conquered? Japanese intelligence reports secured after the war showed that Tokyo's rulers, political and military, were well informed about *most* Philippine activity. They knew, at least roughly, how many radios guerrillas had, how relatively accurate their radio reports to GHQ SWPA were, what were both the short- and long-term objectives of individual irregular groups, the morale of these "bandits," their inveterate quarrelsomeness, and their tactics.[16] The Japanese's reports to their superiors at home were generally factual and frank, not stuffed with propaganda puffery. Yet they persistently underrated guerrilla *numbers* to an incredible degree, and their ludicrous misperceptions of American and Filipino psychology have been pointed out repeatedly in this narrative. Furthermore, Nipponese army, navy, and civilian authorities worked at cross purposes throughout the war. Sometimes they seemed to be bewildered by the very magnitude of their own early successes. How to explain it?

Of course in any major war military needs and purposes often clash with political objectives, and either or both frequently conflict with the seeming short-term needs of propaganda. Also, *all* peoples misunderstand the psychology of others to some degree, and sheer confusion is inseparable from war. Thus are many wars more truly lost by the ineptitude of the vanquished than won by the valor of the victors.[17] Perhaps the cynic was right who said, "If you shake all the nonsense out of human affairs only 10 percent remains."

Other developments were far more grim than periodic bizarre Japanese behavior. Early in December 1942, the enemy forces in Cagayan were heavily reinforced. On December 8 a Japanese battalion occupied Tuao and began preparations to march on Kabugao. Reports from Abra and Ilocos Norte indicated that enemy forces there intended to mop up those areas while containing Apayao.

After completing his judicial labors at Pamplona, Captain Jones arrived back in Kabugao about December 15. Although Praeger was seriously ill, the two of them and Major Adduru spent the next day in laborious consideration of their precarious situation. What had to be decided specifically, and soon, was whether to stand and fight the enemy or retreat farther back into the mountains. Most of the men in Troop C were away collecting intelligence information. Those left in Kabugao had only about thirty-five rounds of ammunition per man, supplemented by about two hundred of James Needham's improvised dynamite grenades. This modest arsenal was not likely to discommode any Japanese force larger than a company.

Comparatively, the CAF radio was a far more important possession than these meager armaments. Yet the transmitter, receivers, batteries, generators, gasoline, and miscellaneous parts were collectively so heavy that about forty cargadores would be needed to move it all. Even so, it seemed a better bet to fade away into the hills and try to drag the communications gear along than to engage the enemy. Also, the matter of retaliation against the civilian population had to be weighed. The people had already run great risks and made many sacrifices to support the guerrillas, and doubtless would have to continue to do so for the foreseeable future. It seemed morally incumbent on CAF leaders to endanger them only to the minimum absolutely necessary. The savage Japanese reprisals taken after Barnett's ill-advised attacks in La Union were fresh in everyone's mind, and reports were filtering in from the upper Cagayan Valley that enemy mopping up there was being conducted with fearsome brutality. Since the CAF officers were by then convinced that MacArthur's forces could hardly be expected to return before the end of 1944—two full years away—it seemed highly unlikely that any CAF operations beyond mere security and reconnaissance could be conducted for long.

Yet war is filled with intangibles—factors that cannot be counted, weighed, or measured but which are often more important than those that can. Napoleon is supposed to have said that in war moral factors are three times as important as material. Kabugao had come to represent to thousands of people the last well-organized center of resistance in North Luzon. Two provincial governments were based there, and a third was not far distant. It was the only place on Luzon where American and Philippine flags still flew. To abandon Kabugao without a fight would cost heavily in prestige, especially among the older natives who had no understanding of the value of a radio but who understood war in the sense of combat. Guerrillas elsewhere who had been assigned intelligence missions and forbidden to fight, but had then disobeyed their orders subsequently came under heavy criticism. For instance, Col. Ruperto Kangleon, the foremost guerrilla leader on Leyte, gave more support to his combat units than to his coastwatchers, who reported their observations of Japanese shipping to GHQ SWPA. He was reproached for it. Yet successful guerrilla warfare is impossible if human feelings about it are disregarded by regular military establishments. The lives of Kangleon's men, combatants and observers alike, depended on the support of the people of Leyte. Even the mildest of people, if called upon to risk their lives to feed soldiers in occupied territory, want those soldiers to strike blows at the enemy now and then. It may be illogical, and it may result in serious harm to the people themselves, but their hearts are filled with outrage and they want to see the foe punished—at least until his reprisals grow unendurably severe.

Only a few weeks later a test case occurred that vividly highlighted the dilemma facing the officers of the CAF. Their coastwatchers reported a convoy of 125 ships moving south off eastern Luzon. The news was sent at once to GHQ SWPA. The convoy was subsequently bombed heavily, quite likely because of the information supplied by CAF radio. But those who sent the message knew well enough that the people in and around Apayao would never feel the same pride about the radio message they would have felt had a couple of CAF patrols knocked off a Japanese company in their immediate locality.[18]

There are hard decisions that must be made in all spheres of life, but few are as excruciating as those that sometimes come up in war. Captain Praeger was not primarily an intelligence officer. He was a fighter from a sense of duty, as his separation from Colonel Horan to raid Tuguegarao had demonstrated nearly a year before. But he was also an intelligent, cautious man who did not love fighting for its own sake, as some reckless adventurers and abnormal human types do. As instructed from Australia, he had issued orders forbidding ambushing the Japanese, but a larger question loomed: Could one let Kabugao fall to the enemy without defending it? After carefully weighing all the factors involved, Praeger recommended to Major Adduru that they withdraw quietly. Adduru approved and GHQ SWPA was notified.[19]

The Japanese patrolled the area around Kabugao for several days but captured only a few women and one man, who escaped a few hours later. The man had been taken by surprise, and during his brief stay with the Japanese had revealed nothing, but local Filipinos demanded that he be executed at once for his crime. When Captain Jones asked a local barrio lieutenant what "crime" the man had committed, the lieutenant replied that he had permitted himself to be captured alive—which surely was crime enough. Filipinos might be westernized in some respects, but these primitive mountaineers were as oriental as any Japanese in their attitude toward war. To them, a man fought to the death, for if he was captured alive he would be executed anyway! They could never understand why the Americans did not execute their handful of Japanese prisoners. Captain Jones finally managed to persuade the natives that the poor fellow should not be executed— or perhaps it would be more accurate to say that he reduced them to silence on the matter. Who could know how many of them underwent conversion in their hearts? If Japanese thought pro-

cesses often baffled Americans, American ideas and ways sometimes seemed similarly inscrutable to the Nipponese and Filipinos.

As the Japanese neared Kabugao, Lt. Feliciano Madamba,
who had been Roque Ablan's chief military commander and who
still headed the guerrilla force in Ilocos Norte, telephoned and
offered to move his men to Kabugao at once if they were needed.
The offer was declined with thanks. Had help been needed
Madamba would have been warmly welcomed, for he had
gathered together some soldiers and was operating in La Union
and northern Abra. A mountaineer by birth and a forest ranger
by profession, he knew every trail in the mountains and jungle
of the region, and his exceedingly mobile forces were a thorn in
the side of the Japanese. But Captain Praeger had made his
decision to take the radio and its supplies and move deeper into
the mountains instead of defending Kabugao.

As for Madamba, for months the Japanese had exerted every
effort to capture him, without success. As a consolation prize
they stooped to one of those acts of spectacular villainy that did
so much to blacken their national reputation all over the Orient:
they captured his girlfriend and paraded her naked in the capital
of Abra. Furious, Madamba slipped into town to try to rescue
her. The effort failed so he shot her to death to prevent the enemy
from heaping further humiliation on her. The Japanese then
denounced *him* as an animal, not a tao (man), and offered fifty
thousand dollars and thirty tins of gasoline to anyone who would
kill him. So determined were they to capture Madamba that they
assigned six thousand men to the task. They lined the few roads
for miles around with sentinels every hundred yards to prevent
him from slipping through. After months of such pressure
Madamba and his remaining men, by then sick and worn out,
capitulated under the terms of an amnesty in March 1943. Like
Guillermo Nakar and Candonia Gaerlan, Madamba was one of
the true heroes of the resistance movement in North Luzon.[20]

During these same weeks another sequence of comparably
terrible events began to unfold in northern Abra. At the turn of
1943 the Japanese there were operating against the 121st Infantry
and attempting to capture the few Americans on Mount Bawao.

On January 1 David Foster, an American veteran of the Spanish-American War who had stayed in Juanita's grandfather's house the preceding night, left in the morning to go farther up into the mountains to Naglibacan. A few minutes after Foster departed, a company of Japanese entered Aximao and noticed his shoeprints leading away from the house. They knew the prints must have been made by an American because none of the natives wore shoes. They at once seized Juanita's grandfather and demanded that he tell them where the man had gone. The old man refused to answer. The soldiers began to club him and, despite his piteous cries, continued to beat him for an hour until he died. His son, Juanita's uncle, soon learned of his father's demise. That afternoon the Japanese left Aximao. One of the soldiers fell behind the column marching along the trail and was captured by Juanita's uncle. The Filipino stripped the Japanese of his arms and took him to Barrio Lanoc, near Aximao. There he tied the luckless soldier to a stake and, while the townspeople watched, beheaded him to avenge his father's death.

At first the Japanese assumed the soldier had wandered off and gotten lost in the jungle, but by March they had learned the truth. On March 31 a small Japanese patrol of eighteen men entered Aximao. Almost at once they captured two guerrillas who were leaving Juanita's house after eating lunch there. Without harming the guerrillas, they entered the house, seized Juanita, and cut her throat with a bayonet. The patrol swiftly proceeded to Barrio Lanoc, where the slaying of the Japanese soldier on January 1 had taken place. There the Japanese called the people together for a meeting and then led them off, two by two, down to the river's edge, where they held their hands over the victims' mouths to muffle their cries as they stabbed them to death with bayonets. The corpses were then thrown into the river. Dozens of people were killed before those at the "meeting" site became aware of what was happening. Panic stricken, they tried to flee, but the Japanese mowed them down with rifle fire. As soon as news of the massacre circulated, the entire population of the Aximao district fled into the hills.

If that had been the end of the whole bloody tale an outsider might simply have concluded that the Filipino thirst for vengeance had been repaid with interest by the Japanese. But it was not all. Many times during World War II the Japanese demonstrated that they were stupefyingly bad psychologists when it came to gauging the feelings and responses of other peoples. In this instance they sent a message to the mayor of Aximao stating, "Justice has been satisfied. There will be no more killing. Please have all the people return to their homes and we will have a party together and be friends." Felipe sent a message of his own to Corporal Heuser: "Among the dead is my beloved mother. I buried her and Juanita today. The people are going to stay in the mountains for a time, and if possible we would appreciate it if you and the other soldiers would go somewhere else for six weeks as there is not sufficient food even for the people to feed themselves. Please come back then."[21] War is often enough hell for soldiers—it can be even worse for civilians. After the massacre, seventy-one bodies were recovered. How many more were carried off by the river remains unknown.

The CAF's fortunes along the north coast were better. In December 1942 the Japanese sent a forty-man patrol from Aparri toward Pamplona. The detachment was met at Lubban by Lieutenant Bowen who, with only four or five men, took up a position on the west bank of the Abulug River and directed enough fire across the stream that the enemy force went back to Aparri. But no such luck occurred in Abra or around Kabugao. On December 26 the enemy burned the barrio of Malabanig on the outskirts of Kabugao, as well as the Philippine Constabulary and officers' quarters in the town. When they left, CAF patrols followed. The Japanese, anxious to avoid the pursuing patrols, fell into ambushes set by civilians at Lenning and Telefugo. Three enemy soldiers, including a company commander, were killed, at the cost of one Filipino *cargadore*. In January the enemy organized the Faire-Tuao-Rizal area in southwest Cagayan and made occasional forays into Apayao from that base. Farther south and west they mopped up Abra, capturing Captain Peryam, C.O. of the 121st Infantry, and his principal staff officers on January 4, 1943.[22]

If Captain Praeger had ever been tempted to reverse his decision to withdraw and save the radio rather than stand and fight, his ardor would have been dampened by a message from GHQ SWPA in mid-January. It was directed to all guerrilla forces on Luzon, and it spelled out once more with unmistakable clarity what General MacArthur wanted everyone to do: Try to improve intelligence gathering; send GHQ SWPA as much detailed information as possible; try to unify all guerrilla groups on Luzon; avoid hostilities with the Japanese; and be brave and patient for ultimate victory is certain.[23]

The CAF began to come apart at the seams following the evacuation of Kabugao. The government of Cagayan set up its new headquarters at Grace Park, halfway down the Abulug River toward the north coast, and the government of Apayao at Cagawaddan, a small barrio hidden behind the Abulug River some miles north of Kabugao. Both places were less than ideal. Living conditions at Grace Park were primitive, although all concerned carried out their duties efficiently. Governor Adduru sought authority to induct five thousand men in Cagayan as guerrillas but GHQ SWPA disapproved, explaining that it was impossible to send them arms.[24]

At Cagawaddan the old, faltering figurehead governor of Apayao, Milton Ayochok, was visibly going to pieces. He drank more with every week that passed. His wife, an admirable Bontoc woman, did everything she could to keep him going, but the burden of serious administration fell on the treasurer, auditor, and other members of the gubernatorial staff.[25]

The only ray of sunshine that penetrated the thickening gloom was receipt of a radiogram from Australia on January 12, 1943, promoting Captain Praeger to major. Everyone was pleased. Lieutenant Tomas Quiocho also received a well-deserved promotion to first lieutenant, and Sergeant Arnao, having demonstrated his courage and reliability for a year, was appointed a second lieutenant.[26]

The brief good news of the promotions was soon counterbalanced by more bad news from the north coast. There, unlike the areas around Kabugao and Tuao, the regular Philippine government still operated openly, but enemy operations clearly impended. Praeger sent a message to Lieutenant Bowen ordering him not to take any foolish chances, but Bowen, as ever, interpreted orders to suit himself when he was out of range of effective authority. This time he seized upon an illness as an excuse to remain in Nummuao, although Japanese occupation of the place was expected momentarily. On February 3, three hundred enemy troops from Aparri moved into Lubban, near the mouth of the Abulug River.[27]

11

The Clouds Gather: Spring 1943

On February 6, 1943, Lieutenant Colonels Martin Moses and Arthur Noble arrived in Kabugao accompanied by twelve men. Dressed in shorts and wearing civilian felt hats and patched shirts, they attempted to keep their identities secret by calling themselves "Sergeant Smith" and "Sergeant Brown." The effort was not a success. Every native in northern Luzon knew exactly who they were, as did even the Belgian missionary priest in Kabugao. He recognized their West Point class rings and remarked dryly that he thought graduates of the U.S. Military Academy were given commissions.

The two colonels had been on the run ever since the war began, chased out of every place where they had paused on their trek from Bataan to the northern mountains. After the vicious Japanese response to their October offensive, they had fled to Ifugao. There they were attending a Christmas party at the headquarters of local guerrillas when enemy patrols surrounded the place and attacked it from all four sides. Moses and Noble managed to slip into the rain forest and hide for three days, after which they had gone off to the north coast, hoping to recuperate there for a few weeks. No such luck. The Japanese occupied the area and the fugitives fled to Kabugao. Moses was clearly exhausted and spent most of a day just sitting in a chair in the sun. Noble seemed to be losing his sight in one eye. Yet both were in basic good spirits and went readily with Captain Jones to

Praeger's radio station the day after their arrival. For months they had been collecting intelligence information throughout the Mountain subprovinces and sending it by runners to Praeger's headquarters in the hope that he could transmit it to Australia. Now, at last, they could communicate directly with GHQ SWPA. For the next two weeks they bombarded General MacArthur with information about northern Luzon and requests for assistance for themselves. They said the Ganaps (pro-Japanese Filipinos) had become numerous and active, that civilian morale was deteriorating, that local action was needed to reverse this trend, and that the accomplishment of virtually all guerrilla missions was growing increasingly difficult. They requested[1] and obtained authority to induct the equivalent of one regiment into the service of the United States, to be armed and supplied locally—a classic example of acting first and asking permission afterward since they had already been inducting so many men for so long that only eleven days later they assured SWPA that they had unified all the guerrillas in northern Luzon and now controlled six thousand men![2] They further requested that propaganda leaflets be dropped over the Philippines by plane, even if it involved the sacrifice of the plane. They added that supplies of every sort—but especially transceivers, medicine, ammunition, and money—were urgently needed.[3] Yet another message the same day incongruously exuded pride at the great successes of the guerrilla offensive of October-November 1942. It claimed that two thousand Japanese and many Ganaps had perished, that large stocks of arms and ammunition had been seized, bridges had been destroyed, and food dumps burned—all with small USAFIP losses. The colonels noted in passing that they had suspended operations for the time being per SWPA orders, but added that civilian morale was high (where it had been low only eleven days earlier!), that many Filipinos wanted to become guerrillas, and that civilians would support guerrillas in all possible ways.[4] Small wonder that GHQ SWPA seemed confused. Accurate information about events on Luzon was always late and in short supply,[5] but these messages were different in tone as well. What to do? What *was* done was to reply blandly that requests for outside aid could not be filled "for some months" due to a shortage of planes and gasoline.[6]

Undeterred by either their own failures or the tepid enthusiasm of GHQ SWPA for their varied and often conflicting schemes, Moses and Noble resurrected that perennial notion so popular with ambitious guerrilla leaders: unite all the Luzon guerrillas under one leader (invariably the dreamer himself). They discussed it at some length with Adduru and Praeger but, as ever, nothing tangible resulted.

Throughout February the CAF's outlook grew steadily darker. The Japanese who had occupied Lubban on February 3 began to drive westward along the north coast while other enemy forces simultaneously made a series of surprise landings by barge, covered by destroyers, at Ballesteros, Abulug, Pamplona, Sanchez Mira, and Claveria, all along the north coast. The whole operation was well planned and executed, and although no guerrillas were killed or captured in the first day or two, only a few nights later the Japanese surrounded the 3rd Company, Cagayan Force, and either killed, captured, or chased off every man in it. The 4th Company, which had only recently been organized, then broke up. The Aparri Company of the Philippine Constabulary, commanded by a regular PC officer, Captain Gonzalo, had the good fortune to have a fine first sergeant, and managed to go underground and hold together against the Japanese.

The overall C.O. on the north coast, Lieutenant Bowen, remained in Numuuc, near Sanchez Mira, with his staff. With typical nonchalant bravado he stayed under the very noses of the Japanese who occupied the town, deigning only to move his abode back and forth across a highway from time to time. But everyone has his breaking point somewhere, sometime. By April it was clear that the Japanese were preparing to execute the families of Bowen's enlisted men, so he surrendered. By then his legs were so badly ulcerated that he was unable to walk. The Japanese, out of respect for his courage, chivalrously sent Bowen to their own hospital in Tuguegarao for treatment. Bowen had done a magnificent job on the north coast, both maintaining law and order and keeping up the morale of the Filipinos, who idolized him.[7] For a long time his mere presence had kept the Japanese bottled up in Aparri. Fearless, modest, generous, indifferent to promotions or personal honors, and always considerate of his men, he was one of the finest of the guerrilla leaders.[8]

Meanwhile, the Japanese were preparing to tighten their noose around the beleaguered garrison in and around Kabugao. Information from the 121st Infantry indicated that the Nipponese in Abra to the southwest were preparing to drive down the Dagarra Valley to Kabugao. News from Lieutenant Madamba in Ilocos Norte disclosed that a Japanese battalion would soon leave Solsona and proceed eastward. Finally, information from Tuao indicated that a drive westward from there would begin early in March. In an effort to evade the doom that seemed impending, the CAF underwent a fast reorganization. Captain Jones was assigned command of a western Apayao-Abra-Ilocos defense force, Lieutenant Camp was assigned a similar command in southern Apayao and southern Cagayan, and Lieutenant Quiocho was assigned one in the Luna-Abulug area to the north. On February 25 the Japanese at Solana near Tuao began to move. Ten days later they were also on the move southward from Luna, and northeastward from Sapol in Abra Province. Information from several quarters indicated that the total enemy strength was about a thousand and that their objectives were to capture Governor Adduru, seize Praeger's radio, and destroy the CAF and the governments of both Cagayan and Apayao. Major Praeger cut off contact with Australia on March 8 and began to move the radio to a new location across the river, about a mile from Kabugao. A year and a half later this would have been a practical project, for by then field radios had been improved sufficiently that they could be carried on the back of one man, but in March 1943 transceivers still weighed hundreds of pounds, and auxiliary equipment was comparably heavy. Thus the move was not completed before the Japanese entered the area.[9]

These melancholy developments also set the luckless Moses and Noble on their travels once more. By now the two "old colonels" were close to being overborne by their hopes and imaginations. Some thought they wanted to go to Abra to look for

Ablan and the remaining elements of Walter Cushing's old outfit. (Cushing himself had been dead for five months, and nobody had seen Ablan for a year.) According to Thomas Jones, their intention was quite different: to go south and set up a new headquarters in Kalinga Subprovince. There they would collect information to be channeled to wherever Praeger should set up his new command post in Apayao. They would also have their agents collect additional information in Manila and around Baguio, all to be relayed ultimately to Australia. The latter idea itself was not unsound, but the Japanese mop-up in the next six months was so effective the system never got into operation.[10]

The information that the enemy had given the capture of Governor Adduru highest priority in the impending mop-up operation—higher even than seizure of the radio or the American officers—indicated that the Japanese had at last begun to realize that the widespread resistance they were encountering stemmed not from any artificial stimulus by the Americans but directly from the Filipinos themselves.

In the center of North Luzon, Governor Adduru was the core of that resistance movement. The aid he rendered the Americans was beyond measure. A skilled politician, he saved them from many blunders they might otherwise have committed from inexperience. A quarter of a million people depended directly on the guidance and protection they had received from the provincial government allied with the CAF soldiers. That they had, so far, lived in relative tranquility, subject neither to enemy retaliatory measures nor to the depredations of bandits and scoundrels of their own nationality who sometimes posed as guerrillas, was due largely to the wisdom and foresight of Marcelo Adduru. A man of great energy in addition to his other gifts, he worked most days from dawn until 10:00 or 11:00 P.M. Sometimes, when business was particularly pressing, he got practically no sleep at all. In December 1942, when the decision to eventually evacuate Kabugao was made, he oversaw twelve delegations from various government agencies and municipalities. He worked all night. By dawn, all the paraphernalia and supplies necessary to run even a rudimentary government in a war area could be quickly loaded into barges. The physical substance of the government of Cagayan Province then floated downstream in a long convoy, the governor propped up in a boat still studying documents.

The Japanese had repeatedly promised Adduru that they would retain him as governor of Cagayan if he would go over to them. To add sharpness to their appeal, they said he would be executed if he did not. By the autumn of 1942 he was convinced that they meant it, but he did not waver. Nonetheless, the long-term threat of death weighs heavily on any normal human being. Marcelo Adduru coped with it by initiating a daily Bible study program at his command post in which all personnel participated. It was moving to see this brilliant, stout-hearted man lead his staff in prayer and ask the help of Divine Providence in a situation which was, temporarily at least, beyond the help of the most powerful nation in the world. His people looked to him not merely as the governor of a province, but as the highest remaining officer of a nation at war. The Americans trusted him implicitly.[11]

These remarks point up one of the most serious errors the Japanese made in attempting to crush the guerrilla bands. All too often they directed their efforts against the Americans to whom, in many cases, had fallen the command of guerrilla units. But command is not the same thing as leadership, and neither command nor leadership could provide the basic ingredients of the guerrilla movement. When American leaders were competent, the guerrillas operated more effectively than they would have otherwise. However, some of the Americans were ill-suited for the task, and the guerrilla movement would have been better off without them. Cushing, Praeger, Jones, Volckmann, Barnett, Bowen, Camp, even Moses and Noble in aspiration and effort— to mention a few—made major contributions to the resistance movement in Northern Luzon, as did Lapham, Hunt, Anderson, Hendrickson, and others farther south. But Governor Adduru, Governor Ablan, Lieutenant Madamba, Colonel Nakar, Colonel Enriquez, and many other Filipinos made contributions that were no less valuable. As for the rank and file, all were Filipinos. And it is worth remembering that the guerrillas could exist only as long as the Filipino populace was willing to accept the risk of maintaining them. For a long time the Japanese seemed to think that if the Americans were rooted out and eliminated, resistance would collapse. By 1943 they had begun to learn better, as their concentration on Adduru indicated.[12]

The net finally closed on March 12. Three hundred and fifty Japanese troops from Ripang (near Tuao) and another company from Luna in the north entered Kabugao. Still another enemy advance patrol of company strength, this one from Ilocos Norte, effected a junction with a similar force from Cagayan at Tulungtung, eight miles north of Kabugao. The enemy then began an intensive mopping-up operation in Apayao that lasted until September. They thoroughly sketch-mapped the whole province and air-mapped the Kabugao area. Every effort was then made to destroy the CAF. Nevertheless, the mopping up in Apayao was done humanely, in sharp contrast to the brutal methods employed elsewhere. A large part of the credit for this is due Capt. S. Takahashi, who became commander of the Japanese Kabugao garrison. An extremely hardworking and efficient officer, he drove his troops to the point of exhaustion; yet it was not until the last few days that he used force against civilians, and then only to a limited extent. So impressed was Major Praeger by the superior qualities and civilized behavior of this Japanese officer that he reported his opinion by radio to GHQ SWPA.

The soldiers used in the mop-up operation were several cuts above ordinary Japanese occupation troops—both physically and in general efficiency. In only one notable area were they deficient: that perennial bugaboo of armies, sickness. In North Luzon, captured American officers were told by a Japanese interpreter that the Japanese sick rate around Kabugao was 50 percent and that there had been a complete turnover of personnel in their units every month. The principal reason for this had been drinking contaminated water and taking insufficient precautions against malaria. The CAF sick rate had been comparably appalling in the first months at Kabugao in 1942.

The native mountaineers must have gradually developed

an immunity to malaria in their long and obscure history, because few of them ever suffered from it. Down in the lowlands, though, malaria was common enough among Filipinos. There, at some time in the past, they had developed an effective home remedy against it. It consisted of taking the bark off a delapauan tree, a relative of the cinchona tree which produces quinine, soaking it in water, and then boiling the solution down to a tenth of its original volume. Even so, lowland Filipinos seldom actually drank the stuff, probably because of its foul taste. Doctor Irenio Reyes, the CAF medical officer and official surgeon for the whole province, was familiar with this elixir and knew how to prepare it. Every day he required that a bucketful of it be carried down the ranks while the men were in company front, and each man was made to drink some of it. Atrocious taste aside, malaria rates fell off sharply after July 1942.[13]

Captain Jones thought Takahashi and other Japanese officers adopted more humane methods of reducing Cagayan and Apayao Provinces than those employed elsewhere because the Allies had functioning, lawful, humane governments in both provinces. Although enemy propaganda vilified CAF men as bandits, rapists, and conscienceless exploiters, it was obvious that the Japanese did not believe this themselves, nor did they make any serious effort to force Filipinos to believe it. In other areas where the regular Philippine government had collapsed, life for guerrillas was harder, and harder still for hapless Filipino civilians. Down in the lowlands especially, civilians were often pillaged, plundered, raped, tortured, and had their houses burned, or suffered some combination of these atrocities. Sometimes they were looted and abused by Japanese occupation troops, sometimes by Filipinos who posed as guerrillas but were really bandits. Often they were victimized by Hukbalahap guerrillas and lawless USAFFE personnel. The USAFFE guerrillas were ordinarily well behaved if their commanders were able and sensible, but many a unit was led by men who lacked judgment or character or both. Two sentences in a radiogram from Praeger to GHQ SWPA summarize much that was amiss among USAFFE irregulars more than a year after the war began: "USAFFE ABUSES IN

AREAS WITHOUT CENTRAL CONTROL ARE EXCESSIVE. COMMANDEERING, EXECUTIONS WITHOUT TRIAL, AND RAPE."[14]

A couple of examples of the sort of thing that often took place, and how such matters were sometimes dealt with, illustrate the point more sharply. On one occasion, Lieutenant Bowen detained a large number of guerrillas who had come into northern Cagayan from an adjacent province. They had commandeered whatever they wanted, and three of them raped a Filipina who had been married to a Japanese before the war. Their commander was sufficiently grateful to Lieutenant Bowen for instructing him in the proper conduct for soldiers that he gave Bowen two of the rapists for trial. The third had abruptly absented himself but was finally apprehended. His commander, by then disgusted by all the trouble the miscreant had made for him, simply caused the man to "disappear." A simple wooden marker bearing the legend, "Here lies Pvt. Juan de la Cruz, Rapist," testified to the disposition of his case.[15]

On another occasion, three Troop C soldiers were assassinated by a rogue guerrilla band that wanted their weapons. So many persons had been murdered by this particular organization of scoundrels that one of the CAF Philippine Scout sergeants killed its commander on the spot. That officer *might* have been mad. Before he was killed, one of his men had deserted and come to CAF headquarters to ask if he might transfer to the CAF. He was an Ifugao, from one of the bravest tribes in Mountain Province. Exceptionally big and husky for a Filipino, he bore the name Kalafu, a rough Philippine equivalent of Tarzan. What follows is a remembered conversation between Kalafu and Major Praeger. Kalafu spoke very slowly throughout. An onlooker could readily imagine wheels turning in his head before he answered a question. The dialogue went approximately thus:

PRAEGER: Kalafu, why do you want to leave your organization and join us?

KALAFU (after a long silence): Because, sir, I do not care for the customs and habits of my commanding officer.
PRAEGER: Why, what are his customs and habits that you don't like?
KALAFU (after a long wait): Because he kills too many people.
PRAEGER: Japanese?
KALAFU: No sir, Filipinos.
PRAEGER: Why does he kill Filipinos, Kalafu?
KALAFU: He says they are bad, sir.
PRAEGER: Well, then, why do you object to his killing them?
KALAFU (the wheels go around again): Well, sir, it is I who must do the killing. Although my commanding officer is a fine man, still I do not like to be always killing Filipinos.
PRAEGER: How do you kill them, Kalafu? Do you shoot them?
KALAFU: No sir, I don't shoot them.
PRAEGER: Well, do you bolo them?
KALAFU: No sir, I do not use a bolo.
PRAEGER: Well, then, how do you kill them, Kalafu?
KALAFU (after long silence): I wring their necks, sir. That is why I want to join your outfit, because you do not wring people's necks here.

Major Praeger thereupon enlisted Kalafu in Troop C, writing under "Remarks" that in his opinion Kalafu was innocent of any crimes he might have committed at the direction of his former commanding officer. Kalafu certainly proved to be a hardy man—and a handy one too, on occasion. When the radio had to be moved, Kalafu, because of his great strength, was given the task of carrying the block for the generator, which weighed nearly two hundred pounds.[16]

As for the radio itself, there were many reasons why it was never a dependable means of communication. The most obvious was that it was too heavy to be transported readily. When it and all its auxiliary equipment were being transferred from Gok-Gok to a new location in March, the men carrying the transmitter were intercepted by the enemy and forced to drop their burden in some bushes, where it lay in the rain for several days.

Meanwhile, reports of Japanese massacres elsewhere in North Luzon came in regularly and weighed heavily on everyone's mind. Although the Japanese in Apayao were operating in accord with the laws of war, nobody ever doubted that they were quite capable of committing the same atrocities there if they failed to attain their objectives—especially if Captain Takahashi were transferred elsewhere. Other dangers seemed quite as serious. Suppose the enemy should capture the radio? How would the intelligence reports GHQ SWPA seemed to value so highly then get to Australia? Much worse was the ever present danger to the civilians who were feeding and sheltering the troops. All the people working for the Japanese in Apayao were either CAF agents or watched by CAF agents. They risked their lives and their families' lives every day—and put the Americans, at least, in their debt to a degree that could never be repaid.

The radio itself was located in the barrio of Bulu, less than a mile from the enemy garrison in Kabugao. Nearly every Filipino for miles around knew where it was. The Japanese tried all sorts of ploys to learn its location—offering large monetary rewards, giving people quinine, other medicines, or soap, all mixed with periodic dire threats—yet it was late August before they got what they wanted.

The constant pressure broke some civilians eventually, but for a long time it had the opposite effect of driving civilians and the CAF closer together. Formerly, food and supplies had been paid for with newly manufactured scrip, but by the spring of 1943 many people refused to accept payment at all on the ground that in difficult times it was not proper to take money from their army. The extreme generosity of this gesture can be appreciated when it is recalled that only a handful of families in Apayao ever possessed more than ten pesos (five dollars American) during a year in peacetime, and that all of them lived permanently on the very margin of existence. Before the war, Apayao had the reputation of being the most inhospitable province in the Philippines. That certainly was not so during the war. The poverty-stricken people there gave whatever they had merely for the asking.

CAF control over the Cagayan Valley really ended on April 1, 1943, when Major Adduru, with his family and most of his staff, was caught behind Grace Ridge. The Allied forces who had been there for a year as something less than soldiers but more than mere guerrillas soon became entirely guerrillas—and ones limited solely to underground operations at that.[17]

On April 9, Cpl. Louis "Apple" Heuser, Philippine Air-Warning Company, and Pvt. Ng Lai "Lee" Soo, 121st Infantry, reported to Captain Jones at Dibulu and briefed him on conditions in Abra. Mopping up there had been extremely brutal. The 121st had suffered severely. Lt. Edward Zaija had been captured and Lt. William Arthur had surrendered. Heuser and Lee also told Jones about the horrible massacre in Aximao. Privately, Lee informed Jones that the highly emotional Heuser had nearly gone berserk when he heard about the grisly deaths of his Filipino friends. Half mad with grief, he had wanted to attack the Japanese at once. Felipe, the schoolteacher and agricultural expert, and Sergeant Barcelona, had barely dissuaded him from doing so by pointing out that the only result would be that the Japanese would come back and kill all the remaining people they could catch. Heuser knew this was true but, consumed with rage and sorrow, he had shouted that it made no difference since the villains would come back and kill them all anyway. He also knew that some of the 121st's automatic rifles had been left in the care of a native in the district who was supposed to keep them safe and well oiled. When the massacre occurred, the man issued the weapons to his own family. Then he, his wife, and two girls—aged ten and twelve—took up positions on the trail in front of their house to guard against any approaching Japanese. Corporal Heuser lamented bitterly that if such people could fight the enemy he saw no reason why he shouldn't as well.

Heuser was still suffering from the shock of the Aximao massacre when he arrived at Captain Jones's command post. He was obsessed with it for days. He reproached himself bitterly because he had let others dissuade him from attacking the Japanese. He repeatedly asked rhetorically what there was to live for when all his friends were dead. The memory of little Juanita, with whom he had traded so many jokes and who had brought nice cakes to him and Sergeant Brazelton, flooded his mind—as did her grandfather's promise that they would all die before they betrayed the Americans to the enemy. Heuser brooded on these memories and talked about them incessantly.

All that consoled him, and likely saved his sanity, was his Bible. He taught both Lee and Captain Jones, neither of whom was overly conversant with Scripture, all the great biblical passages. Heuser was able to find an appropriate passage in the Bible for everything that happened. Of the Filipinos who fed and protected them, he quoted Acts 28:2: "And the barbarous people showed us no little kindness: for they kindled a fire, and received us every one, because of the present rain, and because of the cold." It wasn't cold in the Apayao jungle but it was indubitably wet, and the "barbarous people" truly had shown American and Filipino guerrillas alike "no little kindness."[18]

One of the most intelligent and interesting men to join the CAF during the war was Chinese private Ng Lai Soo, or Lee, as the Americans called him. He had lived in the Philippines before the war, and in peacetime had been employed as a master mechanic at the Minuri Mine, owned by Manuel Concepcion. Concepcion seldom paid his bills or his employees on time, and so owed Lee a large sum in back salary. When asked why he didn't quit such an employer, Lee gave a reply that may seem puzzling to Occidentals who assume a narrowly economic view of life: "With a Chinese it is different. If we like a man we stay with him. True, Concepcion owes me much money, but I like him and I like my work, so if I leave and go elsewhere maybe I will have more money but I won't be as happy. So I will stay where I am even after the war."[19] When one considers how many people in the Western world spend years in jobs they hate merely because the pay is good, one would have to wonder who was wise and who was eccentric. Of course this common Occidental attitude is not universal: it is an American adage, after all, that if you find a job you love you will never work a day in your life. Maybe Lee's response was just a personal idiosyncrasy.

Lee spoke good grammatical English, but his accent was poor and he realized it. It happened that there were a few of Shakespeare's sonnets, copied from a child's notebook, around camp. Lee would often read these to try to correct his pronunciation and acquire a feel for each word. One day he was repeating the lines, "Golden lads and girls all must as chimney sweeps, come to dust," when suddenly their beauty broke upon him and his face lighted up.[20]

Lee was also a good cook. Many of those connoisseurs who regard eating as one of the fine arts have claimed that our planet enjoys only two truly distinctive forms of haute cuisine: French in the West and Chinese in the Orient. The Filipino cooks in the CAF were competent in a pedestrian sense, but no one would confuse them with the grand chefs of five-star French restaurants. This was not good enough for Lee. He cooked rice with great care so it would be done exactly right, and he scoured the jungle for anything edible that would add flavor to the rice and salt that constituted everybody's dietary staple in the spring of 1943. He found all sorts of interesting comestibles: antibun (heart of palm but not the coconut), bamboo shoots, rattan, and many more odd delights. These were supplemented periodically with prawns caught in streams or honey pilfered from the hives of wild bees.

After being forced to flee from Kabugao the men lived, for the most part, in little lean-to bamboo huts in the jungle, which could be thrown up in a couple of hours. They seldom stayed in barrios anymore because it would have been too exhausting to keep a constant watch out for the Japanese, who entered and left without warning. Living in the jungle was not especially difficult, but it was dispiriting. In northern Apayao it rained virtually every day from September 1942 until May 1943.[21] Those who have not experienced it can hardly understand the depressing effect of continuous rainfall on a hunted man. Between rain and jungle, everyone lived in perpetual gloom, not seeing the sun for weeks at a time. Clothing molded and rotted away, and leather shoes—or what was left of them—became almost unwearable. They could be polished with banana peels to temporarily destroy the mold, but this did not preserve the leather. Canvas shoes also rotted to tatters. Thus it was that after a year nearly everyone had joined Major Praeger in going barefoot.

General disintegration seemed to accelerate in a dozen different ways. The Japanese seized over two hundred kilometers of CAF telephone line in a few weeks, making practical control of the district by what little that was left of provincial government far more difficult. No longer were there towns to live in nor flags to fly from buildings.[22] The supply of radio news was suspended from March to June because the transmitter had been temporarily abandoned when it was being moved to Gok-Gok. There it had lain in grass and brush for several days and become so thoroughly water-soaked that it took three months to make it usable again. In the interim, the CAF remained knowledgeable about what nearby Japanese were doing but lost all contact with the outside world. Deterioration was also personal. Praeger fell ill in April, and Sergeant Brazelton became so sick he nearly died.

On the same day that Corporal Heuser and Lee arrived at Captain Jones's CP, the enemy made a mad dash from Kabugao to Cagawaddan—the temporary seat of government in Apayao— hoping to catch the figurehead governor, Milton Ayochok. But he and all his officials escaped. Ten days later, April 19, the enemy's luck was better. With both Ayochok and Adduru in Japanese custody, Captain Jones became the de facto administrator of what was left of the government of Apayao.[23]

As if all these disasters were not sufficient, the CAF then had some bad luck of its own. One evening Cpl. Julio Mamba was leading a patrol in an effort to contact an enemy unit. In the growing darkness they suddenly came upon a group of men carrying what looked like rifles. Thinking they were Japanese, Mamba and his men opened fire. Three men were killed and two more wounded before they discovered they had shot up a band of inoffensive Filipino civilians carrying spearfishing guns. Such tragic foul-ups are common in all wars, and this unhappy blunder was the only incident of its type that ever occurred in Apayao.

Even so, the debacle was the last thing the CAF needed in its dire extremity.

Corporal Mamba was held blameless after an investigation. The wounded and the families of the dead were indemnified according to local custom. The wounded were each given property worth thirty dollars, and relatives of the dead received vases valued at seventy-five dollars. Until the settlement was agreed upon, though, tribal honor required what amounted to a virtual state of war between all the kinfolk of the deceased on one side and Mamba and all his relatives on the other. Captain Jones saved the day by hurriedly arranging a truce of sorts, and then appealed to all parties to keep the peace because of the presence of the Japanese. To their credit—perhaps out of concern for self-preservation as well—they did so.

During the latter part of April Jones visited Lt. Charles Arnao's patrol, then stationed at Maragat. Arnao had gotten no radio news since early March, and was endeavoring to keep up the morale of the local people by inventing and publishing his own news reports. He had North Africa falling to the Allies in April—not a bad guess as it actually fell in May. Captain Jones returned to Dibulu and the next day went on to Cagawadden, a few miles away. Right after Jones and his group left Dibulu the Japanese encircled the barrio and took it. They captured one old man, to whom they administered the "water cure" to make him talk. This was a horrible indignity that consisted of forcing water down a victim's throat until he nearly burst, then stomping on his stomach until the water was forced out all the openings of his body. The old man could speak only the native dialect, so the Japanese used a young Isneg to translate his statements into English, which a few of them understood. The old man told the truth to the Isneg interpreter—that Jones had gone to Cagawaddan —but the interpreter rendered his reply in English somewhat as follows: "Oh, Your Excellency, this old man has dwelt here all his life and has never seen an American. Because of his great age he asks you to be merciful to him. He says you are welcome to search all the barrio and the surrounding area and he will show you the way, but that there are no Americans here." After some hesitation the Japanese decided to accept the offer and stopped the torture.

The whole sordid episode is mentioned here mainly to illustrate how difficult and uncertain the transmission of information is when one or both parties have to depend on interpreters —and also how sly the Filipinos could sometimes be in getting around the Japanese. In this particular case the interpreter was simply following orders that CAF officers had given to all the people in Apayao: that they should use only their Isneg dialect when speaking to the Japanese. This permitted the unavoidable interpreters, who were all CAF agents, to check their responses and edit their replies as the situation required. Other Filipinos are known to have played the same game. It required not only linguistic ability but great courage as they never knew when one of the Japanese they were attempting to bamboozle might happen to know the Filipino dialect in question and penetrate the sham. If that happened the interpreter's fate was far from enviable.[24]

By May it had become impossible to use normal security measures against the enemy because this placed too great a burden on the CAF's dwindling numbers. The Japanese patrolled almost constantly, and in all directions. This forced the guerrillas to take chances they would not have taken under normal circumstances. If the enemy was five hundred yards away, CAF troops simply ceased paying much attention to them, beyond occasionally looking at the Japanese and wishing that the CAF was a real army that could fight openly instead of hiding in the woods when a human being approached. This lack of alertness soon resulted, as it usually does in war, in disaster.[25]

Early in May, Lieutenant Colonels Moses and Noble came to Lieutenant Arnao's camp, located in one of the most remote corners of Apayao. As usual, they were on the run. They had been driven out of Kalinga and pursued for weeks thereafter by a Japanese patrol. They had been hoping to rest there, but were chased out the next day. Two days later the Japanese patrol reached Arnao's camp, surrounded it, and opened fire. Lieutenant Arnao, Cpl. Silvestre Vaggas of Troop C, and Capt. William Ebert of the

206 / Intrepid Guerrillas of North Luzon

Philippine Air-Warning Company, were captured. Private William Carroll, also of the Air-Warning Company, escaped in a hail of bullets. Corporal Feliz Domingo of Troop C was out rustling supplies when the attack took place. On his return he saw the Japanese before they saw him and was able to escape into the jungle. Vaggas also escaped three days later, the second time he had given the Japanese the slip.[26] He found Captain Jones and identified Arnao's captors as *Kempeitai,* the much-feared Japanese secret police. He said those captured had been well treated but that the Japanese were chagrined that Moses and Noble had managed to evade them once more.

This particular Japanese patrol had been based at Bontoc, perhaps a hundred miles south in a straight line, but they had traveled at least twice that far over rough mountain trails before reaching Arnao's camp. All Japanese troops in North Luzon at that time were sparing no efforts to catch or kill every American in that whole sector. They largely succeeded in Kalinga Subprovince in April and May.

On May 19 Captain Jones moved from Cagawaddan to Tuyangan, at the junction of the Abulug River and the Ilocos Norte Trail—a spot from which he could watch Japanese from both Ilocos and Cagayan, and communicate easily with Major Praeger as well. A few days later the enemy searched the area and Jones was cut off. He managed to escape and set up a new command post about a mile away on the south side of the Abulug River. There river and trail could be watched easily, but in order to reach the place one had to travel for half a mile in full view of a trail on the opposite bank being used by the Japanese. Moves were coming at ever shorter intervals and with no long-term advantage accruing from any of them.

On June 2 a devastating blow fell. After a relentless pursuit lasting fifty-two days and ending back in Kalinga, Moses and Noble were captured at last—probably because the Japanese were able to seize Moses's orderly and torture him until he revealed his superior's hideout. Since it had been the two lieutenant colonels' reckless determination to make open war on the Japanese eight months earlier that had galvanized the enemy into action, the capture of Moses and Noble did not damage the few remaining guerrillas in any personal or material way. Nevertheless, symbolism is often more important than tangibles. Moses and Noble were the highest-ranking American officers in the north, they had asserted their command over all guerrillas there, they were indubitably brave personally, and they had tried to carry the war to the enemy. Now they were gone for good. It was profoundly dispiriting, and it would not be long before the few scattered guerrillas still at large in the north would be gone, too.

12

The Curtain Comes Down

As Captain Jones remembered it years afterward, the month of June 1943 around his camp near Tuyangan in northwest Apayao was superficially quiet and not unhappy. The food was better than it had been in recent months, and everyone regained some strength. Even better, the everlasting rain finally stopped. Just to see and feel the sun again buoyed up the spirits of many. Corporal Heuser continued to read his Bible, and Lee faithfully studied English. Jones himself alternately read his Greek texts and the intelligence reports of the western Apayao-Abra-Ilocos Norte sector. Major Praeger managed to get his transmitter working again and sent Jones and party the latest news. The situation in New Guinea was obscure because the CAF had been for too long without a working radio and so had no context in which to fit what it was hearing. In Tokyo, Premier Tojo declared that the Allies would launch a great offensive in Burma in October or November, a delay Corporal Heuser found profoundly disappointing. Radio San Francisco was quoted as suggesting that an invasion of continental Europe was at hand. Everyone hoped it would take place in June, and wondered aloud if Germany might be defeated by November 1943. If that should happen, then the Americans marooned seemingly forever on South Pacific islands might get back to the Philippines before the end of 1944, which the CAF's officers had long assumed would be their time of deliverance.

Jones's camp was set in a little copse amid high cogon grass that screened it from the trail used by the Japanese across the river. They could look out across the hills to the Ilocos Mountains some twenty miles to the west. The sun went down directly over those mountains, lighting the sky with a brilliant red that was replaced by a dark purple. It was scenically magnificent yet a singularly appropriate backdrop and time for a poem that Lee, the Chinese scholar-aspirant, was currently studying—Edward Arlington Robinson's "Dark Hills," which begins, "Dark hills at evening in the west, Where sunset hovers like a sound . . . ," and ends, "You fade—as if the last of days were fading and all wars were done." Watching the sun go down over the Ilocos Mountains and their peaks disappear into the darkness night after night seemed to lend special significance to the poem. As Jones remembers it, one night Lee—half remarking, half questioning—observed pensively, "Someday this war will be done, Captain." To which Jones replied, "Yes, someday it will, Lee. That we can be sure of."

But the time when there would be no war seemed as remote as another world. A time when there was no enemy, when one could walk along a road without pulling up abruptly at the sight of another human being, when the sound of an airplane engine did not inevitably mean Japanese were overhead. A time when one had bread and butter, could sleep on a mattress, or could simply lounge about aimlessly without fear—such a time seemed illusory. Those at Jones's Tuyangan camp did not exactly feel sorry for themselves, for in their situation there was reason to be grateful to have enough to eat, to have a lean-to to sleep under, to merely be alive and free. But all the same, they longed deeply to be secure from the enemy for even a short time. If only there were a rear area where one could go to a movie, and have a sandwich and beer in the post exchange! Reading the Psalms of David, who had been a guerrilla of sorts in his day, it was easy to understand why he had talked so much about danger and appealed to his God so often for protection and security.[1]

Many weeks earlier, Major Praeger and Captain Jones had agreed to keep apart as much as possible so that if one of them was captured the other would be left to carry on. But at the end of June Praeger summoned Jones to Bulu for a conference. Jones and his entourage left Tuyangan in the late afternoon, preceded by an advance patrol, which was in turn preceded by a lone native lad clad only in a G-string. It was his business to give the first warning if any Japanese were encountered en route. Beyond Tulungtung, where flowers still bloomed around the burned-out site of their former outpost, they came to a deserted barrio and set up for the night. All the inhabitants had fled into the mountains. A stream ran through the center of the barrio. While the guerrillas slept on the south bank, the Japanese moved into that part of the barrio on the north bank during the night. It was an ominous development, but the guerrillas had the good fortune at dawn to spot the newcomers before they were themselves discovered. They moved out quickly and had their breakfast a few miles away. That same day they received a message from Praeger saying a Japanese patrol was in Bulu looking for the radio station. It seemed wise to delay another day. The enemy departed the following day, and Captain Jones reached the radio station on July 4, 1943.

The station itself was secreted in a bamboo house built just below the crest of a mountain so that a person walking along the ridge could not see it. It was further camouflaged by high cogon grass. It had been sited with a view to obtaining good transmission to Australia, but for some reason Australian communications never proved as satisfactory as contact with the United States.[2]

The new station was no larger than the old one and had even more people living in it. It was not possible to enlarge it without ruining the camouflage, so a cellar had been dug underneath to house the additional people plus a chicken coop. About half of the main room was taken up with radio equipment and writing tables. Maps, radio news, and bulletins were posted on the walls. Natives often traveled from the remotest parts of Apayao to find out the latest news and to watch the magical way in which Sergeant Brazelton talked to General MacArthur. In their minds, when Australia sent messages, General MacArthur was actually at the key, or at least standing nearby. They had also picked up some vague talk about direction finders, and there was a rumor that a man who had owned a receiver down in the lowlands had been captured by the Japanese by means of a direction finder.[3]

Captain Jones was shocked to find Major Praeger badly run down, both physically and mentally. He was certainly suffering from malnutrition, and quite likely from a mild case of beriberi as well. Brazelton, the operator, was in even worse shape. He had lost about seventy pounds and had nearly died a few weeks before. Only Praeger's constant nursing had pulled him through. In order to keep him alive, the last few cans of C rations had been opened. This supplemented the dreary diet of rice and salt on which everyone had been subsisting for months. Recently, the food had improved—now there was ample rice, a good number of chickens, some vegetables, and some fruit.

Food aside, Captain Jones thought the radio station personnel were not getting enough sleep. During the daytime there was much traffic at the command post—messengers arriving and departing, and recruits to be enlisted. Much of this could have been sidetracked, but Major Praeger wanted the men to come to the radio station to be reassured that they were full members of the organization. If they had been barred they might have felt that they were not entirely trusted. Praeger, of course, had a point. But the easy entry of outsiders at all hours inevitably reduced the efficiency of the people permanently stationed there. Radio contact was at 11:00 P.M. daily, and usually lasted about two hours. This meant that it was well after 1:00 A.M. when the people in the shack got to sleep. It was especially hard on Sergeant Brazelton, who was so weak that he lay on the floor all day, getting up only to operate the key. Jones tried to persuade Praeger to go somewhere—anywhere—else for a time to build up his health. Praeger remained unconvinced of the necessity of this, but did promise to take it a little easier in the future. Despite this halfhearted assurance, Jones remained sufficiently worried about Praeger's condition that he stayed at the radio station throughout the month of July.[4]

Despite poor health and poor working conditions there was considerable optimism among those at the command post in the summer of 1943. Perhaps the foremost reason was that the CAF, like other guerrilla organizations farther south, was able to place numerous agents among the Japanese. Capt. Silvino P. Garcia of the Apayao Company and Lt. Joaquin B. Flores, headquarters commandant of the CAF, surrendered in order to undertake espionage for the CAF. Furthermore, Praeger obtained GHQ SWPA's authorization for Flores to take to the Japanese sixty thousand pesos in emergency money (which the Japanese would of course burn at once) in order to better convince them that his surrender offer was sincere.[5] Lt. Buenaventura Queroligo of the Cagayan Force proceeded to Manila on an espionage mission. His brother, who commanded the puppet Constabulary in the Cagayan Valley, also became a CAF spy. Eventually most of the Constabulary came to sympathize with, then covertly cooperate with USAFFE forces, and finally to go over to them en masse when Allied forces landed at Lingayan Gulf in January 1945. Locally, the CAF was kept fully advised of every enemy movement by the new nominal governor of Apayao, Domingo Gusman, and by the new mayor of Kabugao, Conrado Batlong, who had accepted office under the Japanese in April 1943 at Praeger's specific request.[6]

Such men displayed patriotism and courage to a degree just short of incredible. They looked like traitors to any Filipino, yet they managed to successfully complete missions for which they risked their lives and those of their families and for which their only reward was criticism by persons who did not understand their true status or purpose. Captain Garcia even took his family with him. Thousands of cases like these made for hopelessly intractable problems at the end of the war and immediately afterward, for those who had acted thus were true patriots who deserved back pay and other rewards for guerrilla services. Yet their claims were inextricably mixed with those of *real* collaborators, or mere poseurs claiming to have been guerrillas in hope of securing money or recognition that they could employ as an avenue to some desirable postwar job.

Personal heroism among some Filipinos went even beyond what has been described. One sort of information that GHQ SWPA always wanted was the numbers and names of Japanese troop units. Sometimes a CAF patrol would capture Japanese documents that might have had such information, but no one could know since no local American or Filipino knew Japanese. So the mayor of Luna, a town just inland from the north coast, not only volunteered to spy for the CAF but to persuade his niece to marry a Japanese soldier in order to find out what Nipponese military unit he belonged to. The girl did her duty valiantly, but it was to no avail for Japanese troops in North Luzon had been told repeatedly that whatever they told any Filipino civilian would soon be reported by radio to MacArthur. Thus the husband never told his wife to what unit he belonged.[7]

By midsummer the number of men actually on duty with Major Praeger had dwindled to less than twenty-five, with others being absent on intelligence gathering missions. Most of those at headquarters were specialists of some sort, or men physically unfit for duty. Yet both Praeger and GHQ SWPA remained resolutely confident, at least outwardly. MacArthur's headquarters authorized the enlistment of one hundred men into Troop C, singled out eight sergeants who were to undertake espionage, and directed Praeger to promote eight other deserving enlisted men. Superficially, U.S. forces and procedures in this forlorn part of the world had remained unchanged since December 8, 1941.[8] Locally, official optimism was exemplified by a radiogram from Praeger to SWPA in mid-August. It excluded the Cagayan Force and Company B, 14th Infantry, because their strength returns were not available, but proclaimed routinely that the Apayao Force currently consisted of one Filipino and three American officers and ninety-two enlisted men (Philippine Scouts), armed with twenty-seven rifles and twenty-four pistols—all in Troop C, 26th Cavalry. Attached to this force were five American enlisted men and eight Filipinos. The Apayao Company of the Philippine Constabulary had no officers but thirty-nine enlisted men. They were armed with ten rifles, three pistols, and twenty shotguns, although there was no ammunition for the latter. In all other cases, varying amounts of ammunition were available.[9] Despite this aplomb, all these numbers indicate how depleted both Troop C and the whole CAF had become. At various times in the preceding eighteen months they had numbered as many as six hundred officers and men.

Much information was dispatched to Australia by radio in the last weeks before the destruction of the CAF. Some of it was unquestionably useful, yet it was not always easy to disentangle facts from rumors and omens. For instance, CAF operatives reported that three thousand Japanese had recently moved from the Cagayan Valley to Aparri; still others reported that an enemy regiment had moved from Ilocos to Aparri. A north coast salt maker reported seeing seventeen large Japanese ships loaded with soldiers leaving Aparri, but it is not certain whether this was a new report or merely repetition of a previous one.[10] In any case, few of the Japanese seemed to remain long in Aparri; and Japanese soldiers there were said to have told local people that they were headed for a combat zone. A Filipino-Japanese interpreter who lived among Japanese troops said most of them by then thought Japan would eventually lose the war, and that they hurriedly dove for cover whenever they heard an airplane. But this did not seem likely since individual planes were all reported to be Japanese. Many bombers had flown southward along the Cagayan Valley until June, after which most observed flights had been northward along the north coast—but nobody seemed to know why. Then, beginning June 28, brand-new planes of a type hitherto unknown were observed flying southward in the Cagayan Valley—at up to three hundred miles an hour![11]

At the end of July, Praeger sent GHQ SWPA an extensive evaluation of Manuel Concepcion, the mine operator who owed Lee so much back pay. He sketched Concepcion's strength of character, shortcomings, background, habits, and services to the Allies thus far in the war, concluding that he was considered reliable for intelligence work.[12] This was followed by a laudatory evaluation of Marcelo Adduru, the former governor of Cagayan taken prisoner by the Japanese. He also included news about Lt. Charles Arnao, also a captive, and what had been heard of Roque Ablan, who was still thought to be alive. Not all such information was accurate. Ablan was almost certainly dead by the summer of 1943, and the feckless governor of Apayao, Milton Ayochok, was described as remaining loyal to the Allied cause even after his capture,[13] when he had probably already succumbed to Japanese blandishments. An August 17 message provided detailed information about the size and location of several Japanese garrisons and the names of their commanding officers, and the number of planes at various enemy airfields. It added ruefully that such information was extremely difficult to come by.[14] One of the last such transmissions was routine at that time but in retrospect seems filled with pathos. It reported that the Japanese had offered seven thousand pesos and twenty cans of gasoline to anyone who could kill Lt. Feliciano Madamba, the most popular guerrilla hero in Ilocos Norte. Much smaller rewards were offered for information leading to the capture of Lieutenant Colonels Moses and Noble (who had been seized more than two months earlier). Oddly, though, no reward at all was offered for Praeger.[15]

One of the knottier administrative problems that guerrilla leaders faced during the war was keeping records. Their response varied widely. At one extreme Capt. Ray Hunt refused to keep records at all on the ground that if they were ever seized by the Japanese every Filipino named therein, and his whole family, would probably be robbed, tortured, and killed.[16] This fear was not imaginary. One major kept a diary in which he injudiciously listed all those brave and generous Filipinos who had aided him. When the enemy captured him they also got the diary and proceeded to kill everyone named in it.[17] At the opposite extreme, Russell Volckmann kept detailed records of every sort and presented these to American military authorities a few days after U.S. landings on Luzon in January 1945, thereby risking the life of every Filipino who had ever aided him but insuring for himself more than his rightful share of the credit for guerrilla contributions to the Allied war effort both before and after the American landings.

Major Praeger was well aware of the danger of keeping records and attempted to find a compromise solution. He kept careful records of enlistments and other important matters, and of documents he knew GHQ SWPA wanted kept; but he also took precautions to protect their secrecy, prevent the Japanese from getting them, and thereby safeguard from reprisals all those Filipinos mentioned in them. Every six months he would gather all paper he thought should be saved and either pack it into a five- or ten-gallon gasoline can, or seal it in a square tin box and put the box into the can.[18] One person would then be detailed to bury the sealed can and report its location. Among headquarters personnel, only Praeger and the radio operator who handled the coded messages knew the exact burial place, which was relayed to Australia. There was also a unit policy of sharing as little information as possible among officers, thus limiting what the Japanese might extract by torture from anyone unlucky enough to be captured.

To safeguard daily transmissions in their primitive surroundings, Praeger resorted to a Rube Goldberg procedure remarkable mostly for the imagination that went into it. As soon as a message was sent, the paper was burned in the fireplace across the room from Praeger's table. A copy was also entered in the troop diary, which was filed daily and then buried with all the other significant papers at the end of every six months. For the sake of convenience, two or three of the most current messages, along with parts of the cipher Praeger and the operator were using, were hung on the wall above his desk. A bottle of gasoline hung on a string from a heavy spike alongside the papers. In the event of a surprise raid, the person nearest the messages and cipher was supposed to smash the gasoline bottle against the spike to drench the papers, and then was to ignite them with one of the few precious stick matches also tied to the wall nearby.[19]

As noted before, it is obvious in retrospect that the summer of 1943 was a period of steady deterioration in the CAF's prospects, but it did not *seem* so at the time. Instead, morale was rising among both civilians and military personnel and there seemed sound reasons for it. Major Praeger reported to GHQ SWPA that cooperation from the humblest of Isneg tribesmen was all that could be desired.[20] In reply, President Quezon, who was at Lake Saranac, New York, undergoing treatment for tuberculosis, sent a message praising the efforts of the local people. This was the first time in their history that the people of Apayao had ever been praised for anything by their national government. They were delighted and grateful. Isneg men rushed to volunteer for service in the CAF. Had there been any means of arming, supplying, or feeding them, five thousand could have been enlisted with no trouble.

Meanwhile Maj. Gen. Charles Willoughby, General MacArthur's G-2, had penned a memorandum to his chief in which he pointed out that several guerrilla leaders had been hanging on with great resourcefulness, fortitude, and tenacity against the Japanese without having received any material aid or even any praise or encouragement from GHQ SWPA. He urged MacArthur to recognize their spirit and accomplishments and to boost their morale by giving them promotions, decorations, or both. He especially singled out Thorp, Nakar, Moses, Noble, Praeger, Macario Peralta (on Panay), and Wendell Fertig (on Mindanao).[21] This recommendation again illustrates how fragmentary was GHQ SWPA's knowledge of what was transpiring on Luzon. Nakar was dead, Thorp had been captured eight months earlier, and Moses and Noble three weeks previous. But, in a larger sense, accurate details meant little to Douglas MacArthur, who knew better than most men how to raise the spirits and sharpen the zeal of those he led and those who depended on him. During that ominous summer he weighed in several times with messages couched in his inimitable grandiloquent prose: to congratulate the whole CAF organization, to award Praeger the DSC, to relay praise from exiled Philippine President Quezon, and to embellish promotions for Arthur Furagganan and Silvestre Vaggas.[22] The message of July 20, 1943, addressed to the soldiers of Troop C went thus:

> I gratefully acknowledge and commend the invincible spirit that has held your little band together and permitted you as a unit to so long sustain military operations against the enemy in conquered territory. By so doing you have enshrined your troop guidon in glory

and set a brilliant and inspiring example for soldiers everywhere to emulate. To the ill and depressed among you I trust a merciful Providence will succor and protect you and instill in your hearts new courage and faith and hope in the firm knowledge that your struggle and sacrifice will not have been in vain. I commend your surviving officers, Praeger, Jones, Needham, and Furagganan, for high qualities of leadership, resourcefulness, and unswerving devotion to duty.

Message ND-25 of August 27 began with a sentence of thanks from MacArthur himself, to which was appended the good wishes of Quezon: "Convey to everybody and accept for yourself my good will, admiration, and gratitude. [Then from Quezon:] Have been following your gallant fight and was distressed when no word was heard from you for some time. Am proud of your report about Adduru and his people in Cagayan but was heartbroken to hear of his capture. Hope Ablan will continue his resistance. Have learned the hardships suffered by you and the men in your command. Better days are coming. Keep your faith and courage."

To combat Japanese propaganda, Major Praeger strengthened his own propaganda system. The man deemed most intelligent in each barrio was made responsible for disseminating news of current Allied operations. The striking Allied victories in North Africa, Sicily, and the Soviet Union were explained to the people. They were told again that reinforcements might be expected in the Philippines late in 1944. They were assured that if it was not yet quite dawn, at least the worst of the night had passed. Of course this was true for the overall war effort, but tragically mistaken for their own part in it.

Nonetheless, the intelligence efforts did bear a little fruit. A contact plan was worked out whereby the CAF was to receive money, radio parts, and medicines from Australia, although the CAF was destroyed before anything tangible resulted. Various omens seemed favorable, or at least equivocal. The number of Japanese in Apayao declined and their mop-ups appeared to flag.

The Apayao mint ceased to operate, but other government services continued to function passably. Close liaison was established between Praeger's headquarters and the new puppet governor. The latter was a Japanese appointee, of course, but he had quickly reached an understanding with Praeger. Unhappily, it was all just the last chapter in a tragic tale.

Early in August Captain Jones returned to western Apayao. He was still concerned for the health of Praeger and Sergeant Brazelton, but Lieutenant Furagganan had promised to inform him if Praeger began to overwork himself again.[23]

It was only a day or two before the cold rain of reality began to fall. Just before Captain Jones reached Tuyangan, the enemy occupied the place and sent out patrols to scour the area—so Jones had to stay a mile away for five days. His meals were cooked for him by the family of one of the Isneg recruits, Pvt. Dawila Longkennon. Once when Longkennon's sister was bringing Jones his breakfast carried in a plate on top of her head, a Japanese patrol stopped her. The food looked good to the leader so he asked the girl if he might taste it. He and his compatriots then ate all of it. Private Longkennon, who had witnessed the whole proceeding from a distance, raced to Captain Jones to tell him the bad news. Jones, recalling the fate of poor Juanita, who also had fed visiting soldiers, heaved a sigh of relief that Longkennon's sister had not been harmed.

A few days later, Cpl. Julio Mamba arrived from western Apayao, where he had been on patrol. He was both disconcerted and displeased to find Captain Jones in other than an approved and expected place. He grumbled that the local people were not his relatives, hence there was no way to know whether they could be trusted. He really did not mean that the only trustworthy people in the world were his kinsmen, what was on his mind was whether these strangers would be more afraid of him or of the Japanese. Mamba was the native "boss man" in the district. His view of other people was simplicity itself: when he spoke, everybody should jump. And jump they did. Whenever something was needed—guards, runners, food, shelter, wine, tobacco— he simply nodded his head and somebody procured it. Mamba distrusted intangibles. He did not believe loyalty could be developed by arousing patriotism. He felt confident of obedience and support only if he was certain that others feared him more than they feared the Japanese. In this respect he was not so different from other successful guerrillas, for in the last analysis they cannot command the public support necessary for their existence if their supporters do not fear them more than the enemy. It was just that Mamba was more blunt, direct, and demanding than most others. His personal followers were handpicked from among the bravest men of his district. He told them to their faces that they must commit suicide rather than surrender, and he promised that he would personally kill any among them who were ever taken alive.

When Captain Jones found out about this he called Mamba and his squad together and told them that in an extreme situation they had the right to surrender, and that their corporal might not punish them for such action. On many other occasions Jones had to lecture Mamba not to shoot Filipinos for flimsy reasons. Mamba, being a faithful soldier, obeyed the order—but he did not disguise his conviction that it was senseless. On one occasion a schoolteacher in a nearby barrio asked, "Do we still have democracy in Apayao?" The remark was reported to Mamba, who immediately regarded it as an aspersion on the government. He wrote to Captain Jones to ask if he should shoot the teacher immediately or await Jones's order.[24]

Mamba had a wife, a quiet, gracious woman named Nina. Ordinarily, she was patient with her husband, but when he sent a letter informing her that he was bringing a second wife to her house she was hurt and indignant. Although she was a native of the province, she had been raised a Christian and did not believe in polygamy. She asked Captain Jones to intervene. Jones was able to persuade Mamba to at least keep his new wife in a separate house. The newcomer was a black-eyed siren with a sultry countenance rather like that of the postwar American movie actress Raquel Welch. Jones showed his disapproval of Mamba's behavior by eating in Nina's house and ignoring the second wife. Soon Mamba sent her to a different barrio.

While Mamba was absent on patrol, and no doubt visiting his second wife, Nina gave birth to a child. Mamba did not return for the event, but sometime afterward came back to the barrio on official business. He then entered his house and looked at the baby coldly. It was a strong, healthy boy, and squalling loudly. Soon nature overcame the hitherto indifferent father. A look of pleasure and pride broke over his face, and he gave an order that wine be brought and all the people in the surrounding barrios be summoned. A great party followed, during which everybody except the guards got drunk. Captain Jones christened the child Early in honor of John C. Early, an American who had served as governor of Mountain Province in the 1920s. When he had arrived, Early had discovered that the province was being wretchedly mismanaged by twelve clerks, one of whom was officially classified as a social secretary. He had fired ten of the dozen, and markedly improved both the honesty and the efficiency of the provincial government.

About a week after the christening, an alarm was sounded that the Japanese were climbing up the mountainside and would soon be at Mamba's house. Captain Jones, Mamba, and all the soldiers raced through the barrio. Nina was sitting in the sun, drying her hair. Jones rushed up and told her she had better go. Although she was not brutal like her husband, Nina was, in her own way, no less simple and direct. She said she would stay because it would not look suspicious. As for Mamba, he fought in the war to its end, and soon afterward (August 21, 1945) wrote a letter to Captain Jones that epitomized his spirit still.

Dear Sir:

Having nothing left except ourselves [his squad] without a commander, we had to return home to my family at their evacuation place and beyond the reach of the Japs. We had always been uneasy. We could not rest peacefully because the Japs were always around us and were always hot on our trail.

I received three letters, one from Mayor Batlong and two from Governor Gusman, asking me to surrender. But

I did not give them a damn. Instead I went further to hide preferring to die rather than to surrender. I also received your instructions through Rackel Mangalao to hide well and never surrender. And this I complied well.

When the Japs could not get me, they were after my family and they could get hold of my brother, Itkitan, whom they killed through manhandling. I was alarmed at hearing the news, so I sent for my wife and children. They were able to leave the place unnoticed even by their neighbors.

All those who were inducted under you reported with me [for duty when the guerrillas were reorganized].

I have also participated in my encounters against the enemy but I have always come out unscratched. It was always my desire to kill as many Japs as I can in order to avenge the death of my brother and also my hardship when they were after me. We were the first ones to clean the Japs out from Apayao to the whole of the Second District of Cagayan. I was also one of those who entered Tuguegarao, capital of Cagayan Province, just a day or two before the U.S. Army Force entered the place. However, we were driven back to the river's edge by the Japs.

> Your faithful soldier,
> Julio Mamba

On August 30, 1943, Ralph Praeger was captured by the Japanese. Just how and why has never been established beyond question. General Willoughby reports[25] that Praeger said Governor Adduru had planned to surrender to the Japanese in order to get a job in the occupation regime from which he could send intelligence back to the guerrillas. Since Adduru and his family were captured by the enemy months earlier (April 1) this must have been just another of those many instances when GHQ SWPA was misinformed about events on Luzon. An undated, unsigned entry under "Praeger, Ralph" in a file labeled "Guerrilla Additions" in the Ernie Pyle Museum attributes this design to Praeger himself and says he planned to go to Manila in June to implement it. As indicated earlier in this narrative, it was just such a scheme that had ruined Manuel Enriquez, although Praeger could hardly have known this. Still, it is extremely unlikely that Praeger harbored any such plan in June. He had, after all, been sick for most of the preceding three months, his radio had been out of commission as well, and Manila was more than two hundred miles away. Captain Jones, his closest associate, calls the whole suggestion fantastic.[26] Manuel T. Hernandez, who served under Praeger and admired him unreservedly, thought Praeger planned to surrender but was caught the day before he could do so.[27] A Filipino journalist, Ambrose Pena, who had a high opinion of Major Praeger, said he surrendered "in order to spare the blood of his men who had stood by him."[28]

Russell Volckmann and Donald Blackburn, who were themselves relentless in eliminating collaborators, insist that Praeger did not surrender but was betrayed by spies and Ganaps. Blackburn says he learned as much from Lt. Tomas Quiocho, who had managed to avoid capture when Praeger was taken and who had, by August 1944, become a member of Volckmann's USAFIP NL.[29] This seems doubtful. Both Blackburn and Volckmann penned accounts of Praeger's alleged betrayal, but these do not mesh in important particulars. Volckmann says that two of his officers—Herb Swick and a Filipino, Maj. Joaquin Dunaun—raided the capital of Apayao Subprovince in May or June 1944, seized the records (which included a letter of appreciation to the governor of Apayao for his aid), and that the 11th Infantry quickly rounded up everyone involved.[30] He does not indicate what happened then.

Blackburn's account indicates that a single individual whom he identifies only as "Felipe" was obsessed from the first to discover who had betrayed Praeger. In the *fall* (not May or June) of 1944 he, backed by a platoon of guerrillas, seized all the pro-Japanese officials in the town of *Ripang* and got their records, among which was a letter from the *mayor of Ripang* (not ex-governor Ayochok) to Hilary Clapp, the governor of Bontoc Subprovince (*not Apayao*).[31] It listed the names of everyone involved in the capture and eventual execution of Praeger. Felipe (Perhaps Major Dunaun?) then *personally* hunted down and killed nearly every one of them.[32] All this seems suspiciously similar to the stories circulated after the betrayal and killing of Walter Cushing.

Finally, Captain Jones says he never heard any of these stories, or anything like them, and doubts them in any version because he does not believe that Ayochok ever became a collaborator.[33] Perhaps—but who can know how many collaborators successfully remained undetected?

Others have pointed out that it took the Japanese a long time to find Praeger's hideout because much of the area around Kabugao was virtually unexplored and there were no topographical maps of Apayao accurately depicting the location of streams, mountaintops, and other obvious reference points. Thus, even though their radio direction finders were of good quality and were used with skill, the Japanese still had only a rough idea of where anything was.[34] Moreover, a dead spot where Praeger's radio was located made its detection even more difficult.[35] Thomas Jones, who does not believe Praeger was betrayed at all, thinks Captain Takahashi's dogged determination eventually overcame all the obstacles noted above and enabled him, at last, to locate the radio by triangulation.[36]

Wherever the truth may lie among these conflicting claims and conjectures, it is unlikely that triangulation would have snared Praeger fifteen or sixteen months later. By then, radio transmitters coming to guerrillas by submarine from Australia had been sufficiently reduced in size that they could be carried by one man. Thus several broadcasting stations could be prepared in advance and the transmitter moved quickly from one to another after a broadcast or reception.[37]

Arguing entirely from probabilities rather than any hard evidence, it seems to this author that Captain Jones's view is most likely the correct one: Praeger was caught because able Japanese officers worked with skill and persistence to catch him. Lieutenant Colonels Moses and Noble, who had been chased all over the mountains and jungles of northern Luzon and had thus acquired at least a passing acquaintance with most of the irregular groups there, thought the CAF displayed better leadership, order, discipline, administration of justice, and general humanity, and enjoyed better relations with civilians, than did any other outfit they had seen.[38] Captain Jones, who was in a better position to judge than anyone else, concurred, and attributed this condition to the abilities of Praeger and Adduru, and to the high morale that existed among all ranks in the CAF.[39]

Of course all this does not *prove* anything. Some member of the CAF might have harbored a secret resentment and betrayed his outfit and his leader. Somebody, military or civilian, possibly a rival guerrilla, *could have* succumbed to Japanese pressure or bribery. An enemy spy *might* have penetrated the CAF. The possibilities are endless. But, altogether, it seems probable that Praeger's luck simply ran out and Japanese determination was at last rewarded.

Whatever the case, the trap began to close late in August when Major Kia, commander of the Japanese battalion based in Cagayan, assumed command of enemy forces in Kabugao. He announced that henceforth there would be a detachment of troops in every barrio in Apayao, that no interbarrio traffic would be allowed without Japanese permission, and that no food was to be moved from any barrio. Seriously concerned, the guerrillas began to lay in a three months' supply of food and to consider how to evade enemy strictures.

On August 30, Captain Takahashi arrived in Kabugao with a detachment. All the Filipinos in town, including the CAF runners, were locked up for safekeeping. Late in the afternoon the enemy troops left the village and went directly to Praeger's radio station. They surrounded it and captured Praeger, Furagganan, Heuser, and Brazelton. Sergeant Gomes, who had just begun his thirtieth year in the U.S. Army, was killed, and Sgt. Eulogio Gaduang was wounded and captured. All these men might have escaped had they not refused to leave Major Praeger, who declined to run off and abandon the radio.

By inflicting the infamous water cure, the Japanese soon extracted from one of the Americans the location of Captain Jones's command post. A few days later they surrounded the place and captured Jones and Sergeant Camonayan. That same day, Captain Needham and his wife were nearly caught in the Dagarra Valley. They managed to escape and push on across the mountains, but three days without food exhausted them. They were captured on September 8.

Major Praeger had buried unit records only a month before, so there was not much official paper on hand when the Japanese arrived. The enlisted men's service records and other papers had been given to two Scouts who managed to escape when the outpost guards fired warning shots. The Scout carrying the miscellaneous papers was hunted down by the Japanese but was able to destroy his cargo. The service records were hidden in the roof of a bamboo house, where they eventually rotted from tropical heat and moisture. Praeger managed to burn the file of messages on the wall by dumping them into the fireplace. Sergeant Heuser saw the draft of a proposed message on a table when the Japanese herded the station personnel into one room. He calmly reached for both it and a cigar, lighted the message in the fireplace, touched the flame to his cigar, and threw the burning message back into the fireplace. A Japanese officer observing Heuser's performance merely smiled. He knew that he and his compatriots had not really been balked. It was not until weeks later that the Americans learned the Japanese had intercepted every word sent from the station for many weeks and had, in fact, broken all but the most recent American code. Hence the unsent message that Heuser had burned had not seemed to them a great loss.[40]

A few of the Filipino officers and men in Troop C and the other organizations in the CAF were eventually absorbed into Col. Russell Volckmann's USAFIP NL and lived to fight in the campaign for the liberation of the Philippines in the spring and summer of 1945. But for the rest of Troop C, the war was over. The regimental crest of the 26th Cavalry bears the words, "Our strength is in loyalty." Such mottos seldom mean much, but this one did. Not a single man in the unit deserted, none failed in his duty in any significant way, and relations among all ranks were exceptionally harmonious.

As for Major Praeger, in the *short run* he received generous treatment uncharacteristic of American-Japanese relations generally, but which his own character and deeds fully warranted. When Captain Takahashi captured him, the Japanese officer came to attention and remarked, "A very brave thing you have done for your country."[41]

Epilogue

With the capture of Major Praeger and Captain Jones, the CAF
disintegrated. Lieutenant Tomas Quiocho, who happened to be
in the lowlands at that time, subsequently returned and assumed
command of a few of its remnants. Governor Adduru, who had
been seized several months earlier, was released by the Japanese
at Bongabong in Nueva Ecija Province in October 1943. Soon
after, he reorganized other CAF survivors and commanded them
but never undertook any action. He was recaptured on July 5,
1944, but managed to escape on May 9, 1945. In the interim
practically all the remaining CAF personnel joined Col. Russell
Volckmann's USAFIP NL.[1] By the autumn of 1944, Quiocho and
his followers had also gravitated to Volckmann, then the senior
surviving American guerrilla in North Luzon. Quiocho was
promoted to captain, as was Cpl. Silvestre Vaggas. Both were
given command of units of the 11th Infantry Regiment, which
was formed from the remnants of the old CAF. Quiocho's battalion played a prominent role in the capture of Aparri, the chief
port on the North Luzon coast in June 1945, for which action
Quiocho was commended warmly by Maj. Gen. Innis P. Swift,
I Corps commander, and Gen. Walter Krueger, C.G. of the U.S.
Sixth Army.

The capture of Praeger and the breakup of his organization
dealt a heavy blow to the resistance in North Luzon, both ma-
terially and psychologically. It severed radio contact between
SWPA and Luzon for nearly a year until transmitters and receivers could be sent to the island by submarine in mid-1944. During

those long months Luzon became even more of a "closed book" than before to everyone at SWPA headquarters.[2] Volckmann's contact with the CAF, always tenuous, was so thoroughly cut off that Volckmann and Blackburn were still looking for Praeger in May 1945.[3] The loss of Praeger's radio was for them a near disaster since it deprived them of any hope that they might get arms, ammunition, supplies, medicines, and reinforcements from the outside world. The fall of the CAF also greatly increased the difficulty of USAFIP NL extending its control over the far north because Japanese reprisals against the civilians there who had supported the CAF were so savage that survivors were afraid to cooperate with *any* guerrillas and merely wanted to be left alone.[4]

The CAF men captured either on August 30 or September 4, 1943, were Praeger, Jones, Arthur Furagganan, Sergeant Heuser, Sgt. Earl Brazelton (the radio operator), and two sergeants from the 26th Cavalry. They were questioned intensively by the Japanese for a few days but otherwise treated well, even accorded the status of general staff prisoners rather than ordinary POWs. Apparently the Japanese high command had directed that they be regarded as officers and gentlemen because they had earlier treated Japanese POWs well and eventually released them when it became impossible to continue to observe Geneva Convention standards. Unfortunately, this state of affairs did not last long. In a few days the CAF prisoners were transferred to Bilibid Prison in Manila. There, all rules were off. Fanciful tales have been told ever since about the fate of the prisoners, Praeger in particular, but they illustrate mostly the fallibility of human memory and the inaccuracy of much that has appeared in books by or about prominent figures in the wartime Philippines. According to one account, Praeger was tortured to death over a long period in an ultimately unsuccessful effort to compel him to reveal the code he had used in radio transmission.[5] Captain Jones, who was with Praeger for eleven months in Japanese captivity, says they were tortured only once and that the Japanese's objective could hardly have been to compel Praeger to reveal his radio code since they had already cracked it weeks before Praeger was taken. Edwin Ramsey says he learned in April 1944 that Lieutenant Colonels

Claude Thorp, Martin Moses, and Arthur Noble, Major Praeger, and Captain Joe Barker had been executed after being tortured and made to dig their own graves.[6] With respect to Praeger, at least, this is impossible. Jones was with Praeger continuously until July 30, 1944. On that day Jones, who was extremely ill and not expected to live long, was carried by Praeger to a car waiting to take Jones to the prison hospital. Jones relates that Praeger's last words to him were, "Don't talk. Good-bye."[7]

The truth was less melodramatic, although surely bad enough. Jones records that all the CAF prisoners were suffering from malaria and dysentery when they arrived at Bilibid, where they were questioned intensively for three weeks. On one occasion Praeger was suspended by his wrists for sixty hours in an effort to force out of him information about CAF activities. The effort failed. Although the ordeal must have been agonizing, Praeger, always a strong man, recovered within a few days and was not permanently maimed by the experience. It was the only time during their incarceration of three and a half months that he or others with him were tortured. Otherwise, they were segregated from other prisoners and given less than they wanted to eat, but they were not starved.

Interestingly, in his account of his and Praeger's life in prison, Jones does not mention that he was also suspended by his wrists by their captors, although only for eighteen hours in his case, after which he was beaten three times with a baseball bat. This information was recorded by another prisoner, Richard E. Tirk, a naval officer who managed to keep a diary on bits of paper— and to save it in ways he does not mention—from January 20, 1943, to February 5, 1945.[8]

On January 4, 1944, the prisoners' fortunes took a decided turn for the worse. They were transferred to Fort Santiago, which was run by the *Kempeitai*, the dreaded Japanese secret police. There they were treated harshly and fed badly, and Praeger acquired dengue fever. Worse, an array of charges were drawn up and formally presented to him shortly after the CAF prisoners were transferred to an annex of Bilibid reserved for guerrillas and other grievous offenders. About fifteen of the charges were lodged against Praeger, twelve or thirteen against the others. The more important ones were operating a radio transmitter, espionage, maintaining an enemy government, printing enemy currency, resisting the Japanese army, and disseminating Allied war propaganda. Living conditions were as grim as in Fort Santiago. Much of the time prisoners were required to sit with their legs crossed, Japanese style. Talking was prohibited save to answer the endless questions put to them daily by enemy interrogators. It was difficult to sleep at night because lights were left on around the clock and mosquitoes were numerous and hungry. Months dragged on endlessly. Most of the CAF POWs expected to be executed because many who had been there before them had been court-martialed and taken away to an unknown fate. Thomas Jones guessed that their cases might have been so long delayed because the enemy remembered that they had treated Nipponese prisoners well and so could not decide whether or not to treat *them* well. An entry in Tirk's diary for October 6, 1944, says that he was told by another prisoner that Praeger and Brazelton had been court-martialed some time before but had not been given specific sentences.[9] They had then been sent to Fort McKinley, where they were presumably shot not long afterward, perhaps on August 26.[10]

When anyone of some prominence disappeared in the wartime Philippines there usually followed much speculation about his fate—and many claims to have been the last to see him surfaced. This was as true of Praeger as it was of Roque Ablan, Walter Cushing, and many others. In Praeger's case, the mystery was deepened by the consideration that the CAF had only occasional contact with any other irregular unit in North Luzon, so few knew much about Praeger's activities after the fall of 1942.

Praeger received a number of posthumous honors and awards from the U.S. government, including the Distinguished Service Cross, Legion of Merit, and Purple Heart. President Manual Quezon probably intended to bestow on him the much-coveted Distinguished Star of the Philippines, but Praeger never learned of it.[11] On October 26, 1958, a newly created Army Reserve Center at Great Bend, Kansas, was named in honor of Ralph

Praeger. Perhaps what would have meant the most to Praeger, could he have known of it, was a letter of condolence received by his father on December 1, 1945. After some conventional remarks about Praeger's courage, sacrifices, and achievements, it ended thus: "In your son's death I have lost a gallant comrade and mourn with you. [signed] Douglas MacArthur."[12]

Richard Tirk was not in Bilibid Annex at the same time as Praeger, but in 1944 Capt. James Needham was for some months in the same cell in Bilibid Prison Camp Hospital with Tirk and other special prisoners. Talking was permitted in their group, and Tirk noted that Needham took a prominent part in many long discussions about what the postwar world would be like or ought to be like.[13] It mattered little what he thought: the Japanese eventually executed him, perhaps near Laoag.[14] Edda Needham survived the war but never entirely got over the loss of her husband. She returned to her native Maine, lived in London for a time in the early 1950s, and met Thomas Jones once in Bangkok in the late 1960s, but he lost touch with her thereafter.

Praeger tried to protect Arthur Furagganan by insisting to Japanese interrogators that he had nothing to do with CAF radio equipment. It seemed for a time that the effort was successful, for Furagganan was sentenced to only fifteen years imprisonment after his court-martial, and the two Filipino sergeants from Troop C to only eight years each, whereas all the Americans received longer sentences. The three Filipinos were also separated from the other prisoners about the time of Praeger's probable execution and sent from Old Bilibid Prison to New Bilibid at Mutinlupa. Nonetheless, Furagganan's habitual pessimism proved accurate in his own case. For reasons known only to the enemy he was among the last group of twenty-one men led out and shot on February 4, 1945.[15] Governor Adduru managed to live through the war and to pursue a postwar career in the business world.

Lt. Tomas Quiocho joined Volckmann's guerrillas and survived the war, emerging as a temporary captain or major. He had been a Philippine Scout before the war. When the Scouts were officially disbanded in 1949 he was offered the choice of enlisting in the U.S. Army with the rank of Master Sergeant or accepting a commission in the Philippine army. He elected the latter but eventually regretted it and emigrated to the United States, where he married, worked at various jobs, and raised a family in Fresno, California. He later returned to the Philippines, where he lived (1997) in good health near Manila.

The only American in the CAF who survived was Capt. Thomas Jones. By a quirk of fate he owed his life directly to his bad health. When the Japanese wished to punish or humiliate Allied POWs, one of their favorite ploys was to tell their victims that they were not prisoners but captives or criminals and thus not entitled to the civilized treatment enjoined by the Geneva Convention.[16] This had been their message to Praeger, Jones, and the others who had been given over to the *Kempeitai* in grim Fort Santiago.

They remained there for only a month. Early in February 1944, Jones, Praeger, Brazelton, Furagganan, and the two Scouts were transferred to Bilibid Annex, a Japanese disciplinary barracks. It was a regular military prison run by ordinary military men, in this case probably by the Japanese judicial corps. Although it was assuredly no country club, it was less grim than the *Kempeitai* interrogation center and its brutal interrogators at Fort Santiago. There were about two hundred Japanese prisoners in Bilibid, most of them already sentenced, and about two hundred Allied prisoners, mostly Filipinos, awaiting court-martial. The regimen was severe for all inmates, although the Japanese were fed better and allowed the "privilege" of doing such menial work as emptying the latrine buckets. From 6:00 to 6:15 A.M. other prisoners were allowed to polish their own wooden cell floors. Then, from 6:15 A.M. to 9:00 P.M., all sat in silence facing the wall, in the lotus position, hands in the lap, back straight as possible. The latter was torture for the Americans, but the guards often relented a bit and were less strict about their posture than about that of the Japanese convicts.[17] Talking or putting one's hands on the floor were always punished with beatings, but if one followed the rules he was not beaten. At 9:00 P.M. prisoners were allowed to lie down with a thin blanket and a small, hard pillow. Besides their shorts, these were their only possessions. A single light bulb burned all night, and there was twenty-four hour surveillance by guards who peeked through a slit in the wall. It became uncomfortably cold at night even though it was hot outdoors in the daytime. Captain Jones's health deteriorated alarmingly under this tough regimen in these dismal surroundings. By the end of July 1944 he had shrunk from his normal 140 pounds to a skeletal 70 pounds.[18] He was delirious periodically and sometimes went days without eating. Jones was supposed to be included when the other CAF men were court-martialed, but the Japanese ignored him because they thought he would die within a few days anyway. Jones, who credits Praeger with saving his life several times in 1942-1943, says that this was one of those occasions. He says Praeger watched over him carefully and reinforced the Japanese's belief in his imminent demise by insisting to them that Jones must have medical treatment to survive even a few more days. Perhaps for this reason on July 30 the enemy relented and moved him to their version of a military hospital. There, U.S. medical officers among the POWs persuaded the Japanese to give Jones more food.[19] His fits of delirium gradually subsided and his weight inched upward to perhaps eighty-five pounds. Vitamins and drugs were available too, so his eyesight gradually improved until he could read again. He stayed there until the war was nearly over, seemingly because his captors forgot about him. All might have come to naught, however, for he was eventually moved out of the Special Ward to the Dysentery Ward, where everyone was extremely sick with that highly contagious malady and corpses were carried out every day. Jones's turn would surely have come soon had the war not ended abruptly and brought about his liberation.

Jones remained in the U.S. Army after the war and enjoyed a rewarding career. Promoted to major in 1945, and later to lieutenant colonel (1951) and colonel (1960), he served in tank battalions and armored divisions in Texas and Germany, interrupted by a year in Vietnam when the French were withdrawing from their old colony in the 1950s. He later became chief of war plans for the Seventh Army in Germany, and retired to France in 1962, only to return to Vietnam in 1966 as a pacification adviser. He remained in the III and IV Corps areas there until the American withdrawal in 1973. Since then, in his own words, "I've done nothing except read."[20] At this writing (1999) Col. Thomas Jones, USA (Ret.), in good health and good spirits, lives with his wife in Clearwater, Florida. He says he cannot now remember what happened to any of the other special prisoners who were with him.

At least one of them survived: Richard Tirk, the diarist, spent much of his life after 1945 working for world peace with such organizations as the American Friends Committee and Amnesty International. He died in 1994.

Of all the officers in the CAF at one time or another, the one who was by disposition most truly a natural soldier was Lt. William Bowen. Whether the death of one individual is more tragic than that of another is always a matter of opinion, but Bowen's demise was certainly the most bizarre of any member of the CAF. Following his surrender to the enemy in the spring of 1943 to save the lives of the families of his men, the Japanese put him into a hospital until his ulcerated legs healed, then moved him into the Cabanatuan POW camp in early 1944. Throughout the war the Japanese moved prisoners about a great deal, and they soon sent Bowen to Manila. By luck he happened to be dispatched to the same hospital as Captain Jones in October 1944. It was the first time they had seen each other in a year and a half. Bowen's health was by then good and, always a skilled scrounger, he had managed to get hold of some fruit, which, with typical generosity, he brought to Jones, who had not yet recovered from his own assorted ills. The two talked a great deal. Bowen knew he was soon to be put on a ship bound for Japan. Jones later recalled that Bowen had traded his tropical helmet for an over-seas cap, which he thought would cause him less trouble aboard ship.[21] On October 10, in Manila, he was put on the unmarked Japanese freighter *Arisan Maru* along with eighteen hundred other American POWs. The ship did not actually sail until eleven days later. Three days out of port it was torpedoed by a submarine, probably the USS *Snook*, about 225 to 250 miles northeast of Hong

Kong. Only eight POWs survived. It was one of the worst single-day losses of life at sea in U.S. history.

It is thought that another CAF man, Lt. Charles Arnao, perished along with Bowen, but this is not certain.[22] Exactly *how* Bowen died is likewise unknown. Details about the sinking were derived mostly from five American survivors: Pvt. Avery E. Wilber of Battery A, 60th Coast Artillery Battalion, Pvt. Anton Cichy of the 194th Tank Battalion, Cpl. Donald E. Meyer of the 693rd Aviation Ordinance Company, Sgt. Calvin R. Graef, otherwise unidentified, and a civilian named Overbeck. In depositions taken later, they said three torpedoes were fired at the *Arisan Maru*. One missed around each end, but the third hit the ship in the middle and blew it almost in two. Nobody happened to be in the hold that was hit, so probably no one was killed by the *explosion*. The ship floated aimlessly for several hours before sinking. The Japanese seized all the lifeboats in sight, packed them with their own people, then battened down the hatches and cut the rope ladders into the holds in an effort to insure that all the POWs would die. This did not happen at once. Some POWs on deck opened the hatches and dropped ropes into the holds, thus enabling some of the men trapped there to at least climb on deck. Some of these were then able to grab life preservers and jump into the sea. Others just jumped, hoping to be picked up by a boat or at least to grab some floating debris. A few managed to make their way close to two nearby Japanese destroyers. They were beaten off, though none were shot in the water. One man, the civilian Overbeck, managed somehow to get into a small boat. He gradually picked up the other four. They drifted for thirty hours, half-frozen, toward the China coast until they were picked up by a Chinese fishing boat aboard which they were welcomed, fed, and treated well. All were sure that their comrades must have perished from the combination of cold water and cold winds.[23]

In the context of the eons of existence astrophysicists toss about so serenely, it makes little difference how any one individual dies. But in historical time, to die in battle, or even because of the deliberate malevolence of an enemy, has meaning. To perish, as Bowen and thousands of others did, due merely to the negligence, callousness, or indifference of several parties somehow seems worse because it appears pointless. The Japanese habitually packed POWs into trains and ships much as they would coal, rice, or any other commodity. Of course they could say in self defense that they packed their own soldiers in the same way, although they always fed and watered their own men and did not stuff them into holds ankle deep in horse manure as they sometimes did with Allied POWs. Moreover, Western soldiers were bigger physically than the Japanese, so cramming a given number of them into a given space was more severe and painful. Why the Japanese did not mark prison ships with a Red Cross nobody knows. It surely would have afforded them a propaganda advantage if Allied planes or submarines sank such ships rather than unmarked ships. But they did not mark POW camps located next to ammunition dumps either, though to have done so would seem to have made Allied air attacks against such sites less likely. Strictly speaking, they were required by international agreements only to mark *hospital* ships, not prison ships. Other nations, including the United States, did not mark prison ships, either. Both sides in the Pacific War machine-gunned enemy troops in the water after bombings and torpedoings, although it must be said for the Allies that they did this because they had learned from experience that it was often unsafe to keep Japanese POWs aboard ships and always unsafe to put them into submarines. Nevertheless, the Japanese were more flagrant in their disregard for the conventions of war and treated men aboard ship far worse than did others.

Less easy to understand is why the U.S. Navy, in particular, sank so many ships carrying Allied POWs, especially in 1944. By the latter half of that year GHQ SWPA was getting regular information by radio from guerrillas all over the Philippines about the location of internment camps, the movement of POWs from place to place, who or what was being transported into Manila, who or what was being loaded onto ships, and where and when these activities took place. Intelligence summaries were circulated monthly, weekly, even daily, to a wide audience that included the navy. These contained much information about the movements of prisoners. After a Japanese ship was sunk off Mindanao in September 1944, several dozen survivors were picked up onshore, taken to Australia, and debriefed. Thus *knowledge* was not lacking that the Japanese were sending more and more ships packed with POWs to Japan, that such ships moved much more slowly at sea and nearer the coasts than before, and that they were not marked.[24] Knowing this, the death of William Bowen seems somehow less explicable, more enigmatic, than, say, the executions of Ralph Praeger or Arthur Furagganan.[25] It seems more a major instance of that wretched bungling that repeatedly enraged Col. Robert Arnold so much.

Most of the CAF's leaders were killed in World War II. Most of the rank and file also died, or merely went home, although some were absorbed into Volckmann's USAFIP NL to continue the struggle against the enemy. Why, then, should anyone endeavor to record their deeds more than half a century later? Perhaps anticipating such a rhetorical question, Marcelo Adduru, then in the custody of the Japanese, put pen to paper sometime in the autumn of 1944 and composed a four-page statement of the "Activities and Accomplishments of the Cagayan-Apayao Forces." It was signed in longhand by the ex-governor but was undated, and there is no indication for whom it was meant or to whom, if anyone, it should be sent. Adduru seemingly meant it for that glimmering abstraction called posterity.[26] The governor first enumerated the internal accomplishments of the CAF that he deemed worthy to be recorded and remembered: that the enemy had been kept at bay in many areas for a long time; that the authority of the Philippine government in Cagayan, Apayao, and Kalinga had been maintained until April 1, 1943; a mint had been established; radio transmitters built; supplies secured; public health improved; the morale of civilians bolstered; domestic peace and order maintained; a military commission established to insure justice; the mail and telephone system preserved until March 1943; intelligence information collected systematically and transmitted to Australia whenever possible; and Japanese prisoners of war treated justly. Then Adduru listed ten instances in which CAF raids or attacks had done serious damage to the enemy and inflicted upon him anywhere from eleven to two hundred deaths (the last a reference to the Tuguegarao raid in January 1942). He concluded by listing twenty-eight more occasions on which seven or fewer Japanese had been killed and some appreciable damage had been done to enemy installations or materiel—deeds such as burning bridges, staging ambushes, destroying gasoline, raiding supply depots, burning sawmills, wrecking trucks, stealing or sabotaging telephone apparatus and wire, and capturing enemy troops. He obviously thought the CAF had done well, considering its meager resources and lack of outside aid.

These achievements were indeed respectable, measured by any reasonable standard.[27] Yet most of the men in the CAF were captured, killed, or both, while a fair number of other guerrilla leaders—both American and Filipino—survived the war and were acclaimed public heroes. Such was the case with Edwin Ramsey, Robert Lapham, Ray Hunt, Russell Volckmann, Donald Blackburn, Bernard Anderson, Harry McKenzie, John Boone, and others among the Americans. Many Filipino irregular chieftains did even better. Manuel Roxas and Ferdinand Marcos parlayed their ambivalent wartime careers into a stint in the Philippine presidential palace—as did Ramon Magsaysay, an unquestioned war hero. Alfonso Arellano became chief of staff of the postwar Philippine army; Macario Peralta, secretary of defense; and Eduardo Joson, governor of Nueva Ecija. Many others acquired lesser positions. Were they more fearless or more intelligent than their counterparts in the CAF? Not necessarily. Every guerrilla leader came close to being captured during the war, many of them several times. Most of those who were killed or captured succumbed in the first year of the war when they were all learning how to operate. Those who managed to eliminate or neutralize spies and collaborators, who learned how to win the support of civilians, who established effective spy systems of their own, who learned when to hide and when to show themselves, usually made it to the end of the war. But even one of the shrewdest and most successful of them, Robert Lapham, acknowledged that sheer luck was often decisive.[28] Those in the CAF, 150 miles north of Lapham, tried just as hard but were far less lucky. They did not survive even the year 1943.

The ancient Greeks thought human existence was essentially tragic. Surely it must have seemed so to most of the men in the CAF. Their organization was destroyed by the enemy and a high proportion of them did not survive the war. Should they, then, be regarded as failures? Not at all. We who live near the end of the twentieth century are experiencing an age in which abominable personal conduct is passed off as pursuit of an "alternate lifestyle." Worse, it is frequently rewarded with publicity, money, and acceptance. Meanwhile, education is "dumbed down" to avoid undermining the self-esteem of the mediocre and the lazy. Sophists explain away vice and crime by attributing it to unfortunate genes or undesirable environment—whichever of these opposites best suits any particular case. Every sort of corruption from the lowest to the highest political circles has become so commonplace, and so commonly accepted, that more than half the electorate no longer thinks it is worth the trouble to vote.

To such a society the brave men of Troop C, 26th Cavalry, and the CAF constitute a heartening contrast. No matter how unsuccessful they might have been in the short run, all of them risked their lives—and most of them gave their lives—to do their duty. Their deeds deserve to be recorded and their example displayed to a later age, many of whose members can scarcely imagine the meaning of the words valor and sacrifice. Societies and nations live on their memories quite as much as do individuals. Those who leave behind them examples of responsibilities accepted, performance of duty embraced, and blood shed for worthy causes may live only brief lives, but they enrich the national legacy for generations to come.

Notes

Preface

1. Col. Morris A. Marcus, "A Reply to Correspondence from Major Jones," July 9, 1946, p. 144, "History of the Cagayan-Apayao Forces," Folder 500-22A, Box 258, PAC, NA II.
2. As he explained ruefully decades later, "I did not realize that America was so anti-war that it would risk Hitler ruling Europe." (Personal communication to the author.)
3. Jones, "Operations of Troop C," p. 1.
4. Ibid., p. i.

1. The Guerrilla War Begins

1. There are a number of extended descriptions of the Candon ambush. Cf. Jones, "Operations of Troop C," p. 15; Nielsen, *Bank Note Reporter,* May 1976, p. 29; *Guerrilla Resistance*, pp. 6-8; *Guerrilla Days,* pp. 9-10.
2. Definitions of alcoholism are notoriously variable. They range from those of elderly Women's Christian Temperance Union stalwarts who can say, "He's drunk! I can smell liquor on his breath," to the casual observations of carefree souls that "He's not drunk, I just saw his hand move." Although Cushing relished periodic binges, he did not allow drinking to get in the way of serious thought, hard work, or duty. By contrast, real alcoholics like Maj. Everett Warner and Governor Ayochok of Apayao were slaves to booze and, as a result, largely useless for any constructive purpose.
3. *Guerrilla Days*, p. 12.
4. Horan, "1960 Diary," p. 33.
5. Arnold, *A Rock and a Fortress*, pp. 261-62.
6. Jones, "Operations of Troop C," p. 21.
7. Ibid., p. 38.
8. Ibid., p. 39; Nielsen, *Bank Note Reporter*, May 1976, 29-30.
9. Personal communication to the author.
10. Jones, "Operations of Troop C," p. 39.
11. *Guerrilla Days*, p. 16. Volckmann, *We Remained*, pp. 26-36, and

Sanderson, *Behind Enemy Lines*, pp. 196-218, provide extended accounts of Cushing's activities and demise.

12. Horan, "1960 diary," p. 50.

13. Nielsen, *Bank Note Reporter*, May 1976, p. 30.

14. Jones, "Operations of Troop C," p. 39.

15. Vincente G. Erieta and Manuela R. Ablan, "North Luzon Guerrilla Warfare and Governor Roque B. Ablan's Exiled Commonwealth Government," p. 2, File 54-2, Folder 2, Box 297, PAC, NA II. This twenty-eight page description of Ablan's deeds and purposes was coauthored by an infantry captain (Erieta) who was one of his guerrillas, and by Ablan's widow.

16. Ibid., p. 3.

17. There is a sketchy account of Ablan's brief career in Nielsen, "North Luzon: Ilocos Norte, Part I," *Bank Note Reporter*, May-June 1975, 21-22. Volckmann, *We Remained*, pp. 36-39, also provides some information.

18. Six pages of copies of radiograms related to these matters passed among President Quezon, General MacArthur, and Ablan. They are on pp. 7-8, Folder 2, File 54-2, Box 297, PAC, NA II.

19. Ibid., pp. 1-2.

20. For instance, to a Mr. Lopez of the Ilocos Norte government, March 12; to the mayor of San Nicolas, April 15; to the mayor of Pasquin, April 16; to the municipal treasurer of Paoay, April 17; to the mayor of Badoc, May 25; the mayor of Dingras, May 28; the mayor of Burgos, May 29; the municipal secretary of Burgos, June 6; plus mass mailings on April 1 on the appointment of policemen, and on April 25 and May 1 about payment of public officials. (Ibid., pp. 5-6.)

21. "Ablan's Guerrilla Forces," pp. 13-15, File 54-2, Box 297, PAC, NA II.

22. Ibid., p. 17.

23. "Ilocandia's Guerrillas," p. 3, File 54-1, Box 297, PAC,.NA II.

24. Ibid., Folder 1, File 54-2, pp. 5-7.

25. C.N. Geed, ibid. There were later unconfirmed reports that Ablan had been seen in Apayao on February 15, 1943, when a Japanese attack took place there.

26. "Preliminary Investigation Statement Taken from Vincente Erieta," January 7, 1946, Folder 1, File 54-2, Box 297, PAC, NA II.

27. Arnold, *A Rock and a Fortress*, p. 12, suggests the possibility of murder by headhunters. Others speculate that death in action or by betrayal is more likely. Rodriguez, *The Bad Guerrillas*, p. 78, thinks he was killed in Mountain Province, somewhere near LaPaz.

28. File 54-1, Box 297; "Mariano Felipe to C.O. General PHILRYCOM, Guerrilla Affairs Section," March 28, 1947, Folder 1, File 54-2, Box 297, PAC; Thomas J. Brown, CWO, USA, Asst. Adj. Gen., to Baldomero Perez, September 30, 1947, Folder 2, File 54-2, Box 297, PAC, NA II.

2. The Philippines in 1941

1. Morton, *Fall of the Philippines*, pp. 59-60, 69, 72-73.
2. Thompson, et al., *The Signal Corps: The Test*, pp. 11-58, 116, 119, 524-27, and many other places in this long book.
3. One of the most recent and relentless criticisms is in Daws, *Prisoners of the Japanese*, pp. 60-72, 288, 327, 365, 372-73.
4. Whitehead, *Odyssey of a Philippine Scout*, p. 10.
5. Morton, *Fall of the Philippines*, p. 69.
6. Ibid., pp. 102-03, 105-06.
7. Toland, *But Not in Shame*, p. 88.
8. Miller raged at interwar congressmen and the American public alike for their selfishness, indifference to the needs of national security, concern only for elections, and "stupid idealism," pp. 2-3, 10-63, 71-75, 78-79, 86, 88, 116-17, 372-74. The quotations are from p. 374.
9. Col. Richard Mallonee, Bataan Diary, vol.1, 62-63, cited in Morton, *Fall of the Philippines*, p. 136.
10. Morton, *Fall of the Philippines*, p. 131.
11. Agoncillo, *The Fateful Years*, vol. 2, 896-98.
12. Long, *MacArthur As a Military Leader*, p. 69.
13. Ramsey and Rivele, *Lieutenant Ramsey's War*, p. 51.
14. Ralph Praeger to Mrs. Praeger, Nov. 6, 1941, Praeger Papers. Praeger's lament was neither serious nor derogatory. What had happened was that in 1941 some six thousand new Philippine Scouts were gradually added to the U.S. Army. About two hundred of them were eventually assigned to the 26th Cavalry and then scattered among the various troops, while many veteran Scouts were transferred from one troop in the regiment to another. Thus, at any given time, a unit would be a melange of parts of two or more sister units plus a dozen or two "new" Scouts. This was what Praeger meant by "bastard organization." (Thomas Jones, personal communication to the author.)
15. A Filamerican mestizo, familiar with the place, characterized it thus: "while the sun is normally 93,000,000 miles away from most places on earth this time of year at Fort Stotsenburg it was generally conceded to be sitting just a few feet overhead." (Whitehead, *Odyssey of a Philippine Scout*, p. 17.)
16. Troop C's official diarist apparently did not know what had been left unsaid and so dutifully recorded that Praeger and his men had been dispatched specifically to help defend against the expected Lingayen landings. (Vance, "Diary of the 26th Cavalry," December 20, 1941.)
17. In 1946 Praeger's father described Ralph to a potential biographer thus: "He was an active helper in the home and on the farm, a good student in school, and always willing to carry more than his share of the responsibilities of life." (Herman Praeger to Brig. Gen. G.O. Pierce, Sept. 27, 1946, Praeger Papers.) General Pierce was Praeger's last commander at Fort Stotsenburg.

18. Col. Ralph Praeger Jr., personal communication to the author.

19. Devereux, *The Story of Wake Island,* pp. 35, 198, 225; Urwin, *The Defenders of Wake Island,* p. 470 ff.

20. Ralph Praeger to Mrs. Praeger, June 8, June 26, July 6, July 18, August 10, September 29, 1941, Praeger Papers.

21. He clearly had far more than ordinary athletic ability, too. He describes setting a course record of 66 at golf, hitting a drive 330 yards, and having the lowest handicap on the post. (Ibid., June 17, June 26, July 18, August 10, 1941, Praeger Papers.) At bowling he mentions that he had games of 237, 259, and 630 for a three-game series. (Ibid., August 22 and September 19, 1941.)

22. Ibid., July 6, July 16, and July 18, 1941.

23. Ibid., June 17, July 6, July 16, July 24, Sept. 19, October 6, October 31, 1941.

24. Ibid., August 29, September 29, October 16, November 21, 1941.

25. This description of Praeger is drawn heavily from Jones, "Operations of Troop C," pp. 5-7.

26. Horan, "1960 Diary," p. 4.

27. Ibid., pp. 2, 25.

28. Jones, "Operations of Troop C," p. 2. Langdon Gilkey, a twenty-four-year-old English teacher at Yenching University in China when the war began, made a similar discovery. He was captured by the Japanese and put in a compound with some two thousand other generally well-educated and prosperous Occidentals. Life in the camp was not sordid or disfigured by cruelty, but it was hard. Instead of sharing burdens, hardships, and chores, most of the inhabitants did as little as they could, took whatever they could get, exploited any advantage they could gain over their fellows, and ignored all appeals to justice, morality, or even the opinion of others. They acted justly only when force or the threat of it was employed against them. Only a small minority of strong, fair, and upright people—most of them clerics—acted honorably and so held the community together. Gilkey said in 1966 that the experience destroyed all his illusions about the supposed innate goodness of mankind and convinced him that the doctrine of Original Sin, or some equivalent, was true; that, as he put it, ward heelers know more about real people than do professional philosophers. (Gilkey, *Shantung Compound,* pp. 24-34, 42, 71-138, 142-56, 161, 169-76, 179-224.)

Eve Hoyt, a friend of this author, spent three years in Santo Tomas prison in Manila with similar people. Like Gilkey, she was not heartened by the conduct of most of them. (Personal communication with author.)

29. Horan, "1960 Diary," p. 10. Horan complained that the trails were hellishly steep. Negotiating one of them was so exhausting that he lay utterly motionless for an hour after the climb. ("1942 Diary," December 25, 1941.)

30. Horan, "1960 Diary," p. 8.

31. The whole business was deplorably reminiscent of the British defeats in Malaya and the subsequent surrender of Singapore. Prime Minister Winston Churchill was astounded to learn that no fortifications existed on the north shore of Singapore Island to defend it against an attack from the land side. He blamed himself for assuming that they must exist, but blamed even more the high-ranking officers who had known the truth for years but had never told him. He was also outraged at what seemed to him the lackadaisical way both the Malay Peninsula and Singapore were defended by the armed forces of the Crown. (Churchill, *Hinge of Fate*, pp. 44-56, 95, 105.)

32. Lapham and Norling, *Lapham's Raiders*, pp. 82-83.

33. Hunt and Norling, *Behind Japanese Lines*, p. 41. Within a few days, Capt. Manuel Enriquez had two hundred disbanded soldiers fishing arms and ammunition out of the Marang River (Jones, "Operations of Troop C," p. 3), while Horan himself soon admitted that the $7 million worth of materiel destroyed by he and his subordinates was sorely needed. (Horan, "1960 Diary," pp. 8, 10-11.)

34. Jones, "Operations of Troop C," pp. 2-3.

35. Horan, "1942 Diary," January 1, 1942.

36. Horan, "1960 Diary," pp. 5-12.

37. The colonel found some consolation when he learned nearly three weeks later that had he attempted to outflank the Japanese by going eastward he would have failed. ("1942 Diary," January 19, 1942.)

38. Jones, "Operations of Troop C," p. 3.

39. Horan, "1960 Diary," p. 14.

3. The Road to Tuguegarao

1. For a brief consideration of the qualities of Negritos and varied opinions of them *See* Lapham and Norling, *Lapham's Raiders*, pp. 2, 35-36, 49, 101-2, 131, 151. A maverick guerrilla, Henry Clay Conner, who not only lived among the Negritos but married the sister of one of their chiefs, held them in high esteem. (*See* Conner, "We Fought Fear on Luzon," *True*, August 1946, pp. 69-87.)

2. Lapham and Norling, *Lapham's Raiders*, p. 3.

3. Harkins, *Blackburn's Headhunters*, pp. 1-15.

4. A good study of the Ilongots by an American anthropologist is Rosaldo, *Ilongot Headhunters*. *See* especially pp. 5, 9, 46-58, 61-106, 122-54, 232-46, 250-76. June 1945 was a horrible month for the Ilongots. American and Filipino armies drove defeated, demoralized, and hungry Japanese soldiers into the Sierra Madres along the northeast coastal provinces of Luzon. A war to the death between them and the Ilongots at once ensued. The Ilongot population was reduced by about a third; nobody knows how many Japanese lost their heads in the process—certainly hundreds, perhaps thousands. (*See* pp. 36, 113, 125-54.)

A marked upsurge in head-hunting also took place during the peak of Hukbalahap (Communist guerrilla) activity in the early 1950s (pp. 263-76), but by 1972 taking heads had gone out of style.

5. Major Lapham, who lived three years among ordinary Filipinos, led them, and was supported by them, thought their similarities clearly outweighed their differences. (Lapham and Norling, *Lapham's Raiders*, p. 2.)

6. Both Robert Lapham and one of his area commanders, Ray Hunt, had a high opinion of Igorots because they were brave, honest, and loyal—not to mention remarkably strong, tough, and agile. Hunt remembered the Igorot Tom Chengay as one of his most energetic, trustworthy, and pugnacious squadron leaders. (Hunt and Norling, *Behind Japanese Lines*, p. 166.)

Lapham had only praise for another, Sgt. Esteben Lumyeb, a faithful and capable subordinate who once saved Lapham's life. (Lapham and Norling, *Lapham's Raiders*, pp. 2, 22-25, 44-45, 63, 148.) By contrast, Capt. Albert Hendrickson, another of Lapham's area commanders, disliked Igorots because of their persistent unwillingness to come out of the mountains and down into the lowlands.

7. Much of the foregoing discussion of the characteristics of the various Philippine peoples is derived from Jones, "Operations of Troop C," pp. 2-8.

8. Jones, "Operations of Troop C," pp. 3-4.

9. Thomas Jones to Mrs. Helen G. Bowen, December 8, 1945, Praeger Papers.

10. Horan, "1942 Diary," January 11, 1942.

11. Jones to Mrs. Bowen, December 8, 1945, Praeger Papers.

12. Jones, "Operations of Troop C," p. 4

13. Ibid., pp. 4-5.

14. Lieutenant Samuel Grashio, an escapee from a Japanese prison camp near Davao who later became a guerrilla for a time, once employed an inspired ruse to get needed goods from a more conventional Chinese merchant on Camiguin Island off the north coast of Mindanao. The entrepreneur was unwilling to surrender his wares for a mere receipt, although he did waver about the proposal. This man's wife, made of sterner stuff, vehemently opposed the exchange—so vehemently in fact that when she perceived her husband's resolve weakening she took the belt off her dress and tried to strangle herself. The spectacle was so grotesque that Lieutenant Grashio began to laugh. Then he took out his service .45-caliber pistol and offered it to the lady, motioning that it was a far more efficient device with which to end her misery. This was too much for everyone. The husband and their two sons also began to laugh; then the wife herself had to laugh. The lieutenant got his goods. (Grashio and Norling, *Return to Freedom*, pp. 158-59.)

15. Some guerrilla chieftains did not even *want* money. Major

Lapham, C.O. of the LGAF, refused an offer of fifty thousand Philippine pesos for which he would have had to account at war's end. He said he and his organization had gotten along fine for two years without any money at all, and he saw no reason to complicate his life. (Lapham and Norling, *Lapham's Raiders*, p. 153.)

16. Horan, "1960 Diary," p. 20.

17. Marcelo Adduru, Statement to C.G. PHILRYCOM APO 707, July 28, 1947, "History of the Cagayan-Apayo Forces," p. 1, Folder 500-22A, Box 258, PAC, NA II.

18. Col. J.K. Evans, General Staff Corps Chief, Southwest Pacific Branch, to Marcelo Adduru, November 9, 1942. Inclosure 6, p. 18, Folder 500-22A, Box 258, PAC, NA II.

19. Thomas Jones, Notes, "History of the Cagayan-Apayo Forces," p. 118, Folder 500-22A, Box 258, PAC, NA II.

20. Jones, "Operations of Troop C," pp. 9-10.

21. This was noted in an otherwise laudatory article about Praeger in the *Kansas City Times*, March 22, 1946, pp. 1, 8. Ironically, the headquarters of the 26th Cavalry, then on Bataan, did not even hear of Troop C's success for two weeks. (Cf. Vance, "Diary of the 26th Cavalry," January 26, 1942.)

22. *Guerrilla Days* (published by USAFIP NL, Col. Russell Volckmann's guerrilla organization, Camp Spencer, Luna, La Union Province, 1946), p. 31, describes this raid as taking place a whole month later, in mid-February. It is a good example of how little one guerrilla organization often knew about another either during the war or for a year afterward. Similarly, as will be seen repeatedly later in this narrative, at any time before 1945 GHQ USAFFE had only vague notions about what was happening in most parts of Luzon.

This account of Troop C's journey from Aritao to Tuguegarao and the subsequent attack on the airfield is drawn heavily from Jones, "Operations of Troop C," pp. 8-10. *See* also Jones to Mrs. Bowen, December 8, 1945, Praeger Papers.

23. Jones, "Operations of Troop C," pp. 10-11. An excellent introduction to the whole subject of guerrilla warfare: rationale, strategy, tactics, necessities, opportunities, and pitfalls, is Ney, *Notes on Guerrilla War*. Virgil Ney was an active participant in irregular operations in both the Philippines in World War II and in the Korean War.

4. The Road to Kabugao

1. C.M. Nielsen was still circulating the tale in 1975. (*See Bank Note Reporter*, December 1974-January 1975, p. 14.) Theodoro Agoncillo, in *The Fateful Years*, vol. 2, p. 652, asserts that such an action took place, but says it came only two days after the Tuguegarao operation.

2. *Guerrilla Resistance*, p. 11; Horan, "1960 Diary," pp. 19-20.

3. Jones, "Operations of Troop C," p. 13.

4. Agoncillo, *The Fateful Years*, vol. 2, 651.

5. Jones, "Operations of Troop C," pp. 11, 13.

6. Ibid., p. 13.

7. Ibid., pp. 12-13.

8. Interestingly, Ramona Snyder, the girlfriend of central Luzon guerrilla leader Edwin Ramsey, seemed the same to him: a person exhilarated by danger while he, a professional soldier, endured all the doubts and fears that ordinary people experience in such circumstances. Ramsey and Rivele, *Lieutenant Ramsey's War*, pp. 175-90, 201.

9. Edgar Whitcomb remarks bluntly that San Francisco radio broadcasts provided many words of encouragement in the first months of the war—all of them empty. Whitcomb himself had escaped from the Santo Tomas prison camp in Manila and managed to make his way to China where he successfully posed as a civilian for much of the war. He lived on to become governor of Indiana in the 1960s. (Whitcomb, *Escape from Corregidor*, p. 100.)

10. This description of the Rodriguez family is drawn from Jones, "Operations of Troop C," pp. 11-12.

11. Ibid., p. 14.

12. Cf. Dew (an American newspaperwoman in Hong Kong), *Prisoner of the Japs*, pp. 139, 160-61, 179-81, 184-85, 193-96, 198, 205; Townswick (an American guerrilla on Mindanao), *Too Young to Die*, pp. 24-30; Grashio (an American fighter pilot and prisoner of the Japanese), *Return to Freedom*, pp. 103-5; and Keith (an American magazine writer imprisoned by the Japanese on Borneo), *Three Came Home*, pp. 164, 200-206.

13. Monaghan, *Under the Red Sun*, p. 124. Edwin O. Reischauer, an American amabassador to Japan, writing thirty years after the war, was convinced that psychological confusion among Japanese had increased rather than lessened since 1945. The American victory and subsequent enforced revolution in the Japanese political and social system seemed to discredit all traditional Japanese ideas, yet many people were still nostalgically attached to them. Defeat produced something of a national inferiority complex, yet master-race ideas were still common among people so obviously active, well-educated, energetic, and diligent. They had become heavily influenced by the West but at heart believed the Occident was decadent. They were one of the most homogeneous peoples in the world, yet their "economic miracle" underscored their need to be internationalist. They wanted to be rid of American troops and bases but needed U.S. forces for their own security. They abhorred atomic weapons but longed to be politically and militarily strong once more. They were chastened by the hatred other Asians bore them for their wartime excesses but were also aware that they needed once more to become the leaders of East Asia. Finally, their intellectuals were strongly attracted to both irresponsible idealism and Marxism—attitudes quite at variance with most of the rest of the population. Reischauer, *Japan*.

14. Jones, "Operations of Troop C," p. 16.

15. Ibid., p. 17.

16. Horan, "1960 Diary," pp. 18-19.

17. Dozier, *Mountain Arbiters. See* especially pp. 28, 32-33, 40, 46, 50, 55-56, 192-93, 199-212. As with the Ilongots, head-hunting among the Kalingas peaked during World War II and subsided in the 1960s. (*See* pp. 46, 212ff.)

The author, an American anthropologist, thinks most of the people in the Mountain subprovinces were not descendents of ancient immigrants at all, but merely the progeny of lowland Filipinos who had fled into the mountains between 1600 and 1900 to escape what had seemed to them Spanish tyranny. (Cf. pp. 239-53 and Jones, "Operations of Troop C," p. 28.)

Another American anthropologist, R.F. Barton, studied the Ifugaos on several occasions before World War II. He describes them in much the same terms as the Ilongots and Kalingas, noting that they were not averse to selling each other into slavery. (Barton, *Autobiographies of Three Pagans,* pp. 52-57, 149-62, 167-77, 216-23, 241-43.)

18. Jones, "Operations of Troop C," p. 17.

19. Volckmann, *We Remained,* p. 122; Harkins, *Blackburn's Headhunters,* pp. 105-7, 182, 189, 199-200, 219.

20. A claim made for Marcos by his campaign biographer. *See* Spence, *For Every Tear a Victory,* pp. 100-200. It was rejected by Ray Hunt. *See* Hunt and Norling, *Behind Japanese Lines,* pp. 153-55.

21. Lapham and Norling, *Lapham's Raiders,* pp. 59, 113-14.

22. Manzano, "History," vol. 2, pp. 7-12, Anderson Folder, Ernie Pyle Museum.

23. Jones, "Operations of Troop C," p. 29. An article in *The Guidon,* March 29, 1946, pp. 1-2, alleges that Praeger sent both volunteers and other Filipinos to work for the Japanese, and that while there they stole the parts with which Furagganan made the transmitter, as well as the gasoline to power it. Captain Jones says nothing was stolen from the Japanese save some gasoline at Aparri. (Jones, personal communication to the author.)

24. Venancio S. Duque, "Palaruan: the Unknown Symbol," *Legion's Forum,* December 1947, pp. 44-45.

25. Related in Lapham and Norling, *Lapham's Raiders,* pp. 179-81. Even Pajota's death was tragically ironic. His greatest ambition had always been to become a U.S. citizen. When he was finally able to come to America in December 1976, he at once filed for citizenship. He died of a heart attack before his application could be acted upon.

26. This account of Furagganan's character, deeds, and fate is derived mainly from Jones, "Operations of Troop C," pp. 18-21. The quotation is from p. 21.

27. The feelings of Troop C about the surrender of Bataan are described by Jones, ibid., p. 19.

5. The Tribulations of Colonel Horan and Associates

1. As the anonymous author of *Guerrilla Resistance* put it (p. 12), with some malice.

2. Ibid., pp. 12-13.

3. *Guerrilla Days*, p. 6.

4. Horan, "1960 Diary," p. 15.

5. Ibid., pp. 16, 24.

6. Ibid., p. 16.

7. Ibid., pp. 15-18, 23-24, 27-28, 52. Interestingly, Horan's "1942 Diary" says little about all these activities but does emphasize how enthused the miners were about Walter Cushing and his exploits. Horan records that he was comparably impressed when he met Cushing on January 26. Then he acceded to the entreaties of the miners and, without authorization, swore in many of them as U.S. officers so they could support Cushing's efforts more effectively. (Cf. entries for January 20 and January 26, Horan, "1942 Diary.")

8. Horan, "1960 Diary," pp. 18, 23-24, 40.

9. *Guerrilla Resistance*, p. 13.

10. *Guerrilla Resistance*, pp. 14-15; Horan, "1960 Diary," pp. 21-22.

11. Horan, "1960 Diary," pp. 15, 17-18, 23-25, 27-32, 34.

12. Ibid., pp. 32-33.

13. Ibid., p. 52.

14. Ibid., p. 26.

15. Ibid., p. 28.

16. Ibid., p. 18.

17. Ibid., pp. 17, 20, 22-23, 25, 31, 35, 37-38, 42.

18. Ibid., p. 38.

19. In sharp contrast to the "1960 Diary," Horan's "1942 Diary" contains none of this grumbling, whining, complaining, and finger pointing. In fact, his most vivid complaint was highly personal. He broke off a tooth and went to the only "dentist" in Sagado, where he was then staying. The man proved to be rather less than a conventional dentist; he was merely a "tooth puller." Nonetheless, he had an open mind about his profession. After examining Colonel Horan's mouth, he recommended smoothing off the jagged edges of the damaged tooth with a rat-tail file and a small triangular file. Horan rejected the suggestion and insisted that it be pulled. The dental technician then performed his specialty—loosening the adjoining tooth only slightly in the process. (Horan, "1942 Diary," March 27-30.)

20. Horan, "1960 Diary," pp. 20, 38.

21. *Guerrilla Resistance*, pp. 21-23.

22. Horan, "1960 Diary," p. 39.

23. Agoncillo, *The Fateful Years*, vol. 2, p. 657.

24. Horan, "1960 Diary," pp. 40-44.

25. Ibid., pp. 36, 40-49.

26. Ibid., pp. 46-48.

27. Ibid., p. 42.

28. *Guerrilla Days*, p. 25.

29. Arnold, *A Rock and a Fortress*, pp. 110-11.

30. Horan, "1960 Diary," pp. 14, 17-18, 22-23, 26, 28-34, 43, 51-52, 58.

31. *Guerrilla Days*, pp. 18-20.

32. Agoncillo, *The Fateful Years*, vol. 2, p. 658.

33. Ibid., p. 654.

34. Horan, "1960 Diary," p. 19.

35. Nielsen, *Bank Note Reporter*, December 1975, p. 25.

36. As Col. George Barnett pointed out in defense of Colonel Horan on November 21, 1945. (*See* Barnett, "History," RG 407, RAG, Exhibit "D," File 500-41; "Volckmann's Guerrillas," Box 249, PAC, NA II.)

37. *Guerrilla Days*, p. 34.

38. Ibid., pp. 34-35. As one writer put it, "Enriquez organized, Nakar fought, and Warner drank." Nielson, *Bank Note Reporter,* December 1975, p. 26.

39. *Guerrilla Days*, p. 35.

40. Manzano, "History," vol. 2, pp. 9-12, 25, 28, Anderson Folder, Ernie Pyle Museum.

41. Wolfert, *American Guerrilla*, p. 244. Many others concur in these judgments. C.f. Thomas Jones, personal communication to the author, Russell Volckmann, *We Remained*, pp. 69-70; and Nielsen, *Bank Note Reporter*, April, 1976, p. 28.

42. Santos, "Organ II" file, pp. 7-9, Ernie Pyle Museum. Those he had in mind were unnamed but it is clear that they included Maj. Claude Thorp and colonels Hugh Straughn, Peter Calyer, and Gyles Merrill.

43. Hileman and Fridlund, *1051*, pp. 170-77, 193-99.

44. "Brief History of the 141st Infantry AUS," pp. 6-7, Histories of Different Guerrilla Units Folder, Box 258, PAC, NA II.

45. "Collaboration: 6th Army U.S., North Luzon, Headquarters Intelligence Section," April 6, 1945, File 200.6, Book 1, Box 243, PAC, NA II.

46. *Guerrilla Days*, p. 36.

47. "Brief History of the 14th Infantry AUS," p. 10, Histories of Different Guerrilla Units Folder, Box 258, PAC, NA II.

48. Agoncillo, *The Fateful Years*, vol. 2, p. 655.

49. Arnold, *A Rock and a Fortress*, pp. 33-39.

50. Ibid., p. 76.

51. Ibid., p. 83.

52. Ibid., pp. 221-22; *Guerrilla Days*, pp. 37-38.

53. Arnold, *A Rock and a Fortress*, pp. 98, 103, 108-9.

54. Ibid., pp. 113, 122-25, 193-98.

6. The Troubles Worsen

1. Thomas Jones, "Operations of Troop C," p. 3.

2. Hunt and Norling, *Behind Japanese Lines*, p. 83.

3. Report by Richard Evans, WOJG, USA, o/c Project "J" Section to Chief of the Veteran's Bureau, GRLA-30, Annex 1, Box 538, PAC, NA II.

4. Minton claims all sorts of important achievements for Lieutenant Colonel Warner and himself. Furthermore, he maintains that even more splendid plans he and Warner made came to naught because Colonel Horan disliked Warner, and that Nakar and Enriquez blamed every failure of the 14th on Warner and attributed every success to themselves. Minton claims that he personally heard Nakar boast that his refusal to surrender to the Japanese while some Americans did capitulate would make him "famous enough that I will be elected President of the Philippines." (Affidavit from Capt. Warren Minton, "History of the 14th Infantry AUS," p. 7, File 500-43, Box 257, PAC, NA II.)
Nobody else has ever been able to discover either the accomplishments or grand designs of Warner and Minton. Moreover, what is one to think of a thirteen-page account of Warner's brief wartime career that does not once mention his fondness for alcohol? Virtually every American or Filipino who had anything to do with Warner noted that his most significant characteristic was that he was usually drinking or drunk.
On the outside of the file containing Minton's statement someone wrote in pencil, in capital letters "NOT IMPORTANT to PA file." (Double underlining in original. *See* "Volckmann's Guerrillas," Sept. 5, 1945, p. 7, File 500-43, Box 257, PAC, NA II.)

5. Hunt and Norling, *Behind Japanese Lines*, p. 83.

6. *Guerrilla Day*, p. 37.

7. Ibid.; Nielsen, *Bank Note Reporter*, December 1975, p. 26.

8. As related in Lapham and Norling, *Lapham's Raiders*, pp. 63-64.

9. Affidavit by Romulo Manriquez, GRLA-30 Annex 1, pp. 121-25, Box 538, PAC, NA II. The contrast with Lapham's version of this encounter is grimly humorous. Lapham says he stuck his .45-caliber pistol in Manriquez's ribs, following which there were discussions of the sort professional diplomats call "productive." *See* Lapham and Norling, *Lapham's Raiders*, p. 64.

10. Manriquez's affidavit, ibid.

11. Report by Richard Evans, WOJG, USA, o/c Project "J" Section to Chief of the Veteran's Bureau, GRLA-30, Annex 1, Box 538, PAC, NA II.

12. John H. Miller, VA Form 45056 and Republic Act 385, GRLA-30, Annex 1, Box 538, PAC, NA II. See especially Lt. Rufino F. Mejia, Inf. Bn. S2 and Tomas H. Castillo, field examiners, GRLA-30, Annex 1, pp. 102-5, Box 538, PAC, NA II.

13. Miller, VA Form 45056 and Republic Act 385, pp. 102-211.

14. Hunt and Norling, *Behind Japanese Lines*, pp. 164, 166-67, 218.

15. Volckmann, *We Remained*, p. 83.

16. *Guerrilla Days*, pp. 22-27.

17. Harkins, *Blackburn's Headhunters*, pp. 96-100; Volckmann, *We Remained*, pp. 83, 122, 143-44; *Guerrilla Resistance*, pp. 25-26.

18. Colonel Horan remarks ("1960 Diary," p. 53) with disgust that in his writings Volckmann belittles everything done in North Luzon by anyone save himself, an opinion shared by Maj. Robert Lapham and his area commanders, Captains Ray Hunt and Albert Hendrickson. Lapham resented and resisted Volckmann's persistent efforts to incorporate the LGAF into the USAFIP NL. (Lapham and Norling, *Lapham's Raiders*, pp. 119-21.) Hunt and Hendrickson were just as determined to fend off the unwelcome overtures of Volckmann as was their chief, although Hunt acknowledges that Volckmann could have had motives other than the sheer egotistic desire to run all North Luzon's guerrilla organizations personally. (*See* Hunt and Norling, *Behind Japanese Lines*, pp. 162-64, 216-19.)

19. Horan, "1960 Diary," p. 26.

20. *Guerrilla Resistance*, pp. 19-20.

21. Barnett, "History," RG 407, RAG, November 21, 1945, File 500-41; "Volckmann's Guerrillas," pp. 4-5, Exhibit "D," Box 249, PAC, NA II.

22. "Volckmann's Guerrillas," pp. 4-5, Box 249, PAC, NA II.

23. Moses to Barnett, September 19, 1942, Exhibit "VV," Box 249, PAC, NA II. Moses claimed his action was necessary to "beat the Japs to the punch."

24. *Guerrilla Resistance*, pp. 33-34.

25. *Guerrilla Days*, p. 19.

26. This whole evolution is described in detail, ibid., pp. 18-24.

27. Ibid., pp. 22.

28. Volckmann, *We Remained*, pp. 125-26.

29. Harkins, *Blackburn's Headhunters*, p. 159.

30. Rodriguez, *The Bad Guerrillas*, pp. x-xi, 3, 33-34, 38, 40-41, 48, 51, 57-61, 65-70, 72-75, 77-98, 115-32, 137-38, 142.

31. Ibid., pp. 153-86.

32. Agoncillo, *The Fateful Years*, vol. 2, pp. 755-59.

33. Lapham and Norling, *Lapham's Raiders*, pp. 122-23. The elder Marcos's arms and legs were tied to four carabao, which were then driven off in four different directions until they literally tore their victim apart.

34. "Blacklist of Pro-Japanese and Spies in Nueva Vizcaya," 6th Army USA, North Luzon, Headquarters Intelligence Section, April 6, 1945, Box 243, PAC, NA II.

35. Capt. E.R. Curtis to Lt. Col. W.M. Hanes in "Ablan's Guerrilla Forces," p. 3, File 54-2, Folder 2, Box 297, PAC, NA II.

36. "Ablan's Guerrilla Forces," n.p., File 54-2, Folder 2, Box 297, PAC, NA II.

37. Vincente Erieta, "North Luzon Guerrilla Warfare and Gov. Roque B. Ablan's Exiled Commonwealth Government," in "Ablan's Guerrilla Forces," p. 25, File 54-2, Folder 2, Box 297, PAC, NA II.

38. Lt. Charles P. Middleton, Contact Team E, December 30, 1945, as quoted in "Ablan's Guerrilla Forces," n.p., File 54-2, Folder 2, Box 297, PAC, NA II. Cf. also statement by lieutenants Charles L. Homewood, William D. McMillan, and Howard De Silva on the atrocities in Ilocos Norte.

39. Ibid. All five were members of Contact Team E.

40. Harkins, *Blackburn's Headhunters*, pp. 143-44, 147, 154, 158, 165, 174-75, 178.

41. Thomas Jones, personal communication to the author.

42. Hunt and Norling, *Behind Japanese Lines*, pp. 73-74, 231 n 6 and 7. Fenton's diary was in the possession of Morton J. Netzorg until the latter's death in 1995.

7. Interlude at Kabugao: Summer 1942

1. Jones, "Operations of Troop C," pp. 22-23, describes these policy changes.

2. Jones, "Operations of Troop C," p. 23. By contrast, Capt. Ray Hunt, one of Major Lapham's area commanders, was a fashion plate. He wore two pistols and carried an M-1 Garand, behind which were bandoliers crisscrossing his chest and containing as many as 170 cartridges. This outfit was topped with a hat made from a gourd. He describes himself as looking like a Hollywood version of a Mexican revolutionary. (Hunt and Norling, *Behind Japanese Lines*, p. 110.)

Lapham tried to look as military as possible by wearing denim and epaulettes, whenever he could find any, and shaving regularly. (Lapham and Norling, *Lapham's Raiders*, p. 75.)

3. Jones, "Operations of Troop C," p. 23.

4. Richard Lovelace, "To Lucasta, On Going to the Wars," Stanza 3.

5. Jones, "Operations of Troop C," p. 24.

6. Ibid., p. 25.

7. Ray Hunt, who claimed to have sampled most Philippine alcoholic beverages, said tuba, made from palm buds, was the best. He said basi destroyed one's stomach whereas miding, another common wine made from some part of the nipa palm, destroyed one's mind. (Hunt and Norling, *Behind Japanese Lines*, p. 89.)

8. Interestingly, Maj. Robert Lapham, C.O. of the LGAF guerrillas, disagreed 100 percent. Lapham traveled constantly over his domain in an effort to keep track of everything personally and to keep the Japanese from finding out too much about where he was or what he was doing

at any given time. Of course the circumstances of the two men varied markedly. Praeger was located in a jungle-enclosed hamlet high in thinly populated mountains whereas Lapham's domain was centered in the thickly settled flat riceland of the central Luzon plain, where he had to change his residence every seven to ten days because everyone knew everything about everyone else within a short time. They were temperamentally different men though, too, and had quite different ideas about how government should be carried on. (*See* Lapham and Norling, *Lapham's Raiders*, pp. 88-100.)

9. This description of routine life in Kabugao is drawn heavily from Jones, "Operations of Troop C," pp. 23-28.

10. Marcelo Adduru, Statement to CG PHILRYCOM, APO 707, July 28, 1947, pp. 2, 4, and Inclosures 3 and 4, pp. 15-16; "History of the Cagayan-Apayao Forces"; Thomas Jones to C.O. USAF Pacific, November 1, 1946, pp. 122-23; MacArthur to Praeger (radiogram), p. 7; Jones to G-3, 6th Army, Presidio of San Francisco, June 26, 1947, Inclosure 13, p. 27; Jones to Dept. GI and P, Cavalry School, Fort Riley, Kansas, March 19, 1946, Inclosure 5, p. 17, Inclosure 12, pp. 25-26; Jones to MacArthur, May 30, 1946, pp. 149-50, all in Folder 500-22A, Box 258, PAC, NA II.

11. Jones, "Operations of Troop C," p. 29.

12. Hunt and Norling, *Behind Japanese Lines*, p. 129.

13. Jones, "Operations of Troop C," p. 31.

14. Ibid.

15. Ibid.

16. Ibid., p. 32.

17. Grashio and Norling, *Return to Freedom*, p. 74.

18. Volckmann, *We Remained*, p. 65.

19. Hileman and Fridlund, *1051*, pp. 80-88; Conner, "We Fought Fear," p. 72.

20. Lapham and Norling, *Lapham's Raiders*, p. 43.

21. Harkins, *Blackburn's Headhunters*, pp. 109-10.

22. Wolfert, *American Guerrilla*, p. 189.

23. Excesses among some USAFFE guerrillas were so common that even SWPA HQ in Australia had heard of them and condemned them: "USAFFE abuses in areas without central control are excessive. Comandeering, executions without trial, and rape. . . ." (Radiogram WYY to KAZ NR-5 S-75, MacArthur's Archives, January 22, 1943.)

24. Lear, *Japanese Occupation*, pp. 95, 105.

25. Lapham and Norling, *Lapham's Raiders*, pp. 79-80.

26. Jones, "Operations of Troop C," p. 33.

27. In a formal statement to CINC USAFFE, November 1, 1946, Captain Jones pointed out that not a single Filipino in Cagayan or Apayao had ever been put on trial for war offenses or executed for any reason by CAF guerrilla forces—a dramatic contrast to the extreme harshness, even barbarity, so widespread in so many other irregular outfits all over

the Philippines. He attributes this happy condition to the general stability of the CAF, and in particular to Praeger's and Adduru's wise and humane guidance. "History of the Cagayan-Apayao Forces," p. 124, Folder 500-22A, Box 258, PAC, NA II.

28. The word punitive, in this connection, is part of the title Punitive Articles of War. It is not a value judgment.

8. Serious War Returns: Defeats and Losses Accumulate

1. Jones, "Operations of Troop C," pp. 34—35.
2. Baclagon, *Philippine Resistance*, p. 374.
3. Wayne Sanford, "The Organization of Guerrilla Warfare on Luzon," *World War II Chronicle*, May-June 1989, p. 9.
4. Jones, "Operations of Troop C," pp. 36-38, reprints a laudatory letter to Barker's parents from the military intelligence section at General MacArthur's headquarters, dated December 28, 1945.
5. Ibid., p. 39.
6. Ibid., p. 40.
7. Ibid., p. 41. The quotations here are paraphrases. They indicate accurately what the two Chinese speakers meant, but obviously nobody recalls the exact words of conversations five decades in the past.
8. Described in a radiogram, WYY to KAZ NR-5 S-75, January 22, 1943. Note that the radiogram was sent three months after the event.
9. Jones, "Operations of Troop C," p. 42.
10. Dozier, *Mountain Arbiters*, p. 24.
11. Jones, "Operations of Troop C," p. 43.
12. Ramsey and Rivele, *Lieutenant Ramsey's War*, p. 72. Ramsey adds that he was convinced that Wermuth must have been driven by private demons well beyond mere hatred of an enemy. Captain Jones, who did not know Wermuth but did know several POWs who knew him, says they all told him that Wermuth was a phony. (Private communication to the author.)
13. Jones, "Operations of Troop C," p. 45.

9. Civil Government in Cagayan-Apayao: Late 1942

1. Adduru to Quezon (coded message received by Col. J.K. Evans, General Staff Corps, Chief, Southwest Pacific Branch, from WPI in North Luzon, December 3, 1942), "History of the Cagayan-Apayao Forces," Folder 500-22A, Box 258, PAC, NA II. In central and southern Luzon many such officials were controlled or menaced by Hukbalahap (Communist) guerrillas. There were no Huks in the far north.
2. Nielsen, *Bank Note Reporter*, February 1975, p. 18.
3. Ibid., December 1974-January 1975, p. 14.
4. Ibid., May 1976, p. 30.

5. Ibid., April 1976, p. 28.

6. Ibid., February 1976, p. 27.

7. Ibid., March-April 1975, p. 19.

8. Ibid.

9. Ibid., June 1976, p. 33.

10. Issuing homemade money could become complex. On one occasion President Quezon authorized the issuance of fifty thousand pesos in scrip. The permission was channeled through General MacArthur's headquarters and sent by radiogram from the adjutant general's office to Adduru on January 15, 1943. (GTWO-VSM Snrb). A week later a message came from Praeger's radio to GHQ SWPA saying that Filipino morale was sinking due to gloomy war news and effective Japanese propaganda. The sender pleaded that lack of money greatly hampered intelligence gathering, and asked if any money could be gotten in Manila. A marginal note added that Governor Adduru had been authorized to issue scrip—presumably a reference to the permission received a week earlier. (WYY to KAZ, January 21, 1943.) On the same day, an unsigned radiogram (GTWO VSM SrV to WYY) authorized Adduru to issue another fifty thousand pesos. Whether this was an almost instantaneous reply to Praeger's plea, or whether the two messages just happened to cross, is unknown.

11. The money so manufactured was widely accepted all over those parts of North Luzon not under regular Nipponese control. (*See* Radiogram WYY to KAZ NR-8 S-94, January 25, 1943.)

12. Jones, "Operations of Troop C," p. 47.

13. MacArthur to Adduru, January 16, 1943 (relaying a message from Quezon), "History of the Cagayan-Apayao Forces," Folder 500-22A, p. 22 and Inclosure 8, pp. 20-21, Box 258, PAC, NA II. Most of the information about the manufacture and use of emergency currency is drawn from a series of articles under various titles by C.M. Nielsen appearing in *The Bank Note Reporter* between November 1974 and June 1976. In the reprinted collection available to this author, the pages of ten such articles are numbered consecutively from twelve to thirty-three. Page references to this material in foregoing footnotes follow this pagination.

14. Jones, "Operations of Troop C," pp. 47-48.

15. Willoughby and Chamberlain, *MacArthur*, pp. 210-11.

16. Jones, "Operations of Troop C," p. 48.

17. This is the belief of Thomas Jones. (Personal communication to the author.)

18. Jones, "Operations of Troop C," p. 49. Hedy Lamarr was a Viennese actress of extraordinary beauty who had acquired international notoriety around 1930 by appearing nude, at the age of sixteen, in the movie *Ecstasy.*

19. Ibid.

10. The Disastrous Enterprises of Lieutenant Colonels Moses and Noble

1. Lapham and Norling, *Lapham's Raiders*, pp. 43-45.
2. Teodoro Agoncillo, *The Fateful Years*, vol. 2, pp. 658-59.
3. Lapham and Norling, *Lapham's Raiders*, pp. 110-11.
4. Thomas Jones, "Operations of Troop C," pp. 52-54.
5. Ibid., p. 54.
6. Anderson, interview with Douglas Clanin (1985), *Anderson Folders*, vol. 1, pp. 48, 52, Ernie Pyle Museum.
7. Harkins, *Blackburn's Headhunters*, p. 101.
8. Volckmann, *We Remained*, pp. 83-84.
9. For samples among scores of critical comments of particular guerrillas about certain others expressed in communications during the war, in replies to questionnaires, or in personal interviews long after the war, cf. Doyle Decker to Douglas Clanin, March 3, 1985, about Blair Robinett; Decker to Wayne Sanford, October 9, 1984, about Frank Gyovai; Albert Hendrickson to Sanford, May 14, 1984, about Clay Conner, Gyles Merrill, and Peter Calyer; Gyovai, n.d., about Robert Mailheau; Mailheau, n.d., about Joseph Donahey; Leon Beck to Sanford, February 28 and March 21, 1984, and April 1985, about Edwin Ramsey, Robinett, Edward Fisher, and Daniel Cahill; and Beck and James Boyd, April 1985, about John Boone. All are from "Guerrilla Additions" in the Ernie Pyle Museum.
10. Harkins, *Blackburn's Headhunters*, pp. 178-93, 206-7, 223-24, 278.
11. A process described by Volckmann in *We Remained*, pp. 108-10.
12. Jones, "Operations of Troop C," p. 49.
13. Lapham, *Lapham's Raiders*, pp. 213-16. Lapham remarks on the same phenomenon and describes how his own propaganda operatives took advantage of it. (Cf. Cook and Cook, eds., *Japan at War*, pp. 105-11; Hartendorp, *Japanese Occupation*, vol. 1, pp. 485-86, 507-508, 513, vol. 2, 126n; Hernandez, *Not By the Sword*, pp. 102, 129-30; and Kato, *The Lost War*, p. 145.
14. *Whitney Papers*, Intelligence Channels News Broadcasts, October 1942-June 1943 RL 16 W 100, MacArthur Archives.
15. Cf. Calvocoressi and Wint, *Total War*, for a discussion both more general and more detailed of the innumerable inconsistencies and contradictions in Japanese political and military policies throughout World War II, pp. 673-710. Cook and Cook, eds., *Japan at War*, is filled with even more detailed examples.

To some degree Japanese pretense that guerrilla resistance was minor and peripheral represented nothing more than wishful thinking, but their repeated claims that it had been, was being, or would soon be wiped out indicated how irritated they were at its continued existence. (Cf. Jones, Borton, and Pearn, *Survey of International Affairs*, vol. 7, p. 45.)

For perhaps the most careful estimate of guerrilla numbers, broken down unit by unit, cf. Baclagon, *Philippine Resistance,* p. 532, and the official army history, Smith, *Triumph in the Philippines,* pp. 573, 651. There is a brief summary and commentary on numbers in Lapham and Norling, *Lapham's Raiders,* pp. 226-27.

16. Cf. "Japanese Opinions About Guerrillas," RAG, Folder 48, pp. C, D, 3-8, 19-21, 33-36, Box 538, PAC, NA II. These reports are for April-September, 1944 but their content and tone is similar to that of earlier reports.

17. This theme is explored at some length in Lapham and Norling, *Lapham's Raiders,* Chapter 13.

18. A certain amount of mystery about this convoy has never been entirely dispelled. On March 3, 1993, a Letter to the Editor from Thomas Jones appeared in the St. Petersburg (Florida) *Times.* In it, Jones recalled that about fifty years before a large number of Allied planes had shot up a Japanese convoy off the northeast coast of New Guinea. They had disabled ten enemy warships and twelve transports. MacArthur's headquarters estimated that fifty-five Japanese planes were downed in the battle and perhaps fifteen thousand Japanese soldiers were killed. Jones said the attack was set up by Lieutenant Bowen's coastwatchers on the *northeast* tip of Luzon. They had spotted a large convoy moving south and sent a runner to tell Bowen. He relayed the news to Praeger's command post, from whence it was passed on to Australia.

About the same time, however, a Filipina salt maker on the north coast of Luzon reported that she had seen an enemy convoy move out of the port of Aparri and sail *westward.* Presumably, it rounded the *northwest* tip of Luzon and then turned southward. Could this have been the same convoy Bowen's men reported? It might seem so since it was unlikely the Japanese would make up two huge convoys at the same time and send them down opposite coasts of Luzon, or even that they would have had *enough ships* to do it had they so wished.

Still, it is hardly imaginable that Bowen's men could have lived for weeks on Luzon's north coast without *any* of them knowing whether they were on the northeast or northwest tip. And yet, could the lady salt maker not have known the difference between east and west in an area where she had lived her whole life? Perhaps the guerrilla to whom she gave her information thought she said "west" when she had really said "east," and so reported the wrong direction to Praeger's headquarters. Were there really *two* convoys, or only one about whose direction somebody was badly confused?

Thomas Jones thinks there must have been two convoys, one of which was too small to deserve the appellation. Aparri was only a small port and could not have accommodated even one convoy—much less two—as large as that reported by Bowen's coastwatchers. He believes that the latter convoy was the one eventually ambushed and damaged heavily, and that it never came near Aparri. Most likely the salt maker observed some small vessels sailing westward from Aparri and mistook them for a convoy. (Thomas Jones, personal communication to the author.)

19. Jones, "Operations of Troop C," p. 50.

20. Ibid., p. 51.

21. Ibid., p. 44.

22. Ibid., p. 51.

23. KAZ to WYY NR-11, January 23, 1943, GTWO VSM S/nrb.

24. WYY to KFS NR-I S-246, January 4, 1943; KAZ to WYY, NR-11, January 23, 1943, GTWO VSM S/nrb; KAZ to WYY NR-23 GTWO VSM S/nrb, February 21, 1943.

25. Volckmann says that he was only a puppet governor by then, that the Japanese pressured him to collaborate, and that he and lesser collaborators soon betrayed Praeger and Jones to the enemy. (Volckmann, *We Remained,* pp. 151-52.) Jones doubts that Ayochok ever became a collaborator. (Thomas Jones, personal communication to the author.)

26. KAZ to WYY, January 13, 1943, from Col. B.M. Fitch, adjutant general, GTWO-YSM S/nrb. Two months later, Lieutenant Colonel Moses recommended Arthur Furagganan for promotion to first lieutenant "because he built Radio WYY out of junk," but nothing came of it. (WYY to KAZ [Moses to MacArthur], NR-30 S-265, March 3, 1943.) WYY to KAZ NR-19 S-136, February 13, 1943, carried this recommendation, too, It also recommended that Lieutenant Bowen be promoted to captain.

27. Jones, "Operations of Troop C," p. 52.

11. The Clouds Gather: Spring 1943

1. WYY to KAZ NR-14 S-162, February 8, 1943.

2. WYY to KAZ (Moses to MacArthur) NR-23 S-209, February 19, 1943.

3. WYY to KAZ NR-17 S-182, February 12, 1943; WYY to KAZ NR-24 S-208, February 19, 1943.

4. WYY to KAZ NR-24 S-208, February 19, 1943.

5. On February 13, 1943 WYY radioed KAZ that it had at last learned definitely that Walter Cushing had been killed in Isabela on September 29, 1942, nearly five months before! (NR-18 S-186)

6. KAZ to WYY NR-23, GTWO-USM S/nrb, February 21, 1943.

7. One of the reasons Lieutenant Bowen was so admired by Filipinos was that he genuinely liked and respected them. Sometime late in his life, probably when he was confined to the sick officers' quarters in Bilibid Prison in Manila, he composed "A Salute to the Filipino Soldier." It was handwritten and retrieved by someone who lived on after the war. Eventually it made its way into the hands of William E. Bowen Jr., Lieutenant Bowen's son, who made a copy available to this writer. The paean read thus:

Associated as I have been with Filipino soldiers for the past several years, I am firmly convinced of his unswerving devotion and unquestioned loyalty to the cause in which he has faith and in which he believes.

Prewar association taught me of his tenacity of purpose and full attention to any duty to which he was assigned. His devotion to duty was surpassed only by his love of family.

During the war I became more convinced than ever of his loyalty. Notwithstanding the fact that his families safety and well-being may have been placed in jeopardy by his actions, his faithfulness and loyalty were always evident. Regardless of the circumstances in which he found himself: regardless of the position in which his family was placed; regardless of which flag flew over his native land, he would do to the utmost ability of his sincere and simple soul that which he believed to be right. His creed, his religion will always be the same: Loyalty to the Philippines.

Signed, Lt. William E. Bowen, U.S. Army

8. Thomas Jones, "Operations of Troop C," pp. 53-54. Bowen was awarded a DSC for his part in the Tuguegarao raid. Jones recommended him for several other citations, but nothing ever came of it. (Jones to Mrs. Bowen, December 8, 1945, Praeger Papers.)

9. Jones, "Operations of Troop C," p. 54.

10. Ibid., p. 55.

11. Praeger's regard for Adduru was conveyed in the following personal message to General MacArthur: "Adduru's unselfish devotion, wisdom and courage have earned him respect from the Japanese, admiration of American officers and love of Filipinos. By his just and wise provincial administration, avoiding politics and devoting himself to prosecuting the war he proved himself a good leader." (Praeger to MacArthur, June 30, 1943, "History of the Cagayan-Apayao Forces," Folder 500-22A, Inclosure 10, p. 23, Box 258, PAC, NA II.)

Captain Thomas Jones delivered more moving tributes to the governor on several occasions. (Cf. Jones to Pres. Sergio Osmena of the Philippines, February 22, 1945, "History of the Cagayan-Apayao Forces," Folder 500-22A, Inclosure 14, p. 28; and Jones, Certificate for Extraordinary Heroism, 10 December, 1941-2, April 1943, "History of the Cagayan-Apayao Forces," Folder 500-22A, Inclosure 15, p. 29.)

12. Jones, "Operations of Troop C," pp. 55-56.

13. Ibid., p. 56.

14. WYY to KAZ NR-5 S-75, January 22, 1943.

15. Jones, "Operations of Troop C," pp. 56-57.

16. Ibid., p. 57.

17. Ibid., p. 58.

18. Ibid., pp. 58-60.
19. Ibid., p. 60.
20. Ibid.
21. The rainy season in most of Luzon stretches roughly from June through November, but there is considerable variation from one locality to another.
22. Jones, "Operations of Troop C," p. 60.
23. Ibid., p. 61.
24. Minang Dizon, the fearless girlfriend of Ray Hunt, repeatedly fooled the Japanese in this manner. So did Yay Panlilio, the paramour of the leader of Marking's guerrillas and the real brains of that outfit. (*See* Hunt and Norling, *Behind Japanese Lines*, pp. 99, 148.) Panlilio survived the early Japanese occupation by pretending to collaborate with the conquerors as a broadcaster until she was able to escape. (Willoughby and Chamberlain, *MacArthur*, pp. 59-60. *See also* Castillo and Castillo, *The Saga of Jose P. Laurel.*)
25. Jones, "Operations of Troop C," pp. 61-62.
26. Vaggas had been captured in Bataan a year before and assigned to be the driver for a Japanese colonel, but he had gotten away and joined guerrillas.

12. The Curtain Comes Down

1. Jones, "Operation of Troop C," pp. 63-64.
2. This was also true of Robert Lapham's LGAF radio 150 miles south. (Lapham and Norling, *Lapham's Raiders*, pp. 161-62.)
3. Jones, "Operations of Troop C," p. 65.
4. Ibid., pp. 65-66.
5. Praeger to MacArthur NR-1, June 27, 1943; Reply GTWO-VSM Snrb, same date.
6. WWAL to General MacArthur NR-1, July 15, 1943; Jones, Notes, "History of the Cagayan-Apayao Forces," p. 120, Folder 500-22A, Box 258, PAC, NA II.
7. Jones, "Operations of Troop C," p. 66.
8. MacArthur to Praeger NR-72, July 19, 1943. Most radiograms between SWPA and Praeger are identified by the call letters of their stations, KAZ and WYY respectively, but some were not. Likewise, in 1942 and 1943 most were numbered, but some were not. In July 1943 Praeger's call letters were changed to WWAL.
9. Praeger to MacArthur NR-23, August 13, 1943.
10. Praeger to MacArthur NR-8, July 11, 1943. For the uncertainty about the salt maker's report *see* pp. 261-62, n. 18.
11. Praeger to MacArthur NR-9, July 14, 1943.
12. WWAL to MacArthur NR-16, July 29, 1943.
13. WWAL to MacArthur NR-20, August 16, 1943.

14. WWAL to MacArthur NR-36, August 17, 1943.

15. WWAL to MacArthur NR-33, August 18, 1943.

16. Hunt and Norling, *Behind Japanese Lines,* p. 219.

17. Monaghan, *Under the Red Sun,* p. 142.

18. *See* for example, Praeger to MacArthur (no number), August 18, 1943.

19. Jones, "Operations of Troop C," p. 67.

20. WWAL to MacArthur NR-1, July 15, 1943; WWAL to MacArthur NR-20, August 16, 1943.

21. P.R.S., C. OF S. Coordo. G-2, No. 806007, Charles Willoughby, June 27, 1943.

22. MacArthur to Praeger NR-11, July 20, 1943; NR-24 GTWO CW/ tpd, August 27, 1943; ND-25 GTWO CSB, era, August 27, 1943.

23. Jones, "Operations of Troop C," p. 67.

24. Ibid., p. 68. Many people in parts of the world where some form of authoritarian government has always existed have been similarly confused when the well-meaning democrats of the Occident impose democracy on them after defeating them in a war. In the years immediately after World War II, Western newspapermen reported being asked by ordinary Japanese what was the good of democracy if one's party lost in an election?

25. Willoughby, *Guerrilla Resistance,* p. 48.

26. Personal communication to the author.

27. Manuel T. Hernandez to Col. B. Praeger (Ralph's brother), then in Panmunjon, Korea, July 28, 1968, Praeger Papers. In the letter, Hernandez remarks of Ralph Praeger, "We don't hesitate following him if he has to lead us to the bowels of hell."

28. Pena, "The Redoubtable Ralph B. Praeger," *Manila Free Press,* April 3, 1948.

29. Harkins, *Blackburn's Headhunters,* p. 200.

30. Volckmann, *We Remained,* pp. 151-52.

31. Jones, personal communication to the author.

32. Harkins, *Blackburn's Headhunters,* pp. 235, 257.

33. Personal communication to the author.

34. Hartendorp, *Japanese Occupation,* vol. 2, p. 582; Dupuy, *Men of West Point.* (The author had access to only a few photocopied pages of this book without page numbers or bibliographical information.)

35. Dupuy, *Men of West Point.*

36. Jones to Mrs. Ralph B. Praeger, November 28, 1945, Praeger Papers; personal communication to the author.

37. Lapham and Norling, *Lapham's Raiders,* pp. 161-62.

38. "History of the Cagayan-Apayao Forces," p. 10, Folder 500-22A, Box 258, PAC, NA II.

39. Jones, Notes, "History of the Cagayan-Apayao Forces," p. 113, Folder 500-22A, Box 258, PAC, NA II.

40. Jones, "Operations of Troop C," p. 69.
41. Ibid., p. 70.

13. Epilogue

1. "History of the Cagayan-Apayao Forces," p. 9, Folder 500-22A, Box 258, PAC, NA II.
2. Willoughby, *Guerrilla Resistance,* p. 195.
3. Volckmann, *We Remained,* pp. 122, 151.
4. Ibid., p. 151.
5. Hileman and Fridlund, *1051,* pp. 2, 215.
6. Ramsey and Rivele, *Lieutenant Ramsey's War,* p. 240.
7. Thomas Jones to Mrs. Verda Praeger, November 28, 1945, Praeger Papers. This long letter contains a two-page description of Jones's and Praeger's sojourn in Japanese prisons.
8. The notation about Jones's treatment was recorded on August 1, 1944. (Tirk, "Diary," p. 22.)
9. Tirk, diary, October 6, 1944, p. 34.
10. That is the date supplied by Hartendorp, *Japanese Occupation,* vol. 2, p. 583. It should be added that Hartendorp was not a stickler for precision. On two pages alone (pp. 581 and 583) he calls Praeger "Frager," refers to "Apples" Heuser as "Heiser," spells Furagganan "anen," and says Praeger was *sent* to the north tip of Luzon when the war began when, in fact, he asked permission from Colonel Horan to proceed in that direction for the purpose of raiding the Tuguegarao airfield.

Soon after the end of the war, Sgt. Raymond Camonayan, who had been court-martialed with Praeger, wrote to Thomas Jones to tell him that the last day he had seen Praeger alive had been August 22, 1944. (Jones to Mrs. Praeger, November 28, 1945, Praeger Papers.)

Colonel Parker Calvert deposed after the war that Praeger had been executed in August, as Hartendorp maintained. (*See* "Certificate" given at HQ USAFIP NL, Camp Spencer, November 25, 1945, RAG, Exhibit "BB," File 500-41, Box 249, PAC NA II.)

Although these allegations would seem conclusive, Maj. Gen. Edward F. Witsell wrote to Praeger's father on March 7, 1946, that the War Department believed he had been executed sometime in December 1944. (Praeger Papers.)

11. In a letter to Mrs. Praeger dated January 18, 1946, Maj. Gen. Edward A. Williams said that on November 15, 1943, Quezon had radioed General MacArthur to that effect. (Message No. 496, Praeger Papers.)
12. Praeger Papers.
13. Tirk, diary, July 5, 1944, p. 19; August 13, 1944, p. 26; October 3, 1944, pp. 32, 34.
14. This was the opinion of Colonel Horan, "1960 Diary," pp. 27-

28, but he gives no details or date. Thomas Jones thinks Manila was more likely. (personal communication to the author.)

15. This is Hartendorp's account of Furagganan's demise. *See Japanese Occupation,* vol. 2, p. 583.

16. This was the first message survivors of the Bataan Death March heard from the Japanese commandant of Camp O'Donnell—that they were captives rather than prisoners of war. The commandant was as good as his word. Allied soldiers, particularly Filipinos, died by the thousands there.

17. Jones to Mrs. Praeger, November 28, 1945, Praeger Papers.

18. James R. Patterson, "His Spirit and Monument," *Kansas City Times,* March 22, 1946, p. 8. One more indication of how poor, vague, and outdated was knowledge of men and events on Luzon at GHQ SWPA during most of the war that it was believed there in November, 1944 that Jones had been executed. (Willoughby, *Guerrilla Resistance,* p. 481.)

19. Despite the somewhat improved food, Jones records that the prisoners there, like so many in other Japanese camps and prisons, talked incessantly about food, cooking, recipes, banquets, restaurants, picnics, and the like.

20. Jones, personal communication to the author.

21. Jones to Mrs. Helen Bowen, December 8, 1945, Praeger Papers.

22. In the National Archives there is a list of the casualties from the *Arisan Maru* disaster. Neither Bowen's name nor that of Arnao are on it. The list also has a notation that 196 names are missing. Bowen's name does appear on a much longer composite list of all the victims of all sinkings of Japanese ships with POWs on board, although Arnao's does not. (Sunken Prisoner of War Transports to the *Arisan Maru,* RAG, Box 146, PAC, NA II.)

23. Ibid., for depositions from American survivors of the disaster. That of Wilber was taken December 5, 1944. The others are undated but were probably taken then, too.

24. There is an extended discussion of all these interconnected questions in Daws, *Prisoners of the Japs,* pp. 283-99. Daws finds many of them ultimately inexplicable. For instance, in the holds of Japanese prison ships it was oftentimes so hot, cramped, and foul, and the conduct of the guards so cruel and *unreasonable,* that any accurate description of conditions there hardly seems credible to ordinary people. Yet only Americans killed *each other* in these adjuncts of hell—and officers more frequently than enlisted men! Why? He can offer no explanation. Some things surpass understanding, they can only be described. . . .

25. The demise of Lieutenant Bowen was like the others in one respect, though: there was the same uncertainty about his fate. In a letter from Franz Weissenblatt to Mrs. Bowen dated March 17, 1945, the writer begins confidently with the news that Bowen's ship arrived safely in

Japan; but in another letter to her dated July 2, 1945, he backpedals, reminding her that the U.S. War Department gets all its information about American POWs from the Japanese so nobody will really learn the fate of prisoners until the war ends. (Praeger Papers.) Bowen had died the previous October 24.

26. "History of the Cagayan-Apayao Forces," pp. 86-89, Folder 500-22A, Box 258, PAC, NA II. The only clue to the date of composition is the last entry in what appears to have been a diary that Adduru kept. It is October 12, 1944.

27. Roger Hilsman, an American guerrilla in the China-Burma-India Theater, provides an excellent analysis of what it is reasonable and unreasonable for a guerrilla group to attempt in a major war. He warns that guerrilla warfare is the weapon of the weak, that it cannot succeed alone, in the short run, against strong enemy regular forces. Guerrillas are useful for gathering intelligence information, picking off enemy officers, assassinating collaborators, ambushing enemy patrols, propagandizing for their cause, building a political base for their own support, and in every way possible imposing psychological stress on the foe. To succeed in the long run they need outside aid and, eventually, a large army of their own countrymen that they can then join and strengthen. These words fit the situation of nearly all World War II guerrillas in the Philippines before 1945. It was also, in essence, what General MacArthur persistently urged the guerrillas to do. None tried harder to act in this fashion than did the CAF. (Hilsman, *American Guerrillas*, pp. 289-96.)

28. Lapham and Norling, *Lapham's Raiders*, p. 55.

Bibliography

Primary Sources

Archival collections, personal collections, unpublished materials, collected interviews of World War II American guerrillas in the Philippines, and answers to questionnaires. Secured and compiled by Douglas Clanin and Wayne Sanford. Deposited under various designations in the Ernie Pyle Museum in Dana, Indiana.

Horan, John P., "First Five Months of Guerrilla Warfare in Northern Luzon: Diary of Col. John P. Horan." A diary composed by Col. Horan, seemingly from memory, about 1960. Never published. It is referred to in the text and footnotes as "1960 Diary."

———. "Diary." Written day-by-day from December 1941 to April 1942. Unpublished. A copy exists in the Philippine Archives Collection at the National Archives II. It differs in both content and tone from the "1960 Diary." In both the text and footnotes it is referred to as "1942 Diary."

Jones, Maj. Thomas S. "Operations of Troop C, 26th Cavalry, Philippine Scouts In Northern Luzon: The First Two Years." Unpublished manuscript prepared at The Cavalry School, Fort Riley, Kansas, 1946. It is the single most important source for this book.

Manzano, Jaime H. "History of the USAFFE Luzon Guerrilla Army Forces." Part of the Bernard L. Anderson folder in the Ernie Pyle Museum. Unpublished.

Philippine Archives Collection. National Archives II. Boxes 146, 248, 249, 257, 538.

Praeger Papers. A collection of prewar and postwar letters and other materials of many sorts about Maj. Ralph Praeger. They were collected by his family and made available to the author by Praeger's son, Col. Ralph Praeger Jr., USAF (Ret.).

Praeger, Ralph. Radio messages between Praeger and General MacArthur's headquarters. Declassified in 1975, these documents were secured from the MacArthur Archives by Col. Thomas S. Jones and William E. Bowen and made available to the author.

Santos, Alejo, "Guerrilla Activities In Luzon, As Related to Col. G. Atkinson," January 20, 1945. Ernie Pyle Museum.

Tirk, Richard E. Unpublished prison diary. Acquired by William E. Bowen and made available to this author.

Townswick, Carlyle. "Too Young to Die." Unpublished memoir by a wartime guerrilla on Mindanao. Made available to the author by an associate of Townswick.

Vance, Maj. Lee C. (Executive officer and, after January 1942, commander of the 26th Cavalry). "Diary of the 26th Cavalry, December 8, 1941, to April 9, 1942." Unpublished. Acquired by William E. Bowen and made available to the author.

Whitney, Courtney. *Whitney Papers: Philippine Project Praeger, Intelligence Channels, and News Broadcasts,* October 1942-June 1943. MacArthur Archives.

Published Accounts by Active Participants in World War II

Arnold, Robert H. *A Rock and a Fortress.* Sarasota, Fla.: Blue Horizon, 1979.

Churchill, Winston. *The Hinge of Fate.* Boston: Houghton Mifflin, 1950.

Conner, Henry Clay. "We Fought Fear on Luzon," *True,* August 1946, pp. 69-87.

Devereux, James P.S. *The Story of Wake Island.* New York: Lippincott, 1947.

Dew, Gwen. *Prisoner of the Japs.* New York: Knopf, 1943.

Gilkey, Langdon. *Shantung Compound.* New York: Harper and Row, 1966.

Grashio, Samuel and Bernard Norling. *Return to Freedom.* Tulsa, Okla.: Military Collectors' News Press, 1983.

Guerrilla Days In North Luzon: A Brief Historical Narrative of a Brilliant Segment of the Resistance Movement During Enemy Occupation of the Philippines, 1941-1945. Camp Spencer, Luna, La Union, P.I.: USAFIP, 1946. (Historical Records Section.)

Guerrilla Resistance Movement in Northern Luzon. Camp Aguinaldo, Quezon City: Office of Military History, GHQ Armed Forces of the Philippines, n.d.

Harkins, Philip. *Blackburn's Headhunters.* New York: Norton, 1955.

Hileman, Millard E., and Paul Fridlund. *1051: An American POW's Remarkable Journey Through World War II.* Walla Walla, Wash.: Words Worth Press, 1992.

Hilsman, Roger. *American Guerrilla: My War Behind Japanese Lines.* New York: Brassey's, 1990.

Hunt, Ray, and Bernard Norling. *Behind Japanese Lines.* Lexington: Univ. Press of Kentucky, 1986.

Ind, Allison. *Allied Intelligence Bureau.* New York: McKay, 1958.

Keith, Agnes. *Three Came Home.* Boston: Little Brown, 1947.

Lapham, Robert, and Bernard Norling. *Lapham's Raiders.* Lexington: Univ. Press of Kentucky, 1996.

Miller, Ernest B. *Bataan Uncensored.* Long Prairie, Minn.: Hart, 1949.

Panlilio, Yay. *The Crucible.* New York: Macmillan, 1950.

Ramsey, Edwin, and Stephen J. Rivele. *Lieutenant Ramsey's War.* New York: Knightsbridge, 1990.

Sutherland, Richard K. *Guerrilla Resistance Movements In the Philippines.* SWPA, 1945. (A collection of essays previously published by the Philippine Sub-Section of SWPA. An updated version, under a similar title, was published by Charles A. Willoughby in 1972.)

Volckmann, Russell. *We Remained.* New York: Norton, 1954.

Whitcomb, Edgar D. *Escape from Corregidor.* Chicago: Regnery, 1958.

Whitehead, Arthur K. *Odyssey of a Philippine Scout.* Tucson: Arizona Lithographers, 1989.

Willoughby, Charles A. *The Guerrilla Resistance Movement In the Philippines, 1941-1945.* New York: Vantage Press, 1972.

Wolfert, Ira. *American Guerrilla In the Philippines.* New York: Simon and Schuster, 1945.

Secondary Works

Agoncillo, Teodoro. *The Fateful Years: Japan's Adventure In the Philippines.* 2 vols. Quezon City: R.P. Garcia, 1965.

Baclagon, Uldarico S. *The Philippine Resistance Movement Against Japan, 10 December 1941 to 14 June 1945.* Manila: Munoz, 1966.

Barton, R.F. *Autobiographies of Three Pagans In the Philippines.* New Hyde Park, N.Y.: University Books, 1963.

Breuer, William B. *Retaking the Philippines.* New York: St. Martin's, 1986.

Calvocoressi, Peter, and Guy Wint. *Total War: Causes and Consequences of the Second World War.* New York: Penguin, 1979.

Cannon, M. Hamlin. *Leyte: The Return to the Philippines.* The U.S. Army In World War II. Vol. 2 of Part 5, *The War In the Pacific.* Washington, D.C.: Department of the Army, 1954.

Castillo, Teofilo del, and Jose del Castillo. *The Saga of Jose P. Laurel.* Manila: Associated Authors, 1949.

Cook, Haruko Taya, and Theodore F. Cook, eds. *Japan at War: An Oral History.* New York: New Press, 1992.

Daws, Gavan. *Prisoners of the Japanese.* New York: William Morrow, 1994.

Dissette, Edward F., and H.C. Adamson. *Guerrilla Submarines.* New York: Ballantine, 1972.

Dozier, Edward P. *Mountain Arbiters: The Changing Life of a Philippine Hill People.* Tucson: Univ. of Arizona Press, 1966.

"DSC Purple Heart Posthumously to Guerrilla Leader." *The Guidon.* (March 29, 1946): 1-2.

Duque, Venancio S. "Palaruan: The Unknown Symbol," *Legion's Forum,* December 1947, pp. 17, 44-45.

Dupuy, Trevor. *Men of West Point.* New York: Sloane, 1951.

Estrada, William L. "A Historical Survey of the Guerrilla Movement in Pangasinan, 1942-1945," Master's thesis, Far Eastern University, Manila, 1951.

Hartendorp, A.V.H. *The Japanese Occupation of the Philippines.* 2 vols. Manila: Bookmark, 1967.

Hernandez, Juan B. *Not By the Sword.* New York: Greenwich, 1959.

Ingham, Trevor. *Rendezvous by Submarine: The Story of Charles*

Parsons and the Guerrilla Soldiers of the Philippines. Garden City, N.Y.: Doubleday, 1945.

James, D. Clayton. *The Years of MacArthur, 1941-1945.* Boston: Houghton Mifflin, 1975.

Jones, F.C., Hugh Borton, and Brian R. Pearn. *Survey of International Affairs, 1939-1946: The Far East, 1942-1946.* Vol. 7. New York: Oxford Univ. Press, 1955.

Kato, Masuo. *The Lost War: A Japanese Reporter's True Story.* New York: Knopf, 1946.

Lear, Elmer. *The Japanese Occupation of the Philippines, Leyte, 1941-1945.* Ithaca, N.Y.: Cornell Univ. Press, 1961.

Long, Gavin. *MacArthur as Military Commander.* Princeton, N.J.: Van Nostrand, 1969.

Lovelace, Richard. Poems of Richard Lovelace. Introduction by C.H. Wilkinson, 1925, 2 vols.

Luvaas, Jay, ed. *Dear Miss Em: General Eichelberger's War in the Pacific, 1942-1945.* Westport, Conn.: Greenwood, 1972.

Monaghan, Forbes J., S.J. *Under the Red Sun.* New York: Declan X. McMullen, 1946.

Morton, Louis. *The Fall of the Philippines.* The U.S. Army in World War II. Vol. 2 of Part 4, *The War in the Pacific.* Washington, D.C.: Department of the Army, 1953.

Ney, Virgil. *Notes on Guerrilla War: Principles and Practices.* Washington, D.C.: Command, 1951.

Nielsen, C.M. "Emergency and Guerrilla Currencies of North Luzon." *Bank Note Reporter,* November 1974.

———. "Currencies of Cagayan." *Bank Note Reporter,* December 1974-January 1975.

———. "Emergency and Guerrilla Currency of North Luzon: The Mountain Province." *Bank Note Reporter,* February 1975.

———. "Emergency and Guerrilla Currency of Apayao," *Bank Note Reporter,* March-April 1975.

———. "North Luzon, Ilocos Norte, Parts I and II," *Bank Note Reporter,* May-June 1975.

———. "Emergency and Guerrilla Currencies of North Luzon: The 14th Infantry," *Bank Note Reporter,* December 1975.

———. "Currencies of Nueva Vizcaya." *Bank Note Reporter,* February, 1976.

———. "Emergency and Guerrilla Currencies: Isabela." *Bank Note Reporter,* April 1976.

———. "Emergency and Guerrilla Currencies of North Luzon." *Bank Note Reporter,* May 1976.

———. "Financing Other Luzon Movements." *Bank Note Reporter,* June 1976.

Patterson, James R. "His Spirit a Monument," *Kansas City Times,* March 22, 1946, pp. 1, 8.

Pena, Ambrosio P. "The Redoubtable Ralph B. Praeger," *Manila Free Press,* April 3, 1948.

Potter, John Deane. *Life and Death of a Japanese General.* New York: New American Library, 1962.

Reichschauer, Edwin O. *Japan: The Story of a Nation.* New York: Knopf, 1981.

Rodriguez, Ernesto, Jr. *The Bad Guerrillas of Northern Luzon.* Quezon City: J. Burgos, 1982.

Rosaldo, Renato. *Ilongot Headhunting, 1883-1974: A Study in Society and History.* Stanford, Calif.: Stanford Univ. Press, 1980.

Sanderson, James Dean. *Behind Enemy Lines.* New York: Van Nostrand, 1959.

Smith, Robert Ross. *Triumph in the Philippines.* The U.S. Army in World War II. Vol. 2 of Part 16, *The War in the Pacific.* Washington, D.C.: Department of the Army, 1963.

Spence, Hartzell. *For Every Tear a Victory: The Story of Ferdinand E. Marcos.* New York: McGraw-Hill, 1964.

Thompson, George R., Dixie R. Harris, Pauline M. Oakes, and Dulany Terrett. *The Signal Corps: The Test. (December 1941 to July 1943.)* The U.S. Army in World War II. Vol. 6 of Part 8, *The Technical Services.* Washington, D.C.: Department of the Army, 1957.

Toland, John. *But Not In Shame.* New York: Random House, 1961.

Urwin, Gregory J.W. "The Defenders of Wake Island: Their Two Wars, 1941-1945." Ph.D. diss, Notre Dame University.

Waterford, Van. *Prisoners of the Japanese in World War II.* London: McFarland, 1994.

Whitney, Courtney. *MacArthur: His Rendezous with History.* Westport, Conn.: Greenwood, 1977.

Willoughby, Charles A., and John Chamberlain. *MacArthur, 1941-1951.* New York: McGraw-Hill, 1954.

Index

188; surrenders to save his men's families, 191, 236; Japanese respect for, 191-92; popularity with Filipinos, 191-92, 262-63 n 7; meets Jones in prison, 234; death on *Arisan Maru*, 236-38

Brazelton, Pvt. (later Sgt.) Earl, 87, 201, 205, 211-12; as a radio technician, 50, 148; contacts San Francisco, 170; poor health of, 220; captured, 226; questioned by Japanese, 230; executed, 232

CAF (Cagayan-Apayao Forces), viii-ix, xii, 19; and morale problems, 134

Cagawaddan: temporary CAF headquarters, 187; visit by Jones, 204

Cagayan Province, 23, 45

Cagayan Valley, 22, 44-45, 103, 117; bridges destroyed, 54; new planes seen, 215

Caluen, Domi (wireless operator), 148; contacts San Francisco, 170

Calvert, Capt. (later Col.) Parker, 114; leads Horan's troops astray, 41; evades surrender after Corregidor falls, 92; organizes guerrillas, 105-6; becomes Volckmann's executive officer, 106

Calyer, Col. Peter, 96, 171

Camonayan, Sgt. Raymundo, 67, 118; captured, 226; last saw Praeger, 266 n 10

Camp, Lt. Francis A., 54, 63, 172; joins Troop C, 49; "jungle promotion" of 49; hatred of Japanese by, 52-53;

homemade grenades, 57-58, 118, 123; shoots up enemy barracks, 59; shoots up enemy convoy, 70; massacres nine Japanese in Cagayan, 76

Camp John Hay, 20, 25, 50

Camp Karenko, 90

Candon: massacre at, 1-2, 69, 156

Casiguran Bay, 95

Chengay, Capt. Tomas "Tom": and mining cables scandal, 104; praised by Hunt, 105

Chinese: merchant gives shoes to troops, 54, 248 n 14; hatred of Japanese, 76

Choltitz, Gen. Dietrich von, 90

Clark Field, 1, 20, 57

Conception, Manuel: as employer of "Lee," 201; evaluated by Praeger, 215

Conception, Lt. Sofronio Z., 107

Conner, Henry Clay, 139, 247 n 1

convoy, phantom, 182-83, 215, 261 n 18

Cordillera Central, 46, 150

Corregidor: fall of, 55, 88

currency: manufacture and management of, 163-69

Cushing, Capt. Charles, 103, 114, 176

Cushing, Maj. James, 133

Cushing, Capt. (later Maj.) Walter, 167; and Candon ambush, 1-2; schemes of, 2-3, 10-12; and Tagudin ambush, 3-5; dynamites bridges, 3, 6-7; disputes about rank, 4; prewar life of, 5; character and personality of, 5, 11, 13; organizes guerrillas, 6; acquires Robert Arnold, 7; and Narvacan ambush, 7; steals ammuni-

Cushing, Capt. Walter (*cont.*)
tion from enemy, 7-8; and
Balbalasang ambush, 8; as
propagandist, 9; trip to
Manila and back, 9-10; visits
Praeger, 11; death of, 12-13;
and ambush near Lepanto
mine, 70; widely admired,
44-45, 156, 159; and plan to
unify all guerrillas, 74, 171;
disbands troops when
Corregidor falls, 89, 117;
refuses to surrender, 107

Dagarra River, 159-60, 227
Dangwa, Bado, 105
Decasteker, Fr. Gerardo, 127
Devereux, Maj. James, 30
Diesnick, Fr.: generosity to
troops, 53
dita, 139
Dutch East Indies, 65, 75; as
main source of quinine, 138
dynamite: as a potent weapon,
57-58, 84-85, 123-24

Encyclopedia Britannica: value of
articles, 127-28, 142
Enriquez, Capt. Manuel, 82, 176;
organizes and trains guerrillas, 93-95, 101-2; differing
opinions of, 101-02; ex-
ecuted, 102
Erieta, Vincente G., 114
Escobar, Emilio "Sagad": boasts
of atrocities, 111

Fassoth, Vernon: scrounges for
arms, 40
"Felipe," 186, 200; agricultural
expert, 155
Fenton, Harry: legendary cruelty
of, 115-16; executed, 116

Fort Stotsenburg, 22, 32, 48, 57,
126, 245 n 15
Fourth of July: celebration at
Kabugao, 129-31
Furagganan, Sgt. (later Lt.)
Arthur, 220; expertise with
radios, 77-80, 147-48, 262 n
26; feelings about USA, 78,
122; as a true war hero, 80;
promoted, 218; captured,
226; questioned intensively,
230; executed, 233

Gaddangs, 45
Gaerlan, Capt. Candonia:
ambushes enemy, 152;
betrayed and executed, 153;
as a war hero, 184
Galbraith, Col. Nicholas, 89, 107
Ganaps (pro-Japanese Filipinos),
98, 224; late war slaughter
of, 113-14; Moses and Noble
claim to have killed many,
190
Garcia, Capt. Silvino: as a CAF
spy among Japanese, 213
Giitter, Capt. L.H.: ineptitude of,
36-38, 87; disbands 43rd
Infantry, 89
Grace Park: CAF headquarters
established, 187
Grashio, Lt. Samuel, 248 n 14
guerrillas: cruelty of, real and
alleged, 110-16, 196-98, 257 n
23; plans to unify all, 148,
171-72; numbers in various
units, 179; many unsuited
for the life, 194: civilian
support vital, 195, 199-200;
record keeping among, 216-
17; criticisms of each other,
260 n 9

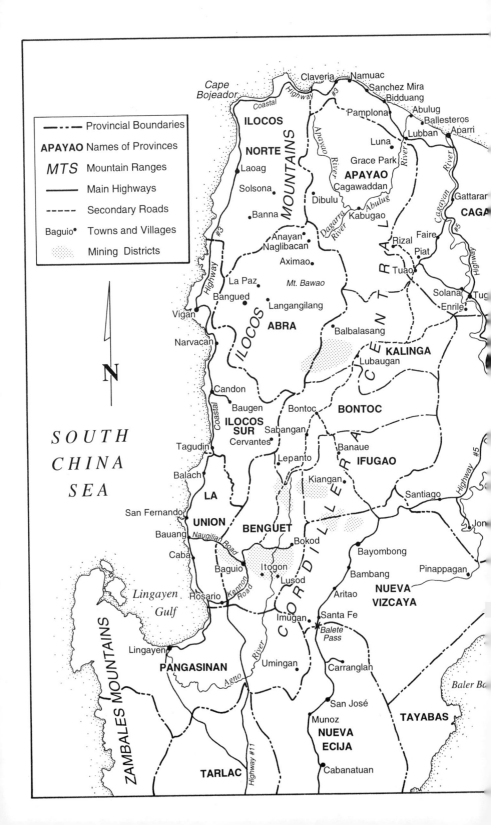